W9-CTO-078

URBAN GUERRILLA WARFARE

URBAN GUERRILLA WARFARE

Anthony James Joes

THE UNIVERSITY PRESS OF KENTUCKY

Publication of this volume was made possible in part by
a grant from the National Endowment for the Humanities.

Editorial and Sales Offices: The University Press of Kentucky
663 South Limestone Street, Lexington, Kentucky 40508-4008

ISBN-13: 978-0-8131-2437-7
ISBN-10: 0-8131-2437-9

Manufactured in the United States of America.

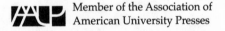 Member of the Association of
American University Presses

for Chris

Contents

Introduction

More than two millennia ago, Thucydides gave us a description of urban guerrilla warfare, involving Theban troops who were occupying the city of Plataea:[1]

The Thebans immediately closed up ranks to repel all attacks on them. Twice or thrice they beat back their assailants. But the Plataean men shouted and charged them, the women and slaves screamed and yelled from the houses and pelted them with stones and tiles; besides, it had been raining hard all night, and so at last their courage gave way and they turned and fled through the city. Most of the Theban fugitives were quite ignorant of the right way out, and this, with the mud and the darkness, and the fact that their pursuers knew their way about and could easily stop their escape, proved fatal to many.[1]

This description of classical Hellenic combat will reverberate remarkably through the urban conflicts to be examined in this volume.

A World of Cities

All across the globe, the human race is crowding into cities. Indeed, "a demographic upheaval of seismic proportions is today transforming almost the entire developing world from a predominantly rural society to an urban one."[2] After the decline of Rome, it required fifteen hundred years for a city to reach a population of one million: that was London. By 1900, perhaps 5 percent of the world's people lived in cities of over one hundred thousand inhabitants; by 2000, that figure had reached at least 45 percent. Most of this explosion of urban agglomerations is occurring in the less-developed areas of the globe: of the four hundred–plus cities with over one million inhabitants, over 60 percent are in the Third World.[3] Among today's largest cities are Manila and Jakarta with approximately ten million inhabitants each, Karachi and Calcutta with eleven million each, São Paulo with fourteen million, Bombay with eighteen million, and Mexico City with twenty million.

Of course, the growth of urban populations is accompanied by an expansion of the physical area covered by them, much of it in the form of sprawling shantytowns, without streets or addresses. Many governments are unable to supply even the most essential services to the inhabitants of these places. In Brazil, one hears of millions of uncared-for children and teenagers on the streets. And weapons abound in the cities of the underdeveloped world. In São Paulo, homicide accounts for nearly 90 percent of teenage male deaths; in such dreadful circumstances, gangs become the families and schools for countless youths and recruiting grounds for criminal and/or insurgent organizations.[4] Providing basic security or maintaining even a semblance of order in many of these urban agglomerations becomes ever more challenging.

While cities in less-developed countries grow larger and more ungovernable, U.S. military technology has rendered traditional rural or mountain-based insurgents more vulnerable than previously to sighting and attack.[5] At the same time, actual or would-be insurgent groups, and especially their leadership, tend to be composed predominantly of city types, a category whose members in the past have not always done well fighting or hiding in rural areas.

All these conditions are combining to shift the locus of insurgency from rural to urban areas, so that "in an increasingly urbanized world, it is likely that soldiers will find themselves fighting in cities."[6] It seems clear that, at least for the intermediate term, the future belongs to urban guerrilla warfare.

Elements of Traditional Guerrilla Warfare

What does such a shift portend? What, if anything, is unique or special about urban guerrilla warfare? How does it differ from traditional or "classic" guerrilla war in the hinterland? With regard to the latter type, "in the ideal, guerrillas are those who fight against ostensibly more powerful forces by unexpected attacks against vulnerable targets, and who are sustained by popular support, high morale, good intelligence, secure bases, and foreign assistance."[7] Guerrilla war is not a phenomenon peculiar to any particular ideology, century, or culture. It is the warfare of the weak, of those who, because of inadequate numbers, weapons, and training, cannot openly confront the regular forces of the opponent. Guerrillas therefore attack small enemy units or isolated outposts. They strike at night, or in the rain, or when the enemy troops are eating or have just finished a march or other exertion. They seek to interrupt the enemy's lines of communications by mining or damaging roads, blowing up railroad tracks, bridges, and trains, and ambushing convoys. Indeed, the ambush is a favorite tactic: for Mao Tse-tung, "the sole habitual tactic of a guerrilla unit is the ambush."[8] Hence, guerrillas will often attack some objective and then lie in wait for the relief column. Moreover, they can indefinitely protract the insurgency by avoiding engagements with the enemy except at times and places of their choosing.

Mao insisted that guerrillas should never fight unless certain of victory, that is, when they enjoy great numerical superiority at the point of contact. It is the element of surprise that allows well-led guerrillas always to outnumber their enemies in a particular combat. Surprise is the primary and decisive weapon of the guerrillas, making up for their lack of numbers and weapons. Sun Tzu wrote, "The enemy must not know where I intend to give battle; for if he does not know where I intend to give battle, he must prepare in a great many places. And when he prepares in a great many places, those I have to fight at any one place will be few."[9] For Mao, "the peculiar quality of the operations of a guerrilla unit lies in taking the enemy by surprise."[10] (But of course surprise has always been "the master key of all the great captains of history.")[11]

Surprise is possible because of mobility and intelligence. "The great superiority of a small guerrilla unit," according to Mao, "lies in its mobility."[12] And the Confederate guerrilla leader John Mosby wrote, "We had to make up by celerity for lack of numbers."[13] Thus, guerrillas suddenly appear and rapidly disperse. But mobility is useless and even dangerous without intelligence—up-to-the-hour information on where the enemy is, in what numbers, and in what condition. Guerrillas are dependent for much of their intelligence on the civilian inhabitants of the areas in which they are active. As a rule, therefore, rural guerrillas should operate in their native districts.

Guerrillas have proved themselves especially effective when they act in a symbiotic relationship with allied regular forces, as did Francis Marion, the Swamp Fox, with the troops of General Greene, or the Viet Cong with the North Vietnamese army. While there are some famous cases of guerrillas achieving impressive results without that kind of symbiotic relationship—Fidel Castro's followers and the mujahideen of Soviet Afghanistan come to mind—such instances are rare.

Outside assistance has been invaluable to guerrilla insurgencies, from the American War of Independence and Napoleonic Spain to Tito's Yugoslavia, South Vietnam, and Soviet Afghanistan.[14] In many cases where outside aid did not reach the guerrillas, as in the Boer War, British Malaya, French Algeria, and the Philippines (twice: after the Spanish American War and in World War II), they came to a bad end.

This subject of outside aid suggests the question of *where* guerrilla operations should take place. Almost two centuries ago, the great Clausewitz identified what he believed to be "the only conditions under which a general uprising can be effective."[15] The most important of those conditions are: (a) the guerrillas should operate over a wide area, so that their movements do not become stereotyped and they cannot be surrounded easily; (b) they should stay away from the seacoast, so that the government cannot make use of amphibious movements against them; (c) they should choose as the center of their activity an area of rough terrain, thus impeding the movements of heavily armed and well-equipped hostile troops while rewarding the lightly armed guerrillas with relative mobility (the Roman word for the baggage a regular army carried around with it was *impedimenta*). And of course, for an uprising to be "general," by definition it has to have the support of most of the population of the affected region, a condition most definitely lacking in some of the cases we shall examine in this book.

A Maoist Perspective

More than a hundred years after Clausewitz penned his advice for guerrillas, Mao Tse-tung emerged as the leader of probably the largest and certainly the most famous insurgency in modern history. He believed the proper objective of guerrillas was to establish control of the countryside and thus surround the cities, forcing them into submission. Guerrilla warfare must be *protracted,* so that the guerrillas have time to build up their strength and skills. (Protraction of the conflict also stems from the guerrillas' conviction that their will to prevail is superior to that of their opponents.) Mao maintained that fulfilling these aims required the guerrillas to possess at least one safe geographical base. That meant some place, some area within the boundaries of the state, that counterinsurgent forces could not effectively reach, or would not attempt, for whatever reasons, to occupy. Such a base would be invaluable to guerrillas: within it they could train and indoctrinate recruits; care for the sick and wounded; and stockpile munitions, food, and medicine. Hence, for Mao protracted insurgency would not be possible in a small country and a fortiori could not be possible *within the constricted area of a city.*[16]

Modern aircraft and satellite surveillance now have made the existence of internal safe bases close to impossible, except in areas where the state has been customarily absent, as for instance in parts of Peru and Colombia. Moreover, insurgencies in small territories like Palestine, Cyprus, Northern Ireland, Sri Lanka, and Chechnya seem to contradict Mao's belief that a guerrilla effort cannot be viable without extensive operational terrain. Nevertheless, there can be no doubt that it was China's vast area and primitive transportation network, as well as the quite inadequate numbers of Japanese troops there, that saved Mao's guerrillas from the armies of Imperial Japan and Chiang Kai-shek. (The number of troops that Japan committed to the conquest of China was proportionately equivalent to President Lincoln's attempting to subdue the Confederacy with an army of nineteen thousand.) And when establishing a secure base has not been possible, guerrillas have sometimes found a substitute for it in the form of a sanctuary across an international border, as with the Greek insurgents after World War II, the mujahideen in Soviet Afghanistan, and the Communists in Vietnam, among others.

Guerrilla Warfare in Cities

Certainly very few would wish to turn the teachings of Clausewitz and Mao Tse-tung, or even clear lessons learned from past guerrilla conflicts, into a rigid and infallible formula for insurgent victory. But what if the insurgents *systematically violate* nearly all such precepts—something that urban guerrillas certainly do? In almost every example we will study here, urban guerillas abandoned the possibility of possessing a secure base or a cross-border sanctuary. Outside help did not arrive (in the case of Warsaw, for very particular reasons). No symbiotic relationship with friendly conventional forces existed (with the instructive exception of Saigon). For urban guerrillas, operating in neighborhoods where they were known could in many instances have been fatal. And perhaps most consequential of all, urban guerrillas exposed themselves to efforts by counterinsurgent forces to surround and isolate them.

But however un-Clausewitzian and un-Maoist, does not urban guerrilla war at least reflect the classic Bolshevik formula: seize the capital city and then conquer the countryside (just the reverse of the Maoist rubric)? No, it does not; the Bolshevik seizure of Petrograd in Red October 1917 took place in a couple of days, really in a matter of hours. The Kerensky regime the Bolsheviks overthrew had been abandoned by everyone, most notably by its own army. Far from being an example of protracted guerrilla combat, the events in Petrograd were a coup d'état. Besides, as we shall see, in Algiers, Montevideo, São Paulo, Saigon, and Belfast, it became very difficult to distinguish urban guerrilla warfare from simple terrorism, that is, violence directed at civilians to frighten, disorient, or punish them.[17] Lenin's voluminous works contain several condemnations of terrorism.[18] Terrorists cut themselves off from the masses through their secrecy and anonymity; they substitute activism for analysis, the individual for the mass; through their bombings of public places and attacks on urban infrastructure they inconvenience, horrify, or kill members of the proletariat, and so on. Partly for such reasons, urban insurgents in Uruguay and Brazil received little public support, and often met hostility from the official Communist Parties of those countries.

To summarize thus far: years ago, anyone who took seriously the teachings of Clausewitz and/or Mao, or studied examples of successful past guerrilla insurgencies, might well have been tempted to conclude that the phrase "urban guerrilla war" was close to being an oxymoron. In any case, it will surprise no reader of this book that all of the urban-based insurgencies examined in it suffered utter defeat. Nevertheless, because of the conditions and processes identified earlier in this introduction, students of irregular warfare are convinced that in the years ahead, conflicts of this type will become ever more common. Such a prospect—especially in light of events from Chechnya to Iraq—surely makes a continuing study of counterinsurgency in urban environments necessary and even urgent.

The Cases We Examine

The urban guerrilla conflicts considered here include Warsaw 1944, Budapest 1956, Algiers 1957, Montevideo and São Paulo in the 1960s, Saigon 1968 (the Tet Offensive), Northern Ireland (mainly Belfast) 1970–1998, and Grozny 1994–1996. Because they all occurred in the twentieth century, they have aspects that are recognizable or even familiar. They are diverse enough chronologically and geographically to ensure that any striking similarities among them will not be time- or culture-bound, but not so numerous as to prevent that consideration of detail and nuance that is usually lacking in large quantitative studies. These cases also present an opportunity to compare the methods of a broad panoply of urban *counterinsurgents*, from Nazi Germany and the USSR to France, Britain, Russia, and the United States, as well as Uruguay and Brazil.

Moreover, these city insurgencies differ widely not only as to when and where they arose but also as to the circumstances of their origin, the nature and number of their participants and sympathizers, their level of intensity, their duration, the consequences of their suppression, and the meaning they may hold for us today. For example, in Warsaw, Budapest, Algiers, Belfast, and Grozny the insurgents fought soldiers who were, or were perceived as, foreign; this was not the case in either Montevideo or São Paulo, and it was only partly the case in Saigon. Another salient distinction among these urban conflicts derives from the nature of the relationship between the guerrillas and the general population of the city in which the fighting occurred. Some of these insurgencies—Warsaw, Budapest, Grozny—were genuinely popular movements. Some—Algiers, Montevideo, São Paulo, Belfast—were distinctly minoritarian and/or elitist. One—Saigon—was waged mainly by outsiders from far beyond the city and even alien to it. In half of the cases—Algiers, São Paulo, Saigon, and Belfast—the majority of the population was clearly hostile to the insurgents. At least three—Algiers, Montevideo, and Belfast—confronted officially democratic regimes. Only two of these urban insurgencies—Warsaw and Saigon—took place in the midst of a general war , and, very notably, only one—Saigon—was waged in the name of establishing an orthodox Communist regime.

Clearly, then, although the military aspects of these conflicts predictably attract much interest, and will receive due consideration in this book, any serious effort to understand urban guerrilla warfare requires close attention to its political elements.

1

Warsaw 1944

Poland was the scene of Europe's largest resistance movement during World War II. The principal act of that movement was the Warsaw Rising of 1944, called by its most recent historian "the archetypal model of urban guerrilla warfare." Although eventually defeated, the Warsaw uprising had the gravest consequences for the emerging postwar world: "The Rising did not cause the Cold War by itself. But it was a major step in that direction."[1] Nevertheless, these Warsaw events, with their complexity, nobility, and tragedy, have faded almost completely from Western consciousness.

Poland Halts the Red Tide

Josef Stalin played a malevolent and determining role in the outcome of the Warsaw Rising. A key to Stalin's attitude toward that struggle can be found in the Russo-Polish conflict following World War I. The 1920 Bolshevik invasion of Poland—the first Soviet invasion of Europe—is one of the least known of modern wars, but its outcome may have been nearly as decisive for the destiny of Europe as Charles Martel's victory at Tours.[2]

The Kingdom of Poland, once one of the largest in Europe, had disappeared at the end of the eighteenth century, partitioned by Prussia, Austria, and Russia. In 1918, with the defeat or collapse of those partitioning empires, a Polish state reemerged. The army of the new state was composed largely of Polish units of the former Tsarist and Habsburg armies. Its principal figure was General Jozef

Pilsudski (1867–1931). He had joined the Socialist Party as a youth was imprisoned or exiled for agitation several times, and organized the Polish Legion under the Habsburgs during World War I. Taking command of Polish forces in Warsaw in 1918, he declared Poland independent.

Pilsudski developed a truly grandiose geopolitical strategy. He wanted Poland's new frontiers to stretch as far east as possible. This extensive Poland would be the fulcrum of an alliance of new states in eastern and central Europe—Ukraine, Finland, and the Baltic and Caucasian republics—that would push Russia away from the shores of the Baltic and Black Seas, undoing the work of Peter and Catherine and setting Russia on the road to second-rank status.

The Russo-Polish boundary was not settled at Versailles. After negotiations with the Lenin regime had clearly failed, on April 25, 1920, Pilsudski launched an offensive. The Polish occupation of Kiev on May 6 aroused Russian nationalist fervor, and in reaction many former Tsarist officers joined the Red Army when its need for officers was most acute. The capture of Kiev dangerously overextended Polish lines. Woefully short of ammunition, and factories to produce it, the new Polish army evacuated the city on June 12. Meanwhile, the British Labour Party forbade workers to load munitions on ships headed for Poland. The French Socialists took the same stance.

The Red Army commander for the assault on Poland was Mikhail Tukhachevsky, twenty-seven years old, like Napoleon in his Italian campaign. Lenin informed the world, "We shall break the crust of Polish bourgeois resistance with the bayonets of the Red Army."[3] Following behind the Russian troops were thousands of horse-drawn carts intended for looting every inch of conquered Poland.

At the end of July 1920, the Red Army established a "government of Communist Poland" in the town of Bialystok, just as Stalin would do years later in Lublin. But as the Red Army advanced into Poland, few Polish peasants joined or assisted it. And as they neared the gates of Warsaw, the Bolsheviks were deeply dismayed to learn that the city's factory workers were volunteering for the Polish army.

General Wladyslaw Sikorski, who would head the Polish government in exile in World War II, commanded the Polish forces in front of Warsaw. Within the city, almost the entire diplomatic corps had fled westward, except for the Vatican envoy, Archbishop Achille

Ratti (later to become Pius XI). In August, when things looked very bleak, the White Russian offensive in the Crimea under Baron Wrangel relieved some of the pressure on Warsaw. More importantly, Tukhachevsky's advance had badly overstretched his supply lines. His long flanks were now exposed to counterattack. Indeed, a copy of Pilsudski's plans for just such a stroke fell into Tukhachevsky's hands, but he dismissed it as a deception.[4] Pilsudski launched his counterattack on August 16; it was the turning point of the war.

A persistent myth holds that French general Maxime Weygand, chief of staff of the famous General Foch, saved Warsaw. This Weygand myth suited the purposes of the Bolsheviks, Pilsudski's Polish critics, and French premier Millerand. But the honors of victory belong above all to Pilsudski, who appeared everywhere on the front line, heartening his troops, some of whom were barefooted and almost without ammunition. Weygand himself gallantly admitted that "the victory, the plan and the army were Polish."[5] (Another French officer in Warsaw, a young captain named Charles de Gaulle, politely declined the offer of a permanent commission in the Polish army.) Late in September Pilsudski attacked Tukhachevsky again, in the Battle of the Nieman River, and completed the Bolshevik defeat. An armistice took effect on October 18, 1920; the Treaty of Riga, signed in March 1921, fixed Poland's eastern frontier until 1939. Polish casualties in the war totaled over 250,000, including 48,000 dead. Red Army losses in casualties and prisoners also exceeded a quarter million, plus scores of heavy guns.[6]

Concerning this battle of Warsaw, the distinguished British military historian J. F. C. Fuller wrote: "The influence of this decisive battle on history . . . was little grasped by Western Europe and has remained little noticed."[7] Yet Tukhachevsky himself declared, "There is not the slightest doubt that, had we been victorious on the [River] Vistula [which runs through Warsaw roughly south to north], the revolution would have set light to the entire continent of Europe."[8] The British ambassador to Berlin, Lord D'Abernon, believed that if Warsaw had fallen, "Bolshevism would have spread throughout Central Europe and might well have penetrated the whole continent."[9] Therefore, D'Abernon continued, "it should be the task of political writers to explain to European opinion that *Poland saved Europe in 1920*, and that it is necessary to keep Poland powerful."[10]

British historian E. H. Carr concurs: "It was not the Red Army, but the cause of World Revolution, which suffered defeat in front of Warsaw in August 1920."[11]

Thus Poland had broken free of the Russian Empire, rejected Bolshevism, and humiliated the Red Army. But the Poles would eventually pay a very heavy price for this victory. Their defeat of Russia, unaided, convinced Polish leaders that they needed to fear neither Germany nor the USSR. And the young Josef Stalin, involved peripherally but not unimportantly in these Warsaw events, conceived a personal hatred for that city and the whole Polish leadership class, including General Sikorski, that he would brutally manifest less than twenty years later.

World War II

Pilsudski had restored a great deal of Poland's historic territory. His success illustrates the illusion that empire means strength and security. The new Poland contained too many ethno-religious minorities: Ukrainians, White Russians, Germans, unassimilated Jews, and others. These minorities were of two types: the territorially concentrated, such as Ukrainians and White Russians, and the dispersed, such as Germans and Jews. Reinforcing these cleavages, most ethnic groups in Poland were religiously compact: the Poles were Catholic, the White Russians Orthodox, the Germans Protestants, and so on. In the 1921 census, only 69 percent of the state's inhabitants gave their nationality as Polish, and that figure is almost certainly too high.

Germans in Poland numbered at least one million. "The central feature of the history of the German minority [in Poland] between 1935 and 1939 was its almost complete conversion to National Socialism [Nazism]."[12] The invasion in 1939 revealed many of them as spies and saboteurs, and almost all of them would collaborate with the Nazi occupation.

The Ukrainians in Poland comprised seven million, almost all peasants, who lived between towns with Polish and Jewish majorities. One million White Russians made up the majority of the population in two eastern provinces; they too were almost all peasants living around towns populated by Poles and Jews.

The 1931 census counted 3.1 million Jews, of whom 80 percent identified Yiddish as their mother tongue. More than 40 percent of these Jews lived in towns larger than twenty thousand. The majority of all lawyers in Poland and nearly half of all physicians were Jews. Nevertheless, by 1939 a large proportion of Polish Jews were dependent on relief, largely private, financed by U.S. Jewish organizations. Polish governments supported Jewish emigration to Palestine, but the British authorities there severely limited the number of newcomers.[13]

Poland was an agricultural country and relatively poor: in 1938, it had one automobile per thousand inhabitants, compared to seven in Czechoslovakia and ten in Italy. Incredibly, the politicians at Versailles had classified Poland as part of the defeated Central Powers; therefore it was allowed no claims for reparations at war's end.

In August 1939 Hitler and Stalin signed their infamous pact, the essential prelude to a renewed world conflict. The Germans invaded Poland without a declaration of war on September 1, attacking from three sides across the 1,750-mile frontier. In hindsight it is clear that at the outbreak of war Polish forces should have been grouped around Warsaw and behind the River Vistula, but the most economically valuable Polish areas were close to the German borders, and thus the Polish Army was mainly deployed there, and defeated there. The Poles had expected help from a French attack on Germany, which never materialized, even though most German forces had been sent into Poland, with only screening forces left on the French frontier. "A French attack against the weak German defensive front on the Siegfried Line . . . would, as far as is humanly possible to judge, have led to a very quick military defeat of Germany and therefore an end of the war."[14] But a French attack never came.

Poland's predominantly infantry army could not pull back eastward fast enough to avoid encirclement by fast-moving German armored divisions. The Luftwaffe, supreme in the air, blasted bridges, roads, and railways to hinder Polish movements, as well as attacking troops on the march. Fifth columnists, mainly members of Poland's Germanic minority, aided these activities. The final blow fell on September 17, when the Soviet army invaded from the east. The next day the Polish government and army high command crossed into Romania (with which Poland had a common frontier in 1939).

Besieged Warsaw held out under a horrendous pounding until September 28. The last important Polish units surrendered on October 5. In the brief conflict 70,000 Polish soldiers died, with another 130,000 wounded. Six thousand had been killed and 16,000 wounded in the defense of Warsaw. German casualties numbered between 45,000 and 60,000, of whom 10,500 were killed. The destruction of the Polish army was a dress rehearsal for the defeat of the French army, "the finest in the world," eight months later. Prostrated Poland was divided into three areas: provinces annexed in the east by Stalin, provinces annexed in the west by Hitler, and the remaining areas, in the center, called the General Government, under Nazi occupation.[15]

The Origins of the Resistance

How, in the aftermath of total defeat and occupation by two overwhelmingly powerful and savagely repressive neighbors, were the Poles able to organize a widespread and sustained resistance? For one reason, the war had been brief, with little loss of life and property compared to what was to come. For another, Polish society was imbued with a "tradition of active resistance and insurrection and the conviction that national identity and sovereignty can be preserved and restored through sacrifice."[16] Besides, there were encouraging prospects of outside assistance: from the Polish government in exile (hereafter called PGE) in Paris, and from mighty allies, first the British and later the Americans, in whom many Poles had a truly pathetic trust. The U.S. government actually did provide millions of dollars over several years to the underground, money that supported sabotage, espionage, and international communications.

But perhaps the most crucial factor in the emergence of a successful resistance was the behavior of the Nazi occupiers: "Nowhere in the whole Nazi empire was the 'Master Race' given such complete control over a conquered nation so comprehensively enslaved."[17] Indeed, "the conditions of German occupation were worse for the Poles than for any other nation except the Jews."[18] German policy was total exploitation; German demands on the Polish people were unlimited and impossible; destruction of the Poles as a people was the aim. All Poles were publicly treated as members of an inferior race, with no gradations of education, wealth, or status. One and a half million Poles were expelled from the provinces annexed to Germany. Thousands of young Polish children were kidnapped, to be raised as Germans. The Nazis imposed compulsory labor, reduced food allowances to below survival levels, and publicly executed hostages. Epidemics of tuberculosis became normal, while the psychological damage, especially to youths, is incalculable. In the words of a famous resistance leader: "We in Poland never met the so-called 'good Germans.'"[19]

The centerpiece of German occupation policy was extermination of the intelligentsia. "The term 'Polish intelligentsia' covers primarily Polish priests, teachers (including university lecturers), doctors, dentists, veterinary surgeons, officers, executives, business men, landowners, writers, journalists, plus all the people who have received a higher or secondary education."[20] The SS murdered priests with special ferocity.[21]

Thus the German occupation was totally illegitimate and destructive, with no serious effort to attract and organize collaborators among any significant element of the Polish population. So indiscriminately and relentlessly harsh was the German regime that, almost uniquely in occupied Europe, "Poland produced no Quisling."[22]

Out of this crucible emerged the Armja Krajowa, the Home Army, or AK. It had its official beginnings in September 1939, when the commander of the troops defending Warsaw commissioned an underground military organization, named the Home Army by prime minister in exile Sikorski in 1942.

The principal aims of the AK were, first, to support the Allies by transmitting intelligence and creating diversions, and, second, to prepare for a national uprising as the hour of German collapse neared.[23] Soldiers of the AK were of three classes: those who led a double life as private citizens and AK members; full-time conspirators; and fighters in the forests, who usually wore Polish uniforms. AK guerrilla units were active wherever the terrain and the local population were favorable.

"Polish nationalism," writes Richard Lukas, "was synonymous with Catholicism. The Church had always provided the foundation of Polish nationalism, especially during periods of oppression."[24]

The religious roots of Polish nationalism were evident in the Home Army oath: "Before God the Almighty, before the Holy Virgin Mary, Queen of the Crown of Poland, I put my hand on this Holy Cross, the symbol of martyrdom and salvation, and I swear that I will defend the honor of Poland with all my might, that I will fight with arms in hand to liberate her from slavery, notwithstanding the sacrifice of my own life, that I will be absolutely obedient to my superiors, that I will keep the secret whatever the cost may be."[25] At the start of 1943, the AK had 200,000 members. By July 1944 this figure had grown to possibly 380,000. Exact enumeration was always problematic because of the secret nature of the organization.[26]

Alongside the AK, the resistance was organized by political parties—National Democrats, Peasants, and Socialists—that had authentic roots in the population, established leadership and organizing experience (sometimes in semi-clandestine circumstances), and no involvement with the now-discredited foreign policy of the prewar regime. Because the defeat and occupation were blamed on the former regime, only an underground organized by the former opposition parties would be able to gain wide popular support. Crucially, the Polish Socialist Party embraced Polish nationalism and hostility to Russia. All these groups accepted the authority of Wladyslaw Sikorski, a hero in the 1920 defense of Warsaw, who became prime minister and commander of all Polish armed forces in France in September 1939.[27] Thus the Polish underground was a collaboration of the government in exile, the Home Army, and the major political parties, some of whom had had their own militias before the war. But the Communists and extreme rightist groups remained aloof from this union.

German mass reprisals for the slightest act of resistance were intended to force the AK to conclude that the struggle was not worth the cost, and also to drive a wedge between the civil population and the AK. But Nazi random shootings, hostage taking, and kidnapping of young men and women from city streets proved that passivity offered no refuge. All Poles came to feel subject to terror, and belonging to the Home Army offered the protection of an active intelligence organization. Many youths fled into the forests and joined the AK there.[28]

Supplying Intelligence

Undoubtedly, the AK's most valuable service to the Allies was providing them with intelligence. Even before the war—as early as 1932—Polish intelligence agents obtained one of the vaunted German Enigma encoding machines. Polish knowledge and samples of Enigma were carried to France in 1939, and then to England after the fall of France in 1940. The ability of the Allies to read Enigma traffic affected the entire course of World War II.[29]

"The Poles in London," wrote William Casey, later director of the CIA, "ran one of the most efficient and ambitious of the exile intelligence services."[30] During the occupation, German supply dumps, prison camps, railroad stations, depots, and airfields in Poland and eastern Germany were under the constant observation of AK intelligence, which provided, among other things, precise warnings of the Nazi invasion of the USSR. The AK discovered the secret activities at Peenemunde, which enabled the Royal Air Force (RAF) to attack factories there on August 15, 1943, setting back German V1 rocket production by several months.[31] In May 1944 the AK obtained intact an entire V2 rocket and sent its detailed description and some parts to London.[32] Polish postal workers randomly opened and photographed letters sent home by German soldiers, a priceless source of information on German army morale and movements. The AK ran a whole series of wireless stations, ingeniously overcoming the dangers of having their radios discovered.[33] (The BBC communicated with the AK via prearranged musical selections.) The resistance also sheltered escaped Allied prisoners of war.[34]

Sabotage was another major AK activity. Between January 1, 1941, and June 30, 1944, the resistance damaged 6,900 locomotives and 19,000 railway cars; destroyed twenty-eight aircraft, 4,300 mainly military motor vehicles, thirty-eight railroad bridges, and 4,700 tons of fuel; and killed 5,733 Germans.[35] AK sabotaging of deliveries of Polish quotas of food and matériel to Germany was worth several divisions to the Allied cause.[36]

Home Army Executions

The AK developed a judicial mechanism for restraining Nazi brutality, at least to some degree, as well as for silencing Polish traitors and spies. Usually, a panel of three Polish jurists would hear an indictment in secret. It could then issue one of three verdicts: guilty, not guilty, or case postponed because of the unsatisfactory nature of the evidence (this last being the most common). A verdict of guilty could carry the death penalty, but a local resistance commander could order an execution without a trial in some grave emergency (for example, if a spy or traitor was about to reveal someone's name to the Gestapo). Naturally, many Polish jurists were quite reluctant to serve on these panels because of the usual impossibility of having the accused person appear in his own defense. But the AK set up the system because of the urgent need both to restrain unauthorized assassination and to provide a legal sanction for reprisals against officials who exceeded even the usual Nazi standards of savagery. To avoid the development of a corps of professional assassins, no AK member could participate in more than three executions.[37]

The most famous AK reprisal involved General Franz Kutschera, who had begun the practice of random street executions in Warsaw. Having warned Kutschera twice that continuing this activity would result in his death, the AK shot him dead in the street on February 1, 1944. His successor evidently took this example to heart, because the Germans stopped performing public executions in the capital.[38] The AK published its own newspaper, which it mailed regularly to the Gestapo. The paper detailed which acts of sabotage and execution had been committed in retaliation for which act of Nazi brutality. AK leaders believed that many Gestapo officials became more circumspect in their actions for fear of reprisals.

The resistance published several other newspapers, some by the parties, one by the local representatives of the PGE. These papers helped to counteract feelings of isolation imposed by the Germans, contradicted German propaganda, issued instructions to the public from the PGE and the AK, and provided a forum for the discussion of problems of everyday life and alternative futures after the war. The resistance also published books—Polish classics, children's textbooks, prayer books—that were forbidden by the Nazis. They were always able to obtain plenty of paper from corrupt Nazi officials.[39]

Because the AK was so large (eventually four hundred thousand men and women), it was not difficult for the Gestapo to capture members of it and, through torture, learn a great deal. Hence most AK members lived in constant expectation of Gestapo arrest.[40] Indeed, prior to the Warsaw Rising, the Germans killed or captured sixty-two thousand AK members.[41] The AK commander in chief, General Rowecki, was betrayed to the Gestapo three days before the airplane-crash death of Prime Minister Sikorski. General Bor succeeded the imprisoned Rowecki, whom SS chief Heinrich Himmler would kill in retaliation for the Warsaw Rising. Cracow, capital of the General Government (the heart of Poland that had not been annexed by either Germany or the USSR), was the headquarters of the Gestapo and a particularly dangerous place, four AK commanders being caught there.

Polish Fighters Abroad

Resistance activities were not Poland's only contribution to the Allied cause. Scores of thousands of Poles fought as regular troops on both the western and eastern fronts. At the time of the Nazi conquest in 1939, many Polish soldiers escaped through Hungary and Romania to France or the Middle East. They comprised one cavalry and three infantry divisions under the French army, and thousands of them were taken prisoner in the fall of France in June 1940.[42] Nevertheless, the Dunkirk evacuation lifted twenty-four thousand Polish troops to England; Polish pilots made up four of fifty-six squadrons of the famous RAF Fighter Command during the Battle of Britain, accounting for 15 percent of German aircraft destroyed.[43] Thousands of Polish soldiers remained behind in occupied France, and many of them became active in French resistance organizations.

In August 1941, an agreement between the PGE and Stalin provided for the formation, on Soviet soil, of a Polish army composed of those Polish prisoners of war whom the Soviets had not yet starved or brutalized to death. The Polish government named General Wladyslaw Anders, hitherto a prisoner in Moscow's infamous Lubianka prison, as commander of this new force. But the Soviets threw every obstacle in the path of organizing his army, so in August 1942, Anders led his troops into Iran.[44]

These soldiers, eventually known as the Second Polish Corps, played a key role in the bloody Italian campaign. The Second Polish Corps would "come to be recognized as one of the great fighting formations of the war, its spirit charged," Harold Macmillan would recall, "with a lighthearted disdain for danger the like of which he had met in no other."[45] The First Armoured Division, formed in Britain of Polish soldiers, played a major role in the fierce Normandy fighting.[46] At the time of Germany's surrender, 250,000 Polish troops were serving in the western theater, and elements of these had fought in Libya, Norway, Belgium, and the Netherlands, as well as in Normandy.[47] The Soviets eventually organized another 170,000 Polish troops, originally under the command of Zygmunt Berling, a deserter from the Polish army.

The Katyn Massacre

In 1940, the PGE in London and Polish military units in Europe gradually became aware that fifteen thousand soldiers, mostly officers —45 percent of the officer corps—were unaccounted for. In February 1943, the German army announced its discovery of mass graves in Katyn forest, ten miles west of Smolensk. These graves contained the bodies of thousands of Polish officers, each of whom had been shot in the back of the head. The dead officers included many hundreds of former teachers, physicians, university professors, writers—the cream of the Polish intelligentsia. At least one of the executed officers was a woman.

Four separate commissions from different countries examined the graves at Katyn, including a Soviet one. From the estimated time of the deaths (on which all agreed except the Soviets), it was clear that the officers had been killed while the Katyn area was still under Soviet control. When the PGE asked the International Red Cross for an investigation, Stalin broke relations with the Poles.

In London, and especially in Washington, the emphasis was on keeping the wartime alliance together at all costs. The Allies rightly feared the possibility of a separate peace between Germany and Russia: recall that Stalin had been Hitler's eager partner until Hitler had abruptly ended the alliance. Thus, the Soviets had to be appeased at any price, which meant swallowing Katyn and anything else the Soviets might do with regard to Poland.[48] The British ambassador to the USSR told the Polish foreign minister that "the easiest way out of this [Katyn] difficulty would be the acceptance of the findings of the Soviet Commission that enquired into the crime."[49]

The Stalin regime always insisted that the Katyn massacres had been a German atrocity. Yet no Nazi was ever charged with the murders at the Nuremburg War Crimes Trials, and there was no protest over this stupefying omission from the postwar Communist regime in Warsaw. "It was decided by the victorious governments concerned that the issue should be avoided and the crime of Katyn was never probed in detail."[50]

In April 1990, fifty years after the deed, Mikhail Gorbachev admitted Soviet responsibility for the Katyn mass murders.[51] For decades after Germany's surrender, punishment continued to be meted out to Nazi war criminals. Nobody has been punished for the countless thousands of deaths resulting from Stalin's deportations of Polish civilians in 1939–1941. No one has been punished for the murders of thousands of Polish officers at Katyn.[52]

The Warsaw Ghetto Rising, April 19–May 16, 1943

In the spring of 1943, the Warsaw Ghetto erupted in revolt, the first Jewish rebellion in nearly two thousand years. "The Uprising was literally a revolution in Jewish history"[53] because "it signaled the beginning of an iron militancy rooted in the will to survive, a militancy that was to be given form and direction by the creation of the State of Israel."[54]

Warsaw had been the greatest center of Jewish life in eastern Europe. In 1939, the Jewish population of the city was 375,000 out of 1.3 million; many Jews were prominent in education, law, medicine, finance, trade, and industry. But in prewar Poland, great numbers of Jews resolutely resisted assimilation, demanding legal recognition as a separate people. "Jews in Poland saw themselves as part of the Jewish people dispersed throughout the world and less as an integral part of Polish society."[55] This was true not only for the Orthodox but for Zionists and Bundists (Socialists) as well. Nevertheless, the defeat and occupation of the Polish state would be an unparalleled disaster for Polish Jews. Unlike other regimes in prewar central and eastern Europe, the Pilsudski government never used the Jews as scapegoats. And before 1939, there was no Warsaw Ghetto: it was the Nazis who began its construction in April 1941 and completed it by November.

Most of the leaders of the Warsaw Jewish community fled east in 1939 (among those departing was the young Menachem Begin). Consequently the future ghetto had no internal direction, and its population was disproportionately composed of women, children, and old men.[56] At its height the ghetto population reached 460,000. The impossible overcrowding and engineered malnutrition produced disease, as well as conspicuous consumption and class tensions.[57] A Judenrat (Jewish council) was organized to run the ghetto (the head of which killed himself in July 1942). High officers of the Judenrat and the Jewish Police were the targets of assassination by Jewish resistance groups. As Stalin had delivered to Hitler those German Communists who had escaped to Russia after Hitler came to power, so he now handed over to the Nazis young Jews who managed to escape to Russian territory.[58] In the midst of all this misery, the German army came to rely on clothing, brushes, and other items produced inside the ghetto.

Many Jews had thought or hoped that the much-trumpeted Final Solution meant the expulsion of all the Jews from German-occupied Europe. As late as July 1940 Hans Frank, governor of the General Government, believed the solution to the "Jewish problem" would be transportation to Madagascar.[59] Armed revolt would only take place when Jews realized what the Final Solution really meant. From January 1942, the announced policy of the Third Reich was the total annihilation of the Jewish people. Between July and September of that year, Nazi deportations reduced the Warsaw ghetto population to around sixty thousand. In a matter of a few weeks three hundred thousand Jews were expelled or murdered, with no resistance. All this occurred because the infrastructure of annihilation—death camps, railway transport, gas chambers—was ready. The Bundists began passing on, through the AK, news to the outside world of the mass slaughter of Jews.

The uprising, when it came, took place not in the ghetto of close to half a million Jews, but among its remnant. Given the constricted area of the ghetto, its much-reduced population, its paucity of weapons, and the total lack of Nazi inhibitions, those who organized the uprising knew it was suicide. The AK was not prepared to participate, nor was there a possibility of a coordinated movement with ghettos in other cities, isolated as they were one from another and the surrounding population, and the whole world. The Jews of the Warsaw Ghetto were all alone—alone with the Nazis.

Nevertheless, "the mute acceptance of their fate and the sense of hopelessness that accompanied the mass expulsions in the summer of 1942 gave way to more defiant attitudes."[60] One participant in the rising wrote her husband, "It was obvious to us that the Germans would liquidate us. We said to ourselves that in this situation we must at least kill as many Germans as possible and stay alive as long as possible."[61]

Even within this doomed little world, unity proved elusive in the face of deep and bitter differences dating from before the war, between the religious and the secular, between Zionists and anti-Zionists.[62] "Even the Nazi threat of total destruction could not unify the Jews"—not that unification would have made any difference to the outcome.[63] Thus, when the Jewish Fighting Organization (ZOB) came into existence in July 1942, several dissident groups formed their own separate units, most prominent of which was the Jewish Fighting Union (ZZW). These different groups obtained weapons from the AK; they also made illegal purchases on the Aryan side of the wall, and produced their own inside the ghetto. Some of their leaders received training in street-fighting tactics from AK officers.

On January 18, 1943, the first clashes between Nazis and armed Jews took place in the ghetto. Like a flash of lightning among Jews and Germans alike, they lit the way to the uprising, which began April 19, the first night of Passover. The ZOB aimed its first blows at Judenrat members and the Jewish Police. It also destroyed materials and goods needed by the German army.

The uprising astounded the Nazis from Warsaw all the way to Berlin. Himmler sent SS general Jürgen Stroop to suppress the troubles in the ghetto. The Germans employed more than 2,000 troops and police on an average day, along with armored cars, tanks, and, of course, artillery. Facing them were some 750 ZOB/ZZW, armed mainly with revolvers; homemade hand grenades; Molotov cocktails; and a few machine guns bought, stolen, or captured from the Germans.[64] The ZOB often released captured German soldiers, but not their SS prisoners.

Many within the ghetto reacted unfavorably to the announcements of a rising.[65] Sometimes Jewish informers guided Nazis to hidden holdouts.[66] The Nazis directed poisonous gases into bunkers occupied by the resistance. Afraid of ambushes, frightened now to go down into cellars, they began to burn the ghetto. "During the day the sky was filled with smoke, and at night with an enormous wheel of fire."[67] Some ZZB members escaped to the woods around Warsaw but were rounded up by German troops. Many in the ZOB killed themselves rather than be captured.

As a symbol of their victory, the Nazis blew up the great synagogue, which was, in fact, outside the ghetto. Stroop described the ghetto fighting in the most dramatic terms, and for his prowess against these few hundred poorly armed civilians, he was actually awarded the Iron Cross.

At the time of the Ghetto Rising, the PGE was preoccupied with revelations about the Katyn massacres. Nevertheless, Prime Minister Sikorski declared on May 5, 1943, that inside the Warsaw Ghetto "the greatest crime in the history of mankind is being enacted."[68] But one week later, U.S. Army major Arthur Goldberg (later a justice of the U.S. Supreme Court) told a Bund activist in London that the Allies could send no aid to the fighters in the ghetto. The man who received this news, Shmuel Zygielbojm, burned himself to death in front of the Parliament building.

The question of direct outside assistance to the ghetto is complicated. The AK watched the inhabitants of the ghetto submit in silence to the massive population removals in 1942. The AK leaders did not believe that any arms they supplied the ghetto, from their own scanty supplies, would be used effectively, given its small area and now sparse population. Besides, the main purpose of the AK was to prepare for a general uprising of all Poland at the most strategic time, not to use up munitions and men at a time and place of the Nazis' choosing.[69] In 1943, the AK was neither equipped nor organized to undertake an effective armed uprising.[70]

Suspicion and dislike of Jews was certainly widespread in Polish society, but that is not the whole story of life under the Nazi boot. Poland was the only occupied country in which the Germans imposed the death penalty for assisting Jews.[71] Many Poles adopted Jewish children to save them; General Bor relates a devastating incident of a mother whose own two children were shot in her home before her eyes by the Gestapo, who then told her, "Now you can bring up your Jewish brat."[72] After the ghetto was destroyed, hundreds of surviving Jews, including members of the ZOB, participated in the AK-led Warsaw Rising of 1944.[73] "General Bor, in his reports to the PGE in London, gave honorable mention to the many acts of Jewish heroism."[74]

Why Did the AK Rise?

In its early years, the AK had not planned to fight in Warsaw, because of fear of German reprisals against the civilian population. Instead, AK units were to move west to attack retreating German columns. General Anders, head of the famous Second Polish Corps, and other leaders were opposed to a Warsaw rising.[75] Apparently Prime Minister Sikorski wanted no general uprising at all without prior agreement on exactly what aid the Allies would provide to the AK. That was also the position of the commander in chief in exile of Polish forces, General Sosnkowski. For their part, the British did not insist on a rising; they were content for the Poles to continue with their intelligence and sabotage activities.[76] The historian Jan Ciechanowski has written that the Warsaw Rising was a grave mistake, because it destroyed the AK and discredited the PGE.[77] Clearly, if faced with an AK uprising, the Nazis could be counted on to respond with the same savagery they had shown toward the ghetto revolt.

Why, then, did the Warsaw Rising occur?

In the first place, the pressures felt by those who lived in an insane Nazi hell-world were increasing every day. The AK was developing an "overwhelming impatience to fight."[78] But there were plausible arguments in favor of a rising. General Bor believed that if the AK did not strike in the summer of 1944, the Nazis would have time to heavily reinforce their hold on Warsaw.[79] Besides, it was known that the Germans were planning to take one hundred thousand young persons out of the city to dig fortifications, and the AK would thereby lose many of its members. The AK also wished to prevent the destruction of Warsaw's population and buildings by retreating Germans. Not least, the Red Army was rapidly advancing across White Russia toward the Polish border, and the AK feared that if it did nothing, the Soviets would brand them as Nazi collaborators. If the Nazis actually abandoned Warsaw without a fight, the AK must be in control of the city before the Russians arrived. And on July 29, Soviet radio declared to the Polish people that "the hour for action" had come.[80]

Polish suspicions of Stalin were well founded. To begin with, the Nazis had gotten into Warsaw through Stalin's connivance. During the Soviet invasion in 1939, the Red Army dispersed leaflets urging Polish soldiers to murder their officers.[81] Between 1939 and 1941, the Soviets had forcibly deported hundreds of thousands of Poles to the east (the total number would approach 1.5 million). Of course, the Katyn murders had become well known within the AK. Significantly, for two years Stalin had been insisting on a "revision" of the Treaty of Riga, which had recognized Polish independence at the end of the Russo-Polish War in 1921.

Besides all this, Red partisans had attacked AK guerrilla units, and the Red Army was arresting and executing AK members in Soviet-occupied provinces east of the Vistula. In Wilno, on July 17, 1944, the Soviets invited the commanders and staff of the regional AK to a conference, and then arrested them.[82] In Lwow, on July 31, the Soviet High Command called a meeting with the AK leadership, whereupon the NKVD, Stalin's political police, seized everyone, including civilian representatives of the PGE in London.[83] Moreover, Soviet informers had penetrated the AK at several levels (the Russians were much more successful at this than the Nazis).[84] The PGE asked Churchill to send British observers to witness Soviet attacks on the AK, but he declined to do so.[85] Neither Britain nor the United States would send any observers into Poland, although they had done so in Yugoslavia and Greece.

The Poles rightly feared that a Soviet occupation would be permanent, while, in contrast, the Nazis were clearly on the way to destruction. A rising was also needed to frustrate the Polish Communist Party's efforts to seize power. General Bor believed that if the AK did not take action, the Communists would proclaim a rising on their own and win much support away from the AK, all of which would make a Soviet takeover of Poland much easier.

Under these circumstances, writes Stefan Korbonski, "it seemed unthinkable that the Home Army, numbering in Warsaw 40,000 officers and men, should stand passively by and not attack the retreating and demoralized German armies. National dignity and pride required that the capital should be liberated by the Poles themselves, and that was accepted without any discussion. Moreover, we had to think what the western world would say if the Russians were to capture Warsaw unaided."[86]

In light of the actions of the advancing Red Army, AK thinking about the best time for the rising gradually shifted from the point of German collapse to that of the Red Army entering Poland. The decision for a Warsaw rising was made during July 21–25.[87] There was no time to increase significantly the AK's woefully inadequate store of weapons, but the rising was expected to be successful within two weeks. The need for secrecy forbade alerting the Warsaw population: "Thus the Uprising broke out in a city which was totally unprepared psychologically and materially for the type of fighting which took place."[88]

The Home Army Rising

In 1944, Warsaw was fifty-four square miles in area, with one and a half million inhabitants. No European capital except Berlin would suffer so much damage as Warsaw, mainly as a result of the 1944 rising.

Beginning on August 1, the rising lasted for an incredible sixty-six days. "The soldiers [of the AK] brought out their arms and put on white-and-red armbands, the first open sign of a Polish army on Polish soil since the occupation."[89] On that first day, the Warsaw AK had at least thirty thousand members, of whom only one in ten possessed a gun. They confronted more than fifteen thousand well-armed German and satellite troops, soon augmented to forty thousand.[90] Perhaps nowhere else in World War II were the adversaries so mismatched.

Most civilians responded wholeheartedly, at first. Polish flags appeared everywhere. "The inhabitants of Warsaw came forward spontaneously, willingly and voluntarily to help; they did not wait to be asked. They were busy putting out fires, repairing barricades, carrying out observation duties on roofs and at entrances, transporting wounded, and handing over stores of food. . . . Children also joined in the fighting, carrying food, arms, and petrol bombs for the Army."[91]

The AK had obtained arms from various sources: caches buried by the Polish Army in 1939, supplies left behind by retreating Soviet forces in 1941, secret manufacture (especially grenades and Molotov cocktails), purchases from the Germans before the rising and captures during it, and eventually some air drops from the British Special Operations Executive (SOE), which had a Polish section.[92] But the AK never had nearly enough weapons or explosives, and lack of ammunition would greatly affect the final outcome.

The AK fought mostly in companies of from fifty to one hundred; each of these groups, of course, had to act with great autonomy. In the early days of the fighting, the AK attacked too many positions and took few of them. The Germans still controlled the main arteries, the airport, and the railway station. AK forces isolated several German strongpoints, but without artillery, without even sufficient light arms, they could not overcome fixed defenses. Neither was the AK able to set up any bridgeheads along the Vistula for the approaching Soviet army to land on. Death, destruction, fire, and smoke from the battle were omnipresent. After two weeks of fighting, eyewitnesses believed everyone in Warsaw had been killed.

Women and girls played a huge role in the unequal fight. Before the rising, eight thousand Warsaw women had taken the Home Army oath.[93] Some were combatants; others nursed the wounded, prepared meals, and carried ammunition, mail, and dispatches. One woman crawled over a wall against German fire to pick a bouquet for a wounded AK soldier. Four thousand girl scouts played their gallant parts. A fourteen-year-old girl set two German tanks ablaze.

On August 4, the Luftwaffe attacked Warsaw for the first time since 1939. Massive bombings and artillery fire totally destroyed the district known as the Old Town, Europe's easternmost extension of baroque architecture and a center of AK resistance. The Germans dropped more bombs on the Old Town than in any other place in World War II, and the AK casualty rate there approached 80 percent.

Clearing the city district by district, German units eventually surrounded the Old Town. After repeated efforts to break out failed, the AK decided to abandon the district and regroup in the city center. Fifteen hundred defenders managed to escape via the sewers, which the AK used for communications between sections of the city they still held. The Germans eventually discovered this subterranean activity and threw hand grenades and gas bombs into the sewers, which often became the scene of desperate hand-to-hand fighting in conditions of indescribable filth. Those wounded who could not be dragged through the sewers had to be left behind; the Germans doused them with gasoline and burned them alive.[94]

In other sections of the city, shattered buildings provided perfect sites for snipers and grenade throwers. Tanks proved of little value in suppressing the rising: in Warsaw's narrow streets, they were completely vulnerable to desperate attacks by young men and women armed with gasoline bombs. These destroyed some 270 German tanks.

On August 14, General Bor called on all armed units in the general area of Warsaw to come to the aid of the city, but Soviet troops prevented many of them from responding.

German Atrocities

Heinrich Himmler, head of the SS, gave orders that everyone in Warsaw should be killed, including women and children.[95] The area military commander, Field Marshal Model, did not want the German army engaged in this kind of activity, so he left the task to the SS and special police. Many of the SS troops involved were neither German nor even spoke German.[96] As will be seen, SS atrocities were so egregious that instead of shortening the rising, they prolonged it. During the battle, the AK captured German soldiers as prisoners of war but began executing captured SS men on the spot.[97] For their part, when attacking AK positions, the Nazis used women and children as screens for their tanks.[98] They deliberately destroyed libraries, priceless works of art, glass, porcelain and the like; they looted and burned hospitals with patients and staff locked inside them. "On 5 August alone, an estimated 35,000 men, women, and children were shot by the SS in cold blood. . . . Indeed the obsession of the SS with slaughtering innocents was seriously hampering the German military effort."[99]

The atrocities in Warsaw are shocking but not inexplicable: the Nazis were profoundly frightened by the rising, as they had been by the revolt in the ghetto the previous year. Besides, Hitler's regime had for years sought to uproot normal human compassion and inculcate unprecedented cruelty, and, of course, to any good National Socialist the Slavic Poles were an especially inferior race.

Nazi savagery was creating masses of refugees from one section of the city to others. The AK had somehow to organize, shelter, and feed these people, lest they become embittered toward the uprising. Indeed, as the battle raged on without electricity, water, or food, and with the diminishing prospect of help from outside, inevitably some sections of the Warsaw public began to turn hostile not only to the approaching Soviets but also to the Allies and the PGE in London, and the AK itself.[100] German reprisals were so severe that the AK feared that the civil population would blame it for their increased suffering, with the consequent strengthening of pro-German collaborationists. The tactics of Polish Communist insurgents—for example, throwing grenades into a German field hospital—were intended to provoke furious German violence against the civilian population, for which the AK was blamed.[101] In the August heat, water became hard to obtain, and food became more scarce, and of the poorest quality. Typhus cases were appearing in various districts. (Yet despite the lack of water in the summer, sanitation discipline was such that no notable epidemics occurred.)

In these circumstances, if the Nazis had conducted themselves with a bare minimum of decency, or even common sense, scores of thousands of civilians—perhaps most of them—would have left the city. Such a mass exodus would have had a devastating effect on AK morale.[102] But Nazi brutality not only prevented any exodus, it also bound the civilians closer to the AK. After the Germans cleared the AK from a particular area of the city, all civilians, including "the wounded lying in the hospitals, together with the doctors and nurses, were summarily shot."[103] Even the elderly cancer patients in the Radium Institute were raped and murdered. Everybody knew that the SS would kill any Pole. All their killing, looting, raping, and burning thus worked against the Nazis. "The Poles were united in their hate and desire for revenge on their German occupiers, and this was to be decisive in the formation of the attitude of the civilian population toward the Warsaw Uprising."[104]

Perhaps even more incredibly, the Germans, despite being pressed east and west by the converging armies of the Grand Alliance, thought it worthwhile to spend precious manpower and matériel and time to raze completely what was left of Warsaw, painstakingly dynamiting the foundations of huge, eighteenth-century buildings.

As the fighting continued, everything approached desperate levels: no food, no water, no anesthetics in the makeshift hospitals. Medical students and novice nursing trainees had to perform amputations. Fainting from hunger and exhaustion was becoming common in the AK.[105] With hardly any milk and even less medical care available, the infant mortality rate approached staggering heights. On August 20 an AK paper published this appeal: "Save the infants! We shall rebuild our buildings, we shall rebuild our churches, but the lost generation we shall not be able to rebuild!"[106]

Throughout all this horror, boy scouts were delivering the mail via the sewers, two thousand to six thousand letters a day. Newspapers continued to appear, including some for children, along with radio programs and concerts, large and small, to keep up morale. Improvised clinics somehow carried on the care of children, soup kitchens fed the most desperate. The fire department, lacking water and often shot at by the SS, continued to perform rescues and evacuations. Religious devotion became more and more intense and open during the occupation, and services were held constantly in private homes. Convents and monasteries sheltered the homeless and orphans and set up soup kitchens and public laundries.[107] And the resistance courts still functioned.

On October 2, 1944, as an act of recognition for the doomed Warsaw AK, the president of the PGE in London appointed General Bor honorary commander in chief of Polish armed forces. On that same day, the Germans agreed to treat AK fighters in Warsaw as prisoners of war according to Geneva Convention principles. Three days later, with his exhausted forces in control of only some parts of the city center, Bor ordered his men and women to surrender. Fifteen thousand four hundred AK members, including women, marched out of Warsaw as German prisoners. The AK had lost around 22,000 killed, wounded, and missing. Civilian deaths approached 250,000. The German commander in Warsaw, SS general Bach-Zelewski, placed German casualties at 20,000.[108] General Bor later wrote that German losses in Warsaw included 10,000 killed, 9,000 wounded, and 7,000 missing.[109]

So ended "one of the ghastliest battles of the war."[110]

On July 31, the day before the rising, Russian armored units were less than twelve miles from Warsaw.[111] In the first days of August, on the east side of the Vistula, Soviet field marshal Rokossovskii and a group of his officers "looked out over a Warsaw covered with roiling clouds of smoke; the burning houses were clearly visible; the city was flecked with bomb bursts and evidently under shell-fire."[112] In the last weeks of the fighting, Warsaw's inhabitants could view the motionless Soviet army across the Vistula. According to the terms of the capitulation, all civilians in Warsaw had to leave the city: "New Yorkers might grasp the enormity of the scene if told that Manhattan was being emptied by the Nazis of its entire population while the Soviet Army stood watching from the other end of a derelict Brooklyn Bridge."[113]

AK leaders had long feared that the Soviet army might pause east of Warsaw.[114] The Red Army was on the offensive in the Baltics (to the north of Poland) and in Romania (to the south). Why didn't the Soviet army come to the aid of fighting, burning, dying Warsaw?

Stalin and the Warsaw Rising

From the very first weeks of the war, the attitude of the Stalin regime toward the Polish resistance was full of menace. In the Soviet-occupied areas, the secret police arrested leaders of Polish society, including academics, jurists, and priests. They deported for slave labor in Siberia and Inner Asia great numbers of the Polish middle class and peasantry from their occupation zone after 1939; many of the departees died.[115] "Nazi repressions in the German zone were not so extensive in 1939–1941 as those perpetrated in [the] Soviet zone."[116] The new Polish Communist Party (Stalin had executed most of the old one) urged the Poles to fulfill the food quota shipments the Nazis imposed on them, while millions of Poles were slowly starving. And then came the massacres of thousands of Polish officers in the Katyn forest.

One needs to remember that Stalin had entered a pact with Hitler to partition Poland, that he was allied with the Nazis while they were seizing Denmark and Norway, defeating and occupying France, bombing London. Stalin punctiliously sent great trainloads of food and matériel to Hitler so the latter could evade the consequences of the British blockade (many of which shipments the AK sabotaged). On Stalin's orders, the French Communist Party opposed their country's war effort. Stalin did not *join* the Allied side, he was crudely kicked onto it by the treachery of his partner Hitler against which Stalin had been warned, to no avail, by his own intelligence agencies.

Apologists for Stalin often maintain that Stalin saved Russia, and indeed all of Europe, by his pact with Hitler because it gave Russia time to prepare for war. True, he did get an extra year and a half of peace, but during that time he was helping feed the Nazi war machine. When on June 22, 1941, the German invasion crashed across the Soviet frontier, it came as a complete shock to Stalin, even though he had been repeatedly warned about the coming attack by the British, the Americans, and his own spies and agents—and despite the fact that the 3.5 million German and satellite troops, with close to four thousand tanks and six hundred thousand horses, that crossed the Russian borders comprised the largest single military force the world had ever seen. As Churchill wrote, "the wicked are not always clever, nor are dictators always right."[117] The "second front" for which Stalin incessantly clamored in 1942–1944 had already been there in 1939. When Stalin finally, predictably, inevitably had to face Hitler in 1941, France had fallen and British troops had been pushed off the continent. What saved the USSR was not Stalin's cunning but Hitler's errors: the invasion of Russia started too late in the year, and German forces were allowed to brutalize civilian populations that at first had welcomed them. And there is the interesting fact that after almost a quarter century of Communism, there was hardly a decent all-weather road in all of western Russia. "If the Soviet regime had given Russia a road system comparable to that of Western countries, she would have been overrun almost as quickly as France."[118]

In any event, "the Polish underground led from London was the largest and the most powerful in Europe; the [AK] thus represented a special obstacle to Stalin, unlike anything he had so far encountered in the war."[119] Stalin's dealings with that obstacle made his plans for postwar Poland perfectly clear. In May 1943 Moscow announced the formation of a Polish Communist army, with Zygmunt Berling as commander; Berling was also named a general of the Red Army. Berling's troops were made to swear an oath of allegiance not to Poland but to the Soviet Union.[120] At the time of the rising this force, ninety thousand Soviet-equipped Polish soldiers, stood just to the east of Warsaw. Stalin also established a Communist underground as a rival to the AK. On July 22, 1944, he set up the nucleus of a puppet Communist regime for Poland, eventually known in the West as the "Lublin government," in opposition to the PGE in London. This absolutely illegitimate, utterly servile bunch of failures and traitors in Lublin agreed to Soviet annexations of prewar Polish territories, and received recognition by the United States and Britain.[121]

During the first week of the rising, while literally thousands in Warsaw were dying, the Polish Communist Party in Moscow denied that there was fighting in the Polish capital.[122] And the Soviet news agency TASS denied the reality of the rising even longer.[123] On August 8, a Polish Communist broadcast from Moscow accused the AK of being Nazi collaborators; this could not have happened without Stalin's approval.[124] On the same day, the Polish Party's central executive committee publicly decreed that all officers of the AK must be arrested, and that anybody wearing the AK white-and-red armband instead of the Communist red one would be shot by the Communists or by the Red Army when it reached Warsaw.[125] (During all this time, the AK could have arrested and/or killed the few hundred Communists in Warsaw, but instead left them alone.)[126] Late in August Stalin referred to the leadership of the AK rising as a "handful of power-seeking criminals."[127] (Who could be more qualified to judge?)

Allied aircraft lacked the range to fly from Italy to Warsaw and back. Thus, if they were going to drop supplies to Warsaw, they needed to land in Russia to refuel. Even if one charitably accepts the apology that the Red Army was "stalled" to the east of Warsaw, what is the excuse for Stalin's refusal to allow British or U.S. planes to land in Russia? Stalin turned down request after urgent request. The Russians told U.S. ambassador to Moscow Averell Harriman that even damaged aircraft would not be allowed to land on Soviet soil.[128] In early September, Churchill wrote Stalin: "Our people cannot understand why no material help has been sent from outside to the Poles in Warsaw. The fact that such help could not be sent on account of your Government's refusal to allow United States aircraft to land on aerodromes in Russian hands is now becoming widely known."[129]

Stalin was aware that his malevolence toward Warsaw was beginning to open a real rift with the British and even the Americans. Besides, Warsaw was by now clearly doomed and the AK all but destroyed. Hence, on September 13, six weeks after the rising began, Stalin permitted the first airdrops to Warsaw by Soviet planes. These dropped supplies in canisters, without parachutes, which smashed to pieces on the ground. This charade went on for several days.[130] Churchill writes: "They [the Soviets] wished to have the non-Communist Poles destroyed to the full, but also to keep alive the idea that they were going to their rescue."[131] General Berling, the puppet commander of Polish troops under Kremlin control, tried to give aid to Warsaw, "for which he was subsequently punished."[132]

Very few Allied flights came to help Warsaw; those that did often had Polish crews. Plane losses were high; British pilots were especially reluctant to fly over Warsaw because they reported that Russian antiaircraft fired at them.[133]

There have always been those who insist that we cannot be sure why the Red Army stopped short of Warsaw during the rising. Observers at the time, however, were *quite* sure. Air Marshal Sir John Slessor, RAF commander for the Mediterranean and the Middle East, called the affair "the blackest-hearted, coldest-blooded treachery on the part of the Russians."[134] For Stefan Korbonski, "the Soviets' conduct during the Rising should be branded as the greatest crime of that war, a worse crime even than Katyn, for two hundred thousand men, women and children paid for it with their lives."[135] And in mid-August 1944, while Warsaw was still fighting, U.S. ambassador Harriman wrote that "the Soviet Government's refusal to help Warsaw is not based on operational difficulties nor on a denial of the conflict, but on ruthless political calculations."[136] Stalin's inaction in the face of the Warsaw Rising was, perhaps, the first major overt act of the Cold War.

Stalin could have won much gratitude and prestige for his miniscule Polish Communist Party if he had saved—or even assisted —Warsaw. But he preferred instead to let the AK (and Warsaw's civilians, including its working class) perish, and then after the war to expel 4.5 million Poles from his annexed territories. And, as Soviet occupation succeeded that of the Nazis, their secret police rounded up all AK members that they could find; many were never heard from again. And Poles were forbidden even to speak of August 1, 1944.

Poland and Her Allies

"Liberation" at the end of the war had a peculiarly bitter, almost insulting meaning in eastern and central Europe: the replacement of the Nazis by the Stalinists.

During World War II, six million Polish citizens perished, half of them Jewish. This was the heaviest loss of any country: Poland lost 220 out of every 1,000 of its inhabitants, compared to 108 in Yugoslavia, 15 in France, and 3 in Norway.[137] Its universities, schools, museums, cathedrals, libraries, hospitals, banks, factories, and railways were in ruins. In return for this appalling devastation, what in the end did the Poles receive?

At the Yalta Conference in February 1945, Poland's allies gave away its eastern provinces to Stalin—just as Hitler had done in 1939—and implicitly withdrew their recognition of the PGE in favor of a new "representative" regime to be formed from the Lublin Communists plus a few others who were acceptable to Stalin. For Poland, Yalta meant dismemberment and Stalinization. Yalta was "our most painful blow," wrote General Bor.[138] "Poland did not fight the Germans for five years, in the most difficult conditions, bearing the greatest losses, just to capitulate to the Russians."[139]

"It was very difficult for the Poles to believe that they who had suffered so much and produced no Quisling, whose forces had fought on all fronts alongside the Allies, should be let down."[140] General Anders, who had been appointed commander in chief of all Polish armed forces in February 1944, had always been sure the Allies would never sacrifice Poland, which had been Hitler's first victim, had remained loyal to Britain, and had made notable contributions to Allied victory in the west. On hearing the results of Yalta, Anders told Churchill on February 21 that he would withdraw the Second Polish Corps from the bitter Italian campaign. Churchill replied that he didn't need Polish troops anymore. But Anders's British Army colleagues begged him not to abandon the war, and he agreed.[141]

Washington offered no assistance, or even sympathy. In May 1945, Roosevelt's personal envoy Harry Hopkins told Stalin, "We had no desire to support in any way the Polish government in London." Indeed, the administration "had no interest in seeing anyone connected with the present Polish government in London involved in the new Provisional Government of Poland."[142] In George F. Kennan's opinion, Roosevelt and Hopkins believed that Poland, and all the countries along the borders of the USSR, had bad relations with Stalin through their own fault.[143] Kennan also offered the opinion that "if there was a conservative regime in Poland, and a conservative Catholic regime especially, this meant, in liberal eyes, *that the Poles were practically like the Nazis.*"[144] "Poland's faith in Churchill and Roosevelt had proved worthless."[145]

Poland had been the first country to defy Hitler, but the PGE received no invitation to the United Nations conference in San Francisco in March 1945. And on June 8, 1946, when the great Victory Parade was held in London, the Polish army was not invited to participate.[146] The Germans were responsible for the deaths of a quarter of a million civilians in Warsaw, by mass execution and deliberate starvation, but no one was arraigned for these crimes (nor for Katyn) at Nuremberg.

Close to a hundred thousand Polish troops in the west refused to return to Stalin's Poland. Stefan Korbonski, the last political chief of the resistance, wondered, in light of Poland's fate after World War II, whether his people's struggle against the Nazis had been worth all the blood and destruction.[147] The Poles had paid an incalculable price for a freedom they did not obtain.

2

Budapest 1956

In 1956, Communist Hungary seemed the very model of a modern Leninist dictatorship. It had a ferocious political police; a carefully recruited and heavily indoctrinated army; a large and disciplined party (10 percent of the total population); and complete regimentation of the economy, the media, the schools, and the labor unions. But in just a few days in October 1956, this apparently all-powerful regime rapidly and utterly collapsed. This Hungarian cataclysm might have alerted the world to the fact that the Soviet empire was perhaps not the omnipotent, inevitable monolith that it seemed—and that in politics, much is illusion, nothing is certain, and anything is possible.

Some Background

The first Hungarians (Magyars, in their own language) settled most of present-day Hungary late in the ninth century and accepted Christianity in the eleventh century. The Turks conquered them in 1526. The forces of the Habsburg crown finally succeeded in liberating Budapest in 1686. After decades of restiveness, Hungarian nationalism burst into revolution against the Austrian Habsburgs in 1848, a year of upheaval all over Europe. Russian troops and the hostility of Hungary's submerged Slavic and Romanian minorities crushed the attempt to set up an independent Hungarian republic. Nevertheless, after their overwhelming defeat by Bismarck's Prussia in the Six Weeks' War of 1866, the Habsburgs came under tremendous pressure to make major concessions to Hungarian national feeling. Accordingly, the Austrian Empire was transformed into the Dual Monarchy of Austria-Hungary. The two states would have their own parliaments and cabinets but continue their union by having the same person as monarch, Emperor of Austria in Vienna and King of Hungary in Budapest. Emperor Francis Joseph was accordingly crowned King of Hungary in 1867.

In 1910, the Dual Monarchy had a population of 50 million, compared to France with 39 million, Germany with 65 million, and Russia with 110 million. The Kingdom of Hungary alone contained 21 million inhabitants, of whom 11 million were Hungarian.[1] These, along with the Germans of Austria, were the most numerous, and the most dominant, ethnic components of the empire, which also contained millions of Poles, Czechs, Slovaks, Romanians, Croatians, and Slovenians. Austria-Hungary was the primary example in modern times of a multinational state. Its principal weakness, however, was not its multinational composition per se but rather the unequal and sometimes quite harsh treatment of its ethnic minorities, especially by the Hungarians.[2]

At the end of World War I, the Dual Monarchy, one of the defeated Central Powers, fragmented into its ethnic elements. Now-independent Hungary achieved the unenviable distinction of becoming the only European state outside Russia to experience a Communist regime. The Hungarian Communist Party was minuscule, but the regular political parties shrank from the responsibility for governing in the light of what they saw as incomprehensible Allied vindictiveness toward Hungary. Thus the Communists came to power in March 1919, not through revolt but by default; they had not carried out a Petrograd-style putsch but rather had been bundled almost overnight from the prison to the palace. Many years before, in his book *Peasant War in Germany*, Friedrich Engels had warned, "The worst thing that can befall the leader of an extreme party is to be compelled to take over a government in an epoch when the moment is not yet ripe for the domination of the class he represents and for the realization of the measures which that domination implies."[3] But who read Engels anyway? Yet it would be difficult to find better evidence for the truth of Engels's words than the tragicomedy of the post-1918 Communist regime under Bela Kun.

Hungary was a pleasure-loving peasant and Catholic society, one of the great wine-producing countries of Europe. On this society Kun imposed persecution of religion, collectivization of agriculture, and—of course, what else—*prohibition*. Kun had expected Bolshevik troops to arrive any day, but a renewed White offensive in the south of Russia against the Lenin dictatorship doomed that prospect. In an effort both to win the favor of Hungarian nationalists and to hasten the Communist revolution in Romania (objectives typically contradictory), Kun sent the Hungarian army into Romania on July 21, 1919; the invasion turned into a rout. Kun informed his cabinet that the Hungarian revolution had failed because the Hungarian proletariat was too soft. He then boarded a prearranged train and escaped to Vienna, leaving his hapless adherents behind to face the counterrevolutionary and Romanian music.[4] What was left of Kun's absurd circus was chased out of Budapest by the Romanian army in August. (Kun himself would be executed in the cellar of a Stalinist prison in 1939.) Mercifully brief though it was, the Kun episode made communism a lasting stench in the nostrils of the Hungarian upper, middle, and peasant classes.[5] Miklos Horthy, commander of the old Habsburg navy (and now an admiral without a fleet), assumed the leadership of the country under the title of regent of Hungary (now a monarchy without a monarch).

One of the most regrettable consequences of World War I was the breakup of the Austro-Hungarian Empire. The destruction of this venerable multinational state had been one of Woodrow Wilson's vaunted Fourteen Points. Its historic position in the European balance of power was filled (or rather, *not* filled) by a gaggle of weak, suspicious states (Austria, Hungary, Czechoslovakia, Yugoslavia, Romania) precariously situated between Germany and Russia. Herein lay a principal root of the renewal of the world war in 1939.[6] The Treaty of Trianon (Versailles) ripped great chunks of territory and population from the Kingdom of Hungary. The rump state was left without a seacoast; worse, of the eleven million Hungarians, three million found themselves on the wrong side of the Yugoslav, Czechoslovak, or Romanian border. All three of these states were allies of the French. Determined to regain Hungary's former lands and citizens, Admiral Horthy drifted into the orbit of Mussolini, and after 1936 toward National Socialist Germany.[7] Hungarian troops fought in Russia during World War II; consequently Soviet armies occupied the country in 1944.[8]

Relatively free, multiparty parliamentary elections in 1945 produced a landslide (59 percent) in favor of the Small Farmers Party.[9] Their victory "was almost certainly due to the open intervention of the Church on their behalf."[10] Despite the presence of the Red Army, only a handful of Communists were elected. A coalition cabinet began to carry out much-needed land reform. But in 1947 the Soviets demanded new elections. In an atmosphere of intimidation by gangs of thugs and the forcible shutdown of non-Communist newspapers, the Communist ticket still managed to garner only 22 percent of the vote. But the party, backed by the Red Army, took over complete power in 1948.[11] In elections the following year, only the names of Communist candidates appeared on the ballot. Thus Hungary began its second experience of Communist dictatorship, one that would last far longer than Bela Kun's.

By 1956, Hungarian society was reaching a critical state. Many Communist bureaucrats ostentatiously enjoyed a lifestyle far above that of ordinary citizens. Most Hungarians deeply resented the overvisible and overbearing Russian military presence. Bitter, even deadly, rivalries inside the Communist Party broke into the open. The too-blatant discrepancy between party propaganda and actual living conditions was increasingly offensive. Khrushchev's so-called Secret Speech to the Twentieth Party Congress of the USSR, in which he "revealed" and denounced the criminality of the Stalin regime, became widely publicized. And in Communist-ruled Poland, massive demonstrations were shaking the foundations of a similarly imposed and similarly detested ruling clique.

The Spark

One of the most reprobate and lupine organizations in the entire Communist empire was the Hungarian State Security Service, known as the AVH. The members of this remarkable force loomed above both the party and the state. According to the chief of the regular Budapest police (an organization totally separate from the AVH), even cabinet ministers were afraid of it.[12] The AVH ran its own prisons, at least one of which had an acid bath wherein prisoners' bodies, dead or sometimes alive, were disposed of; they also had their own crematoria.[13] AVH men received higher pay, wore snappier uniforms, and carried deadlier weapons than other police units. The regime carefully segregated them from society. Many of them had been recruited from the notorious Arrow Cross movement, a pro-Nazi party/militia that had flourished in the 1940s. To this AVH belongs the distinction of being the group that actually ignited the uprising of 1956.

On October 23, 1956, a large and peaceful demonstration of students assembled in front of Budapest's magnificent Parliament building to show support for the reform movement in Poland. Considerable numbers of factory workers and off-duty soldiers joined the students, and the whole demonstration moved to the State Radio Building. (Both places are on the eastern—or Pest—side of the Danube.) It was here that the AVH provoked the uprising. A United Nations report later stated that the first casualty in the uprising was a major in the Hungarian army who wanted to present a list of student grievances to the head of the State Radio.[14] At 9:00 P.M., AVH men in the upper stories of the radio building began firing on the unarmed and still peaceful demonstrators.[15] Possibly as many as six hundred men and women were killed in this massacre

Reinforcements in the form of regular army units were rushed to the State Radio Building. But when these troops reached the scene of carnage, soldiers and officers in the crowd cried out to them not to shoot. Accounts of what happened next vary, but instead of opening fire on the demonstrators, the soldiers actually began handing over their weapons to them. The refusal of army units to protect the security police from the wrath of the people meant that, for all practical purposes, the Hungarian Communist regime was finished. All through that night and into the following days, the demonstrators and the thousands who now joined them received more arms, from soldiers, from army depots, from factory workers' militia centers. The regular Budapest city police (who also feared and hated the AVH) provided additional guns and ammunition to the demonstrators.[16] Many students knew how to handle weapons because of the compulsory military training in the universities.

In contrast to nearly all other similar upheavals, "the almost unique characteristic of the Hungarian Revolution of 1956 may be considered its complete lack of a revolutionary body" to organize and direct it.[17] But perhaps the most shocking aspect of the uprising, from the Communist viewpoint, was the attitude of the Hungarian military cadets. These young men had been carefully selected by the regime according to class background, heavily indoctrinated with Marxist-Leninist teaching, and thoroughly infiltrated by the AVH. Nevertheless, great numbers of these cadets—the favored children and future protection of the regime—openly sided with the revolution.

During those same days, AVH units continued to fire into peaceful civilian crowds. They killed over a hundred civilians in Parliament Square, and yet another eighty in the city of Magyarovar.[18] The responsibility of the special security police for the great effusion of blood that would soon take place in Hungary is undeniable and staggering. "We can see now," wrote George Mikes, "how much of the bloodshed in this revolution was due to the AVO [AVH] opening fire at peaceful demonstrators."[19] Peter Fryer, a reporter for the British Communist *Daily Worker*, wrote on October 26: "After eleven years of 'people's democracy' it had come to this, that the security police was so remote from the people, so alien to them, so vicious and so brutal that it turned its weapons on a defenceless crowd and murdered the people who were supposed to be the masters of their own country."[20]

The years of silent hatred and fear, ignited by the senseless massacres of innocent civilians, now had their condign consequence. It became common in Budapest and other cities and towns to see the bodies of AVH men hanging from lampposts and other hastily selected instruments of popular justice.[21] Fearless when the arrest and torture of single suspects, or even an entire family, was involved, the AVH tended to be much more discreet when confronted by crowds of armed civilians. Its members soon disappeared into their various holes and waited.

Events moved very rapidly. Budapest crowds pulled down the larger-than-life statue of Stalin. The slogan *Ruszkik Haza!* ("Russians out!") appeared everywhere. So did the Hungarian flag, with the Communist red star cut out of it. On October 24 the regime announced over the radio, "Fascist and reactionary elements have launched an armed attack against our public buildings and against the forces of law and order."[22] By smearing the uprising as Fascist, the party was saying that any use of force against it would be justified. Yet on that very day Imre Nagy, an advocate of "reformed" Communism, was installed as prime minister, and Janos Kadar, boss of the Hungarian Communist Party, declared that organization dissolved.

In the wake of World War II, Communist regimes were imposed on several Catholic countries besides Hungary, including Poland, Czechoslovakia, Croatia, and Slovenia. In all of them, Church leaders were imprisoned after grotesque show trials. In the West, the best-known of these churchmen was Cardinal Joseph Mindszenty of Hungary. Imprisoned during the war by the pro-German regime, Mindszenty suffered similar treatment under the Communists. Freedom fighters released him, and the Nagy cabinet declared the charges against him "unjustified."[23] During the second Soviet invasion (see below), the cardinal took refuge in the U.S. embassy, remaining there for many years.

The First Soviet Intervention

As one noted historian of these events wrote, "Had the Soviet Army not been called upon to help, the entire Communist regime would have collapsed within twenty-four hours."[24] But of course the Soviet army *was* called upon, by the outgoing puppet Prime Minister Hegedus, on orders from Soviet ambassador Yuri Andropov (no less).[25] On October 24, two mechanized Soviet divisions crossed into Hungary from Romania. (The Budapest police chief later wrote that Soviet tanks were already moving on October 23.)[26] This first Soviet intervention inflamed opinion, especially in Budapest: "It was the calling in of the Russians which . . . quickly and unequivocally gave the movement its true character—that of a national uprising."[27]

The freedom fighters had obtained a substantial amount of weapons from various sources, including the army and the city police, but the number of persons who wanted to join the fight far exceeded the number of guns available. Soon to call themselves the National Guard, these freedom fighters were students, workers, and soldiers; many of them had, of course, been Communist Party members: "This was the alliance of the workers and intellectuals that Lenin said was indispensable to a revolution."[28] The knowledge gained from courses about Russian guerrillas and partisans, required of all university students, would now be turned by them against their oppressors.[29]

Although organized units of the Hungarian army fought the AVH from the start, the army as such did not resist the invading Soviets at first.[30] For one thing, Hungarian troops did not possess the equipment to withstand the Russians.[31] Nevertheless, many soldiers fought as individuals alongside the freedom fighters. Even more importantly, Hungarian troops refused to protect Soviet tanks in Budapest; this was a most serious situation, because the Soviet T-34 tanks used in the first invasion had clearly marked petrol caps on one side, hence were very vulnerable to Molotov cocktails. Infantry could have offered a good deal of protection to the tanks, but few infantrymen accompanied the invading Soviet armored columns, and those few were reluctant to stay on the streets at night.[32] Another consequence of sending tanks unsupported by infantry was this: since the soldiers in their tanks had very poor visibility, the insurgents could stop a tank column by laying on the streets overturned soup plates, which looked liked mines to the men inside the vehicles. One student of the revolution speculates that the Kremlin sent tanks into Budapest unaccompanied by infantry so that Russian soldiers would not become aware that the Hungarian standard of living, such as it was, clearly outclassed that of the Soviet Union, and also to prevent them from learning that they were fighting to suppress a true national movement.[33] (Forty years later the Soviets would send unaccompanied tanks into Grozny, with the same results.) Soviet tanks in Budapest would shoot at any building that had lights on at night, including even the main city police station.[34]

All sorts of signs indicated that, as they became aware they were fighting workers and students, the morale of many of the Soviet troops sank very low. And there were reports that Russian soldiers sold their personal weapons—and even their tanks—for food.[35]

During these dramatic days, there was no looting in Budapest by Hungarians, only by Russian soldiers. The Russians broke into stores and then forced Hungarians to carry out goods while they were being photographed. These faked pictures then appeared in the Soviet party newspaper *Pravda* to prove that the revolutionaries were nothing but mobs of hooligans and fascists.[36] Hastily assembled insurgent units guarded jewelry stores whose windows had been broken.[37] "Witnesses of all nationalities have testified that there was no looting in Budapest during these ten days, despite the temptation offered by smashed-up windows."[38] Farmers were giving away ducks, chickens, eggs, and potatoes in the streets of Budapest in the days just before the second Soviet invasion, to show their gratitude to the freedom fighters for ending the forced collectivization of agriculture.[39]

All sides agreed to an armistice on October 28. By the next day, when Soviet forces had ceased fighting, two hundred of their tanks had been destroyed or damaged.[40]

The Second Intervention

The establishment of a free, social-democratic Hungary upon the wreckage of a Communist dictatorship would have had the most profound consequences for world politics.[41] Thus the temptation for the Kremlin to crush the Hungarians by force must have been truly powerful; still, one cannot utterly rule out a priori the possibility of a Soviet offer of compromise. But the Anglo-Franco-Israeli attack on Suez distracted and divided the West and encouraged the Soviets to seize the opportunity to reverse events in Hungary by sheer force. If London and Paris had dispatched their ultimatum to Egypt a month later than they actually did (October 30), it is certainly reasonable to imagine that events in Hungary might have taken a dramatically different course.[42]

In any event, the fighting in Budapest and elsewhere made it perfectly clear that to reestablish control of Hungary would require far more than the two armored divisions that comprised the original Soviet intervention. Accordingly, on the night of October 29, new Soviet army units, including three thousand tanks, began entering Hungary.[43] Many of the tanks in this second invasion were T-54s, less vulnerable to gasoline bombs. Now with eleven divisions, Soviet forces in Hungary sealed its western border, surrounded Budapest, occupied all strategic points outside the city, and encircled every airport. AVH men, sniffing their opportunity, guided Soviet tanks into Budapest.[44] "The AVH were in their uniforms again, escorting

Russian soldiers and picking out former insurgents for arrest."[45] Many of these Russian soldiers had actually believed that they were in Germany to fight the Nazis.[46] Aircraft bombed the city, while on the ground the Soviets shelled and burned out many Budapest hospitals, killing or wounding physicians, nurses, and patients.[47] As in Warsaw and Grozny, the insurgents used the sewers for communications. And in this second Soviet invasion, units of the Hungarian army offered resistance to the overwhelmingly powerful Russians.[48] The puppet regime called on Hungarian soldiers to accept amnesty at designated areas; some took the offer, only to be mowed down by Russian troops.[49]

As the fighting raged, representatives of the Nagy cabinet, including Pal Maleter, a Hungarian army colonel serving as minister of defense, were negotiating with the commanders of the Soviet forces in Hungary under a flag of truce. Against all international law, and against every concept of military honor and dignity, the Soviets seized the Hungarian negotiators and cast them into prison, nearly decapitating the revolutionary forces with this one shameful blow.

Withdrawal from the Warsaw Pact

A persistent myth, encouraged by the Soviets, maintains that the Kremlin leaders sent their tanks back into Hungary in November because the Nagy cabinet was going to take Hungary out of the Warsaw Pact and declare neutrality. Since such a move would have had seriously destabilizing effects on the European balance of power, with unforeseeable consequences, the Soviet suppression of the Hungarian uprising was therefore, in this version, actually in the interest of world peace.

Prime Minister Nagy, a lifelong Communist, did indeed declare Hungary's withdrawal from the Warsaw Pact late on November 1. But Budapest police chief Kopacsi, among others, has testified that fresh Soviet intervention forces had begun pouring into the country on October 29. Nagy told Soviet ambassador Yuri Andropov that Hungary would leave the Warsaw Pact *unless the invasion ceased* and all Soviet troops were withdrawn from Hungarian soil.[50] Andropov replied to Nagy that the Soviet troops coming over the borders and taking control of all the airports were doing so in order to facilitate a total withdrawal of their forces.[51] George Mikes presents an overwhelming case that it was not Nagy's declaration of neutrality that provoked the second Soviet intervention, which had, in fact, begun before that declaration.[52] Many other authoritative sources confirm this stance.[53]

In summary, as historian Charles Gati has written: "[T]he Soviet intervention was only marginally related to what Nagy had done or failed to do. It was not caused by his 'provocative' declaration about neutrality and the Warsaw Pact. In fact, the opposite is true: it was the (second) Soviet intervention on the night of October 31 [sic] that prompted [Nagy] . . . to shed his Muscovite past and issue his historic declaration."[54]

Prime Minister Nagy found refuge in the Yugoslav embassy on November 4. The new Soviet-backed Hungarian prime minister, Janos Kadar (the formation of whose government had been announced from Uzhgorod, in the USSR), offered Nagy safe conduct to his home, which he accepted. Immediately upon his emergence from the embassy, Nagy was seized by the KGB, and in 1958 Kadar announced his execution.

Casualties

Armed resistance in Budapest ended on November 14, although fighting continued in mountainous parts of Hungary for several more weeks. Budapest was in worse shape at the end of the second Soviet intervention than it had been in 1945 (when it was the wartime capital of an enemy state). In the country as a whole, at least 22,000 Hungarians had been killed (the proportional equivalent of 750,000 Americans) and many more thousands wounded. Several thousand Soviet soldiers were dead or wounded. Approximately 26,000 Hungarians were imprisoned, of whom 600 were later executed. Eight thousand officers were expelled from the Hungarian army.[55] Over 200,000 Hungarians fled to Austria or Czechoslovakia before November 14.[56] After that, "deportations began, as indiscriminate as 1945, trains full of people packed off at random to Russia."[57]

Reflection

The 1956 Hungarian rising is not mysterious in its origin, its initial success, or its final defeat.[58]

The origins of the rising lay first of all in the manner in which the Communist regime had come to power, having been imposed on the country, against the clear and repeated wishes of the electorate, through the presence in Hungary of foreign troops. That stigma in itself might have been enough, but there was much more: the memories of Russian atrocities during World War II; the provocatively blatant Russian presence; an identification of Communism per se with the detested Russians even in the eyes of those social groups most favored by the regime; the pervasive economic deprivation; a ruling clique remarkable for high living, political incompetence, and personal unattractiveness; and a relentlessly blared official mendacity so crude as to be simultaneously risible and offensive.[59] The homicidal mindlessness of the security police was emblematic of all the regime's pathologies.

The uprising was so successful so quickly because, after the AVH massacres had ignited an already combustible situation, the armed forces not only declined to suppress the popular demonstrations but openly sided with them. That was the master key, the primary and decisive factor, in the collapse of the regime.

Lenin taught, correctly, that no revolution of the masses can triumph without the help of a portion of the armed forces that sustained the old regime. This view, that a revolution can begin but cannot succeed as long as the government possesses the loyalty of the armed forces, has evoked widespread concurrence. Chalmers Johnson wrote that "analysis of the political position of the armed forces always lies at the heart of any concrete study of revolution."[60] Katherine Chorley concluded that "the part played by the army is decisive in any revolution."[61] The Communist bosses of Hungary assumed that their army was completely reliable, because of its social origins and political indoctrination. They might have reflected, but did not, that regimes much more legitimate, historic, and impressive than the Stalinist puppets in Budapest had been swept away when their troops refused to fire upon civilian demonstrators of their own nationality. Examples would include the long-established monarchies of Louis XVI and Nicholas II. (Similar scenarios would topple Iran's Reza Shah Pahlavi and the Philippines' Ferdinand Marcos.)[62] It is a grave error for a government to rely confidently on political indoctrination to counteract the spread of disaffection from civilians to soldiers. It is an even graver error for a government—any government—to command its soldiers to fire into the civilians with whom the day before they may have been talking, eating, drinking, dancing, or praying. The sudden collapse of the Hungarian army in October 1956 is a textbook illustration of these patent principles.

The defeat of the uprising, of course, resulted from the fact that the storm that had swept away the corrupt regime could not prevail against an invasion by great numbers of well-equipped foreign troops with few reservations about killing civilians whose motives and language they could not understand.

As in Warsaw in 1944, so in Budapest in 1956, the freedom fighters believed that the outside world, moved by the justice and heroism of their cause, would assist them. As the Soviet fist was closing around Hungary, Budapest radio sent out this unsettling appeal: "Civilized people of the world! We implore you in the name of justice, freedom and the binding moral principle of active solidarity to help us. Our ship is sinking. . . . Listen to our cry!"[63]

Why did the world not hear this cry? Why did the United States not intervene directly or indirectly to ensure the success of the Budapest uprising, or at least sustain it?

Part of the answer to this disturbing question lies in the fact that, as mentioned earlier, in November 1956 much of the world was convulsed with indignation over the Suez affair. But perhaps the most cogent response is to be found in the words of Dwight D. Eisenhower, president of the United States at the time. A few years after the crushing of Budapest, he wrote:

I still wonder what my recommendation to the Congress and the American people would have been had Hungary been accessible by sea or through the territory of allies who might have agreed to react positively to the tragic fate of the Hungarian people. As it was, however, Britain and France could not possibly have moved with us into Hungary. An expedition combining West German and Italian forces with our own, and moving across neutral

Austria, Titoist Yugoslavia, or Communist Czechoslovakia, was out of the question. The fact was that Hungary could not be reached. . . . Sending U.S. troops alone into Hungary through hostile or neutral territory would have involved us in a general [world] war. . . . Though the [UN] General Assembly passed a resolution calling upon the Soviets to withdraw their troops, it was obvious that no mandate for military action could or would be forthcoming.[64]

And so the Soviet fist closed, and Hungary fell silent.

3

Algiers 1957

Studies of the 1954–1962 conflict in Algeria have long displayed a "Manichean" character—depicting a struggle between good and evil—and perhaps never more so than in recent times.[1] Of course, every war excites controversy, and "the Algerian War was to be the last, probably, and certainly the greatest and most dramatic of the colonial wars."[2] But the conflict was much more than that, because "Algeria was France's Ireland, almost as closely linked to the homeland as Ireland had been to Great Britain until 1922, and with the same problems of a minority population implanted by colonization."[3] In military terms, the French army won an incontestable victory over the insurgents. But this would lead to a near invasion of France by that victorious army, the destruction of the careers of many of its officers, the handing over of Algeria to the defeated insurgents, and the immolation of scores of thousands of France's Muslim allies. The Algerian conflict is thus an instructive example of the primacy of the political, and the ambiguity of victory, in war.

The Setting

The French began their occupation of Algeria in the 1830s. At the time, Algeria was not a nation, or even a real state, but a headquarters of the infamous Barbary pirates. During their reign over Algeria, the French constructed modern ports; built roads, railways, and irrigation systems; and turned large parts of the country into agriculturally productive regions. By 1954, of Algeria's population of about ten million, over one million were of European descent, generally known as *colons*. The colons treated the Algerian Arabs as third-class citizens at best. During World War I and again during World War II, scores of thousands of Algerian Arabs served in the French armed forces, and Algerian territory played a prominent role in the liberation of France. Consequently, as World War II was drawing to a close, demands arose among French-educated Arabs that these services be rewarded with political and economic reforms. General de Gaulle and other French leaders made many promises but delivered few results. The colons and their allies in metropolitan France set their faces resolutely against any concessions to the depressed Arab majority.

Accordingly, armed revolt against the French began on October 31, 1954, when several hundred Algerian Arab insurgents attacked numerous scattered army posts. The insurgency was organized by a group that eventually became the Front de libération national (FLN).[4] In 1958, in Cairo, the FLN proclaimed itself the provisional government of Algeria. (Resentment against Nasser's help to the Algerian rebels had been a major factor behind the Suez invasion of 1956.[5]) The FLN was not Communist-dominated, but like all colonial wars, the Algerian struggle became ensnared in the global schematic of the Cold War. Red China recognized the FLN provisional government three days after its announcement, and arms were reaching Algeria from Eastern Europe and Castro's Cuba.

Perhaps the most important single fact to bear in mind about the war in Algeria is that it began almost immediately after the French army's defeat at Dien Bien Phu in Vietnam in May 1954. The French government's decision to withdraw from Vietnam, after almost eight years of fighting the Communist-led Viet Minh, meant that the army could not keep its repeated promises never to abandon the many hundreds of thousands of loyal Vietnamese.[6] Heartsick and humiliated over what they viewed as the politicians' betrayal of Vietnam, and still preoccupied with the collapse of 1940 and the Nazi occupation, many French officers vowed that the Algerian conflict was one that "even against the will of God or man, must not be lost."[7] And so the flag was nailed to the mast.

The Army Defeats the Rural Guerrillas

To describe Algeria as "large" would be an understatement of Saharan proportions. Algeria is five times the size of France, four times Afghanistan, six times Iraq, six times Japan, seven times Vietnam, and twenty-three times Virginia; indeed within Algeria's capacious borders one could comfortably group Norway, Sweden, Finland, France, Germany, Portugal, and the United Kingdom. At the opening of the struggle in 1954, however, there were in this vast territory only 50,000 French troops, or one soldier for every nineteen square miles. But by 1957 the number had grown to 450,000, the largest French army ever to go overseas. Deploying great numbers of reservists, the French made it extremely difficult for the FLN to operate in rural areas. (Actually, less than 10 percent of French troops in Algeria saw much fighting, the majority being employed in the static defense of installations and settlements.)[8] In addition, French airpower effectively gathered intelligence in Algeria's huge empty spaces.[9] Here lay the origins of the Battle of Algiers, Algeria's capital: the failure of classic insurgency would lead to the attempt to wage urban guerrilla war.

The great number of troops the French deployed in Algeria allowed them to engage in two decisive programs that marginalized the rural guerrillas: closing the borders, and regrouping the civilian population.

Early in the Indochina struggle, the French had abandoned the northern border of Vietnam. Consequently troops and supplies for the Viet Minh insurgents flowed into the country from neighboring Maoist China. In Algeria, the FLN was receiving arms from Communist Czechoslovakia and East Germany, via neighboring independent Morocco and Tunisia. Determined to eliminate this flow, the French constructed major barriers along both borders, variations of the effective blockhouse lines used by the British against Boer guerrillas in South Africa and by Chiang Kai-shek against the Chinese Communists in the 1930s.[10] The truly impressive Morice Line (named for the minister of defense in Prime Minister Guy Mollet's cabinet) ran for more than two hundred miles along the Tunisian border. Its heart was an eight-foot-high electrified wire fence. Minefields ran fifty yards deep on each side of it. On the Algerian side, barbed wire protected a constantly patrolled road, with watchtowers at regular intervals. Monitoring stations could pinpoint the location of any attempted breakthrough and trigger a swift response by aircraft, artillery, and mobile ground units. Eighty thousand troops defended the line, which was completed by September 1957. The FLN suffered so many casualties trying to get across this formidable barrier that it soon abandoned large-scale efforts to do so. But FLN units could still harass the French army with artillery and mortar attacks from their sanctuaries inside Tunisia and Morocco.

Having almost completely isolated the insurgents from outside aid, the French also cut them off from much of the civilian population. Between 1955 and 1961, they moved nearly two million Muslims, from a population of perhaps ten million, out of the zones of guerrilla activity into protected camps. The original purpose of this regrouping was surveillance, but the army soon found itself delivering social services on a mammoth scale to these Arabs. Many French officers became deeply involved in providing public sanitation, medical care, police, education, and even employment to the inhabitants of the *regroupement* camps. All this activity served to solidify the army's commitment to the concept of French Algeria.[11]

And of course, there could be no North African Dien Bien Phu because, in decisive contrast to Vietnam, the FLN never mobilized conventional forces inside Algeria, nor was there a Red China across the border to supply such forces.

FLN Terrorism

Some have expressed the belief that the origins of FLN terror lay in anger against French execution of captured FLN personnel.[12] There are serious difficulties with that explanation. The terror in Algeria was aimed overwhelmingly at civilians, including Muslim civilians; "in both city and country, the FLN relied on terror as its main weapon against settlers and Algerians alike."[13] Besides, the FLN would soon carry terrorism to France itself, mainly in pursuit of Muslims it viewed as enemies. The much more probable explanation of FLN terrorism is this: although the FLN engaged in terror as early as 1954, its massive reliance on urban terror tactics followed from the defeat of FLN guerrilla warfare in the hinterland.[14] The FLN had little choice: "When a committed core of leaders agreed that violence was the only solution to the impasse in which they found themselves, their inability to push the mass of the Algerian people into open opposition or to mount large-scale guerrilla warfare encouraged them to adopt a strategy of terrorism."[15] In the beginning of the terror campaign, the FLN focused especially on killing Arabs of moderate opinion.

Algiers was the epicenter of the terrorist campaign. At the time, its population numbered close to three-quarters of a million persons, the majority of whom were of European origin.[16] Within the city the FLN had perhaps 5,000 members. From among these, roughly 1,500 were involved in terrorism.[17] A notable proportion of the Algiers FLN consisted of real criminals: "petty crooks, tarts, dope peddlers, and thugs."[18] To be admitted into the Algiers FLN, one had to kill a policeman.[19] The hard-core terror activists numbered perhaps 150, but that figure was more than enough to create panic in the city.[20] In January 1956 there were four terror incidents; by December, the number had rocketed to four per day.[21] In January 1957 two hundred persons of all descriptions became terror victims. In June of the same year, FLN gunmen randomly shot forty-nine civilians in the streets of Algiers alone.[22] The number of Muslims killed by the terrorists, purposefully or incidentally, was incomparably higher than the number of their European victims. But "terrorism against Europeans usually took the form of spectacular, high-casualty violence because all Europeans were lumped together as the 'enemy,' and thus all became eligible victims."[23] A dread harbinger of this policy had appeared at the town of Philippeville in August 1955, when the FLN massacred French civilians, including women and children.

Indiscriminate FLN bombings created hideous casualties among innocent civilians of every age, race, and sex. Bombs were left in mailboxes next to school bus stops. Perhaps the single most horrific FLN bombing took place at the Algiers Milk-Bar, a restaurant popular with European mothers and their school-aged children. Among the terrorists' aims in committing such atrocities was to sow seeds of distrust between Europeans and Arabs, and to provoke the French into indiscriminate violence against Muslims in general. Thus, from early in the conflict rural guerrillas would carry out an attack or murder near a village to cause the authorities to impose a blanket reprisal upon the local inhabitants.

The Army Defeats the Terrorists

The heart of the FLN terrorist organization in Algiers was located in the notorious Casbah ["fortress"], about one square kilometer in area with approximately eighty thousand inhabitants, "one of the most thickly populated slums in the world."[24] The fight to eradicate terror emanating from this Casbah, which would become known as the Battle of Algiers, was "arguably the pivotal event in the Algerian War."[25] More certainly, it is a textbook case of what happens when would-be guerrillas systematically violate the advice and example of Clausewitz and Mao Tse-tung regarding how to wage guerrilla war.

On January 27, 1957, General Jacques Massu and his Tenth Paratroop Division, ten thousand strong, arrived in Algiers. A graduate of France's military academy at St. Cyr, Massu joined the Gaullists in World War II and entered Paris during the Liberation with General Leclerc's Second Division. He received the rank of general at the young age of forty-seven. His mission was to restore order to the Algerian capital, which he did: "Between February and October 1957 the Tenth Paratroop Division commanded by General Massu effectively destroyed the terrorist organization in Algiers."[26]

Immediately upon arrival in Algiers, Massu was confronted by an FLN-declared general strike, which he broke by the simple expedient of forcing all the Muslim shopkeepers to keep their stores open. The strike, intended to demonstrate FLN control and French impotence in the city, instead turned out to be "the FLN's gravest tactical error of the entire war."[27]

The most effective and indispensable weapon for uprooting or even restraining any underground organization is intelligence. Massu demanded that all police files on suspected terrorists be handed over to him. From these files he had lists drawn up of persons to be apprehended. Massu then cordoned off the entire Casbah from the rest of the city, establishing checkpoints at all exits. Bomb carriers were usually young, middle-class Muslim women, who quite often were able to pass themselves off as Europeans.[28] Eventually all women attempting to leave the Casbah were searched.

After that, French dragnets ranged over the Casbah day and night, systematically searching the area house by house, looking for the persons whose names appeared on Massu's lists. Massu built up a network of agents and informants from former FLN members and Muslim ex-servicemen. It was not difficult to find Muslims willing to work against the FLN: "In the Casbah of Algiers, [the urban poor] were as much terrorized into lending support to the revolutionary organization as they were converted to its side."[29]

Massu also created commando units from ex-FLN members and gave these a free hand in hunting down their former associates in the Casbah.[30] His men took close to a third of the male population of the Casbah into custody during this campaign. Serious suspects might find themselves confronted by a hooded Muslim, presumably an informant.[31] The French asked everyone whom they took into custody, "Who in your neighborhood collects the terrorists' funds?" They then apprehended those persons and asked them, "To whom do you turn over the money you collect?" Thus the French obtained the identities they needed and methodically closed in on the leadership of the Casbah terror organization.[32]

The French very effectively used double agents to sow distrust inside the FLN: "As a frenzy of throat-cutting and disemboweling broke out among confused and suspicious FLN cadres, nationalist slaughtered nationalist from April to September 1957 and did France's work for her."[33] (One way to disintegrate an insurgent organization is to arrest a known member and soon afterward set him free, whether he provides any information or not.)

Massu's tactics worked. In February 1957 the French discovered the main FLN bomb factory in Algiers. On September 24, 1957, the Casbah terrorist chief Yacef Saadi surrendered. By mid-October, "the terror had been effectively lifted."[34] The terrorists were able to carry out only about one action per month.[35] Thus, "the long nightmare of urban terror came to an end in Algiers."[36]

The Battle of Algiers was an incontestable French victory. Its consequences, however, were not peace or compromise but open, irreconcilable war. French tactics alienated moderate Muslim opinion and provoked much criticism in France, and elsewhere, to be discussed below.

Public Opinion and the War

By 1958, influential elements in France were proclaiming their disenchantment with the Algerian conflict. Significant sectors of the population had not fully recovered from the psychological and spiritual exhaustion following the 1940 defeat, the Nazi occupation, and the Allied invasion. Soon after the liberation had come the disastrous struggle in Indochina. By 1954, French men and women had been involved in some kind of war almost continuously for fifteen years. Now, with a new war in Algeria, opposition to the draft was increasing. Distaste for the intransigent racism of the colons was widespread; certainly the French army did not view its mission in Algeria as one of safeguarding the caste privileges of the colons, many of whom were not even French. FLN terror was increasing among the four hundred thousand Muslims resident in France; seventeen hundred of them were killed in 1957–1958. Leftist propaganda was presenting the insurgency as a movement of the entire Muslim population, a grotesque distortion. And there was the increasingly prominent question of torture.

Torture

The late Raymond Aron observed that "pacification cannot be imagined without torture, just as [a] war of liberation cannot be imagined without terror." Torture was one of the weapons used by the French during the successful effort to contain Algerian terrorism.

What was the extent of this torture? One student of the subject has argued that the French got into trouble because they used it not only against those clearly guilty, which many would have condoned or at least overlooked, but against almost any suspect, that is, almost any Algerian.[37] This is a controversial view. General Massu wrote that the employment of physical coercion was discriminating and relatively rare.[38] According to Colonel Roger Trinquier, a close collaborator of Massu's in the Tenth Parachute Division, torture was usually not necessary; the mere threat of it would make most suspects talk.[39] But the most impressive testimony against the charge of *widespread* torture by the French army comes from General Paul Aussaresses, a career intelligence officer who had joined the Free French in World War II. In 1956 Massu put him in charge of destroying the terrorist apparatus in Algiers. Many years later, Aussaresses published an amazingly frank and unapologetic defense of French counterterrorism in Algeria. Baldly describing his own directing role in these matters, he wrote that torture was both necessary and productive—but not common: "Some prisoners talked very easily. Others only needed some roughing up. It was only when a prisoner refused to talk or denied the obvious that torture was used."[40] Believing that torture had destructive psychological effects on its practitioners, Massu gave orders that no one should be employed in this work for long.[41] Only a very small fraction of the French army was ever involved. "We did everything we possibly could," writes Aussaresses, "to avoid having the youngest soldiers bloody their hands and many would have been unable to see it through anyway."[42] Besides, "most regular army officers never tortured anyone, simply because they were never placed in that sort of situation. As for the draftees, giving them that kind of assignment was out of the question."[43] Both Edgar O'Ballance and George Kelly, among others, concurred in these views.[44]

The justifications for the use of torture were predictable ones. Terror was real and widespread; many women and children, very often Muslims, were victims. Colonel Trinquier blamed the torture on the terrorists: no terror, no torture; this was "a reality which the rebellion should take into account."[45] Certainly, FLN terror revolted and frightened the French army. As Colonel Aussaresses wrote, when the parents of murdered or maimed children come to you and ask why you did not do everything in your power to save them, what do you reply?[46] An anonymous French officer wrote that "between two evils it is necessary to choose the lesser. So that innocent persons should not be put to death or mutilated, the criminals must be punished and put effectively out of harm's way."[47] General Massu justified torture because it brought terror—the killing and maiming of Muslims and Europeans alike—to a halt. (Many have used a similar form of argument to defend the carpet bombings of German and Japanese cities by the British and Americans during World War

II.) For Massu, "The innocent [i.e., the next victims of terror bombings] deserve more protection than the guilty."[48] And he raised this difficult point: "Torture is to be condemned, but we would like a precise definition as to where torture begins."[49]

Colonel Yves Godard maintained that torture was not needed. He said that, if he had been in charge, any terrorist caught red-handed would have been shot within forty-eight hours—unless he revealed what he knew about other terrorists.[50]

In March 1957, with terror incidents having been reduced almost to zero, Massu and his Tenth Paratroopers left the squalid streets of the Casbah for counterinsurgency in the open countryside.

How important was torture in the defeat of the terrorists? Many years ago, Edward Behr wrote that the Battle of Algiers could not have been won without torture.[51] This judgment is difficult to accept: the French brought overwhelming force to bear in a constricted area, against an FLN that by no means enjoyed the solid support or sympathy of the indigenous population, many of whose members were ready to work against it. It is hard to conceive how the French could *not* have won the Battle of Algiers, torture or no. In addition, widespread agreement has existed for many years that torture actually provided the French counterterrorists with little useful information beyond what was obtained from the more usual and incomparably more acceptable means of informants, surveillance, bribery, and public cooperation.[52]

What Did the Politicians Know?

In the waning years of twentieth century, the issue of torture became linked to practically the entire political establishment of the Fourth Republic, especially the leaders of the Socialist Party.[53] Whatever the nature and meaning of torture in Algeria, it was by no means a phenomenon restricted to military circles alone.

The Second Republic had declared Algeria to be not a colony or a protectorate but an integral part of France itself. Leading politicians of the Fourth Republic (1946–1958) embraced and proclaimed the complete unity of Algeria with France. René Coty, president of the Republic, compared the conflict in Algeria to France's desperate struggle for survival in the Battle of Verdun during World War I. François Mitterrand, who would serve as president of the Fifth

Republic from 1981 to 1995, declared to the French parliament, "Algeria is France, and who among you would hesitate *to employ every means* to preserve France?"[54] Pierre Mendès-France, the prime minister who gave up Vietnam in 1954, proclaimed: "The Algerian departments [i.e., territorial divisions] . . . are irrevocably French. Never will France—any French government or parliament, whatever may be their particularistic tendencies—yield on this fundamental principle."[55]

In 1956, facing a crescendo of bloody terrorism in Algeria, Socialist Prime Minister Guy Mollet demanded that parliament approve the Special Powers Law, which conferred "virtually unlimited powers" on the executive.[56] Parliament passed the bill by a vote of 455 to 76; the majority included the Communist members.[57] "It was the civilian government that sent the Tenth Paratroop Division into Algiers with orders to put an end to terrorism by whatever means necessary."[58] Imposing on the army the task of ending terrorism in Arab Algiers made at least some resort to torture almost inevitable. (That same year, the Mollet cabinet joined with the British and Israelis to invade Nasser's Egypt in the 1956 Suez operation. Indeed, managing to stay in office for sixteen months, Mollet's cabinet was the longest-lived of the Fourth Republic.)

In his memoirs, Aussaresses blandly relates that very high-ranking French officials in Paris, including Minister of Justice François Mitterrand, were aware of, and therefore at least tacitly approved, his methods. Apparently the metropolitan police also employed torture against Algerian suspects in France.[59] During the 1960s, de Gaulle's Fifth Republic proclaimed several amnesties for those accused of war crimes committed during the Algerian conflict. And in 1965 de Gaulle appointed General Massu commander of French forces in Germany.[60]

The issues raised in the Algerian conflict will reverberate resoundingly as twenty-first-century terrorism menaces the world's metropolitan populations with weapons and objectives inconceivable a generation ago.[61] How this dread phenomenon will affect the treatment of known terrorists cannot be foreseen. But the distinguished student of international politics Walter Laqueur predicted that "when terrorism becomes a real danger, those engaging in it will no longer be able to run and hide, but will be treated by those attacked as they see fit, as a *hostis,* an enemy of humankind, and thus outside the law."[62]

1958: The Army Rebels

By the end of 1957 the French army was clearly defeating the insurgents. It had almost eliminated terrorism in the large towns, and had choked off outside assistance to the guerrillas. The *regroupement* of two million rural Arabs broke the ties of the FLN with the peasantry and was starving it of food, recruits, and intelligence. There were perhaps twenty-five thousand insurgents outside Algeria, but only fifteen thousand within it (one Muslim out of every six hundred people). Bloody internal rivalries within the FLN were becoming public knowledge. Nevertheless, in part because of domestic agitation over the issue of torture, the politicians in Paris began moving toward accommodation with the FLN. In spite of the near-hysterical clamor in the press and academia, there is reason to believe that public opinion supported the army in the spring of 1958.[63] Certainly, the French electorate had little confidence in or loyalty to the Fourth Republic.[64] At any rate, deeply embittered at what it saw as its betrayal by the politicians in Vietnam and Suez, incredulous at the thought that the latest revolving-door cabinet in Paris would throw away its victory over the FLN, the army in Algiers refused to obey the constitutional civilian authorities (just like de Gaulle in 1940).[65] On May 9, commanders of the army in Algiers telegraphed to the war minister in Paris a thinly veiled warning that the army could not abandon its commitment to the numerous and vulnerable pro-French Muslims. On May 13, massive demonstrations by colons in Algiers occupied the government buildings. The crisis neared a climax on May 24,1958: army units from Algeria landed unopposed on Corsica, clearly demonstrating what they might do if further provoked. The politicians capitulated: on June 1 parliament invested Charles de Gaulle as the Fourth Republic's twenty-fifth (and last) prime minister, armed with the emergency powers he demanded. De Gaulle then appointed General Massu as prefect of Algiers. On September 28, 1958, de Gaulle submitted to a referendum his proposed constitution for a Fifth Republic. The "yes" vote was overwhelming, including in Algeria, where, despite FLN threats, Muslim voters turned out in great numbers, giving clear proof that the army and not the FLN was in control there.

Meanwhile, under the command of General Maurice Challe, the military campaign against the remaining guerrillas accelerated. Challe augmented the number of guerrilla-hunter units, supported by "tracker" units of loyal Algerian soldiers (called "Harkis": see below) and increased the number of Muslims in French uniform, making them a personal promise that France would never desert them. Moving from west to east, Challe methodically chased the guerrillas from their refuges, driving them ever closer to the Morice Line. By October 1959, the FLN was short of weapons, losing up to five hundred men per day (including desertions), and reduced to the most primitive stages of guerrilla warfare.[66]

Nevertheless, French Algeria was doomed. Like Napoleon, de Gaulle saw himself as the heir of Charlemagne, not of Louis XIV: in his vision, France's vocation and destiny lay across the Rhine, not across the Mediterranean. Determined to create a militarily powerful France, viewing the Algerian situation as too expensive financially and politically, de Gaulle moved toward independence for Algeria.[67] Some elements of the army in Algeria attempted to stop him by force, but, isolated from French society and even within the army itself, they failed.[68] Hundreds of French officers resigned from the service, were dismissed, or went to prison. Algeria received its independence on July 4, 1962.

In an ugly epilogue, some officers and ex-officers formed the Secret Army Organization (OAS). This group, seeking a partition of Algeria into European and Muslim areas, tried to incite race war and anarchy through a terror campaign that briefly rivaled that of the FLN in brutality, if not in scope. The OAS tried several times to assassinate de Gaulle and in a final paroxysm of rage and despair turned its violence against the French army itself. With the capture of its last leaders in 1967, the sad, misshapen thing perished.[69]

The Harkis

As in almost every so-called war of decolonization, the question arises: who was fighting whom, and for what? The sorrowful story of the Algerian Harkis illuminates the complexities that character-ized these conflicts.

Like other colonial powers, France had long found it both de-sirable and possible to recruit indigenous elements into its armed forces.[70] During World War I, 170,000 Algerians served in the French army; many future leaders of the FLN were among them.[71] In World War II, scores of thousands of Algerian Muslims fought under the French colors, from North Africa to Germany.

Strictly speaking, *Harki* refers to special operational units orga-nized by the French army; but it has become the common practice to use the term to refer to all Algerian Muslims who served under the French flag. The first Harki units in the Algerian conflict were formed in November 1954. The colons were always uneasy about arming and training Muslims, but in general they proved quite reli-able. Muslims undoubtedly joined the French forces for a variety of reasons; some were no doubt FLN infiltrators. But "perhaps the most significant motivation for Harki recruitment was revenge against FLN violence."[72] One noted authority maintains that 150,000 Mus-lims fought on the French side.[73] Another close student of the subject writes that "in fact by 1961 there were more Algerians fighting in the French army than in the FLN."[74] Whatever the exact figure, "the presence of tens of thousands of armed Muslims under the tricolor gave credence to the French claim to fight for Algeria rather than against it."[75] In contrast, the FLN was able to mobilize less than one male Algerian out of every two hundred: "Twenty thousand guer-rillas raised from a population of nine million [Muslims] hardly amounts to a nation in arms."[76]

The fate of these Harkis, and their families, was a key factor in the army revolt against de Gaulle in 1961, because many French soldiers were loath to abandon them as they had been forced to abandon their allies in Vietnam seven years previously. FLN propaganda to the Harkis constantly prophesied such a fate.[77]

As soon as de Gaulle recognized the insurgents as the ruling group in Algeria, the FLN and its recent adherents began wreaking vengeance upon those who had fought with the French. Wives and children of Harkis were beaten, tortured, and/or gang-raped in the streets. Executions, both official and impromptu, took place everywhere. The estimates of the number of Harkis killed in the aftermath of the war vary from 30,000 to 150,000.[78] Those French troops in Algeria awaiting transportation home received explicit orders not to interfere in these appalling massacres.[79]

At the time of the peace agreement, de Gaulle forbade any Harkis to seek refuge in France. Nevertheless, through the efforts of sympathetic French army officers, sixty-eight thousand Harkis and family members managed to reach that country. De Gaulle ordered these to be rounded up and returned to Algeria. Even to mention the fate of the Harkis was forbidden in Gaullist circles. Over the years, surviving Harkis and their families kept arriving illegally in France; most were confined for years to facilities little better than concentration camps. Today, perhaps four hundred thousand of these persons and their descendants live a very precarious life in France, where they suffer astonishingly high rates of unemployment.

Up to now, the various regimes in independent Algeria have been silent about the fate of the Harkis "because such brutality [toward them] muddies the image of a heroic FLN *maquis* [guerrilla struggle]. The Harki question has been ignored because its true dimensions would reveal that the struggle of 1954–1962 was in reality a civil war."[80] In any event, over the past forty years and more, the Algerian Republic has been the scene of large-scale internecine fighting, including firing into civilian crowds by the Algerian army and the routine use of torture against suspects. Many Harkis have pointed to the political repression and economic failure of the Algerian Republic as vindication of their support of France decades before.

Casualties

At his October 1958 press conference, President de Gaulle stated that the fighting in Algeria had taken the lives of 7,000 French soldiers, 77,000 insurgents, and 1,500 European and 10,000 Muslim civilians.[81] By 1962, French military deaths, including Muslim auxiliaries, had reached perhaps 17,500 (6,000 from noncombat causes), with another 65,000 wounded. The army claimed to have killed 141,000 insurgents, with an additional 12,000 dead through internecine fighting. European civilian casualties numbered at least 10,000. Estimates of

Muslim civilians (not Harkis) killed by the FLN reached 16,000, plus another 50,000 "missing" as the result of FLN abduction.[82]

Reflection

Algeria did not become independent through the victory of its insurgents. On the contrary, their military failure was patent, and nowhere more so than in the Battle of Algiers. Independence was the result of political and diplomatic calculations and maneuvers on a global scale, in France, in the United Nations, in the United States, in the Arab world. Two political factors played primary and perhaps decisive roles. The first was the growing opposition in metropolitan France to the costs—financial, military, moral, and diplomatic—of holding Algeria against the wishes of an increasing segment of the population there who wished to be rid of a colonial system whose time had clearly passed, or who had been terrorized into supporting the FLN. The second was de Gaulle's aspirations to dominate the emerging Western European community, incompatible with France's traditional African colonialism. And as during World War II de Gaulle eventually established his leadership over the resistance groups within occupied France, so the FLN politicians outside Algeria imposed their supremacy over the hapless insurgents within it.[83]

4

São Paulo 1965–1971 and Montevideo 1963–1973

During the 1960s, outbreaks of rural insurgency swept across Latin America, inspired by the success of Fidel Castro's Cuban revolt—or, rather, by a grotesquely flawed understanding of that success. The resounding failure of these efforts in the countryside, culminating in the 1967 execution of Ernesto Guevara in Bolivia, resulted in a turn by would-be revolutionaries toward urban guerrilla warfare.[1]

What Really Happened in Cuba

In the 1950s Cuba was in the grip of the dictator Fulgencio Batista. This decidedly uncharismatic figure succeeded in simultaneously antagonizing the Catholic Church and the business community, and eventually the U.S. State Department as well. His unpopular, corrupt, and isolated regime was supported only by its hirelings, who proved to be completely inadequate.

In 1956, Fidel Castro, a lawyer and son of a plantation owner, landed in Cuba at the head of a revolutionary force of about eighty members. Encountering army units, Castro escaped to the Sierra Maestra with a few dozen survivors. Waging a small-scale guerrilla and a large-scale propaganda war against Batista, Castro promised that if he were victorious, he would restore the democratic constitution of 1940 and hold free elections.

However unpopular and unappealing Batista's regime, his army of fifteen thousand should have been quite adequate to deal with Castro's band, but it was, in fact, less an army than a uniformed extortion ring, with little counterinsurgency training, its leadership "a demoralized gaggle of corrupt, cruel, and lazy officers without combat experience."[2] In two years of desultory fighting, the army suffered an average of three fatalities per week, about the same number that could have been expected to lose their lives in street accidents or barroom brawls. Entire units would surrender without a shot having been fired. Then in May 1958 the Eisenhower administration imposed an arms embargo on Cuba. This refusal to sell arms to what had hitherto been an internationally recognized government signaled to everyone that Washington wanted, or at least expected, Batista to fall. On December 10, the U.S. State Department withdrew its recognition of Batista's government. On New Year's Eve, Batista fled, even though a large proportion of his army had not yet engaged in battle. Hence, what happened in Cuba was much less a Castro victory than a Batista collapse.[3]

Clearly, then, it would have been both logical and prudent to expect that attempts to overthrow other Latin American regimes that were more popular, legitimate, competent, and/or energetic might well meet with an outcome very different from the Cuban affair. But quite beyond even that vitally important consideration, the would-be imitators of Castro promised not democracy but a Leninist state, mass executions, and a disruptive confrontation with the United States; that is, they promised not what Castro had promised but what he had actually delivered once in power. The Castro regime had shot great numbers of Cuban army officers; appalled and frightened by this spectacle, officer corps all across Latin America galvanized themselves to meet the Castroite threat. Presidents Kennedy and Johnson vigorously assisted such preparations with money, supplies, intelligence, and training.

Predictably, efforts to export the Castro revolution came to frustration across the whole spectrum of Latin American states, from dictatorships to democracies.[4] One of the earliest efforts took place in Venezuela between 1960 and 1963. That country was under the leadership of Rómulo Betancourt, who had attained the presidency in 1958 through a free election. The Venezuelan Communist Party launched an urban insurgency to overthrow Betancourt, even though it represented less than half of 1 percent of the population, and despite Guevara's warning that "when a government has come to power through some form of popular vote, fraudulent or not, and maintains at least the appearance of constitutional legality, the guerrilla outbreak cannot be promoted, since the possibilities of peaceful struggle have not yet been exhausted."[5] The insurgents, mainly university and even high school students, carried out robberies, terror bombings, and sniper attacks in many Venezuelan cities. The random shooting of ordinary policemen, most of whom came from working-class families, was perhaps the insurgents' greatest blunder. As the December 1963 presidential election approached, the guerrillas threatened to shoot down anyone, even women and children, found out of doors on election day. Voter turnout, however, reached 91 percent. After this humiliating rebuff, the insurgents turned to guerrilla warfare in the countryside. To assist them, Castro landed some Cuban guerrillas on the coast, but the campaign proved futile, and by 1969 at the latest the whole country was free of noticeable guerrilla activity.

At the opposite end of the political spectrum from Venezuela was El Salvador. Beginning in 1979, the government of that small country faced a guerrilla insurgency led by the Farabundo Marti National Liberation Front (FMLN), whose birth had been announced in Havana. The Salvadoran regime was undeniably oppressive, but a determined anti-Communist solidarity tightly bound the upper and upper middle classes and the army together against the FMLN. Presidents Carter and Reagan provided assistance to the Salvadoran army, while under Washington's prodding the regime slowly but visibly made progress toward democratic reforms. In 1992, with United Nations supervision, most elements of the FMLN agreed to give up revolutionary violence for political participation. Its candidates did poorly in the internationally observed 1994 elections.

The only place in all Latin America where self-described acolytes of Castro came to power was Nicaragua, when in 1979, after years of fighting, the pro-Castro Sandinistas replaced an isolated kleptocracy very much like Batista's. There were, however, at least two very notable differences between the Cuban and Nicaraguan cases. First, the Nicaraguan army, well equipped and well trained, was probably the best one in Central America. Its officers were quite aware of the fate of Batista's army. The fighting, therefore, almost certainly would have gone on indefinitely, but in July 1979 the Carter administration helped broker a cease-fire that included guarantees against mass executions of the former regime's soldiers. The second notable difference between the two cases was this: in 1990 the overconfident leaders of the Sandinista regime, intoxicated by their own propaganda, allowed an internationally observed presidential election to take place. The Sandinista candidate suffered a defeat as resounding as it was unexpected and experienced another decisive rebuff in the elections of 1996.

Thus, would-be revolutionaries eventually sought to develop urban guerrilla warfare in Latin America primarily because classic guerrilla insurgency in the countryside had failed almost everywhere, or could not even be attempted because of unfavorable circumstances. There were, of course, additional contributing factors: The seeming successes of urban guerrillas in Cyprus and Algeria influenced Latin American revolutionaries; everyone began to realize that the majority of Latin Americans were living in or around cities (Latin America has perhaps the highest proportion of urban dwellers in the world—over 75 percent);[6] and last, but important, most aspiring guerrillas were students or other city types, who could neither adapt easily to life in the countryside nor communicate effectively with the peasants they encountered there.[7]

But whether rural or urban, the fundamental idea of Latin American insurgencies since Castro has been that a mass following is not a prerequisite, or even a concomitant, of the outbreak of revolutionary violence. Instead, mass support would inevitably manifest itself *as the result of* the armed action of the guerrilla group and government efforts to suppress that armed action. This approach to revolution came to be known as *foquismo*.[8] Urban guerrilla warfare replicates the fundamental concepts (and weaknesses) of foquismo: an armed nucleus substitutes for an organized party, and violent acts create revolutionary conditions.[9] It bears repeating that these notions, and the actions that flowed from them, radically contradicted the analysis and advice of Clausewitz, Lenin, and Mao (see the introduction).

Brazil

Urban guerrilla warfare broke out in Brazil in the aftermath of the 1964 assumption of power by the armed forces.

In Latin America, throughout the nineteenth and twentieth centuries, "it [was] often the constitution itself that [gave] the military the right, even the obligation, to intervene in the political process under certain circumstances."[10] Students of the role of the Brazilian armed forces in political affairs have developed what they call "the moderator model." In this model, "the military in a sense assumes constitutional functions analogous to those of the Supreme Court in the United States: they [the military] have the responsibility to preserve the political order and hence are drawn into politics at times of crisis or controversy to veto actions by the 'political' branches of government which deviate from the essentials of that system."[11] (Until the late nineteenth century, this supreme court or moderator role had been the prerogative of the Emperor of Brazil.)

Among the key components of this moderator model:

1. Military intervention per se is not seen as an aberration or an abuse but rather as a natural and desirable phenomenon under certain circumstances.
2. Both civilian and military elites acknowledge the legitimacy of military intervention but not the legitimacy of extended military rule.
3. All major civilian groups seek to use the military for their own purposes.
4. The principal aspect of the military's moderator role is to check the excesses of the chief executive or simply to remove him from office.[12]

Demands from civilian politicians and other elites that the army perform its moderator role always preceded its intervention in political affairs. Thus, "a coup would be seen as a movement of the army *with* civilians rather than *against* them."[13]

The 1964 Coup

In 1930 Getúlio Vargas, governor of the state of Rio Grande do Sul, had almost certainly been victorious in the presidential election, but the entrenched political machine that had run Brazil for the previous forty years decreed that he had been defeated. With army support, Vargas overthrew the machine and assumed the presidency. Establishing a velvet-glove dictatorship with notable resemblances to the Mussolini regime, Vargas retained power for the next fifteen years. But by the end of World War II, he had become an international embarrassment for many Brazilians. The army pointedly suggested to Vargas that he resign, which he did. In the 1950 presidential election, however, Vargas won with a plurality of the votes, to the deep dismay of the army and the middle class. This new Vargas administration became increasingly demagogic and anti-U.S. After the attempted assassination of a prominent anti-Vargas politician on the streets of Rio de Janeiro in August 1954, the army for the second time required Vargas to step down, whereupon the president shot himself to death.

In 1961, the elected president resigned after only a few months in office, and Vice President "Jango" Goulart succeeded him. Goulart was the very embodiment of everything the Brazilian middle class disliked and feared about Vargas, whose protégé and lieutenant he had been. Worse, Goulart's political ineptitude was of truly Amazonian proportions. He publicly embraced the Brazilian Communist Party and gave inflammatory speeches to labor rallies, while presiding over astronomical inflation and an actual decline in Brazil's GDP. Incredibly, he tried to meddle with the army's sacrosanct promotion policies, and even encouraged indiscipline among its noncommissioned officers. The army leadership now feared that Goulart was planning to make himself a Brazilian Juan Perón.[14] The end came shortly after he threatened to close down Congress and revise the constitution, the very document under whose shadow he could have claimed protection. Powerful politicians and major newspapers were by now openly clamoring for the army to remove Goulart; the governors of the key states of São Paulo and Rio de Janeiro mobilized their large and well-equipped militias against the president. In the first days of April 1964, the army removed Goulart, who was permitted to go unmolested over the border to Uruguay.[15]

Apologists for Brazil's urban guerrillas blamed the military coup, and its straitjacketing of normal politics, for the outbreak of violence after 1964.[16] There was no alternative, that is, to armed revolt. At least three serious problems arise with such an explanation. First, the 1964 coup was in a venerable tradition of Brazilian politics (the "moderator model") and no previous military intervention had been followed by any notable outbreak of insurgency. Second, many of those who organized or participated in urban insurgency after the 1964 coup had been members of the Brazilian Communist Party or students of Communist guerrilla techniques (or both) for years before 1964.[17] This is especially the case with the insurgency's most well-known figure, Carlos Marighella. Besides, the military regime continued in office for many years after the urban insurgency had been crushed. A third problem with the repression-provoked-rebellion theory arises from electoral data. After the coup, the leaders of the military essentially chose the president of the republic from among themselves. But, while barring from active politics certain politicians whom they held particularly responsible for Brazil's problems, they nevertheless allowed competitive elections for other offices to occur with regularity, elections in which the great majority of Brazilian voters participated and which were usually won by candidates, parties, and coalitions favorable (or at least not hostile) to the military regime. In the November 1966 elections for Congress, the pro-government coalition won a substantial victory over the opposition coalition.[18] General Emilio Medici, president from 1969 to 1974, always retained high levels of personal popularity, at least in part because the country's GDP was growing at 11 percent annually.[19] In the 1970 elections for the lower house of Congress, pro-government candidates amassed 48 percent of the vote, while the main opposition coalition received 21 percent, and blank ballots (presumably protest votes) totaled 21 percent.[20] And in 1989, in the first presidential election after the military had reestablished civilian rule, the conservative candidate Collor de Mello defeated leftist Lula da Silva (who did attain the presidency thirteen years later).

Thus the urban guerrillas, by trying to make a revolution against an election-holding regime, violated one of Guevara's fundamental prescriptions for insurgents. But since advocates and practitioners of urban guerrilla war have already dismissed Clausewitz, Lenin, and Mao Tse-tung, ignoring Guevara must have seemed a minor peccadillo indeed.

In any event, it is not unreasonable to conclude that the taking of power by the military was more the excuse than the cause of the subsequent urban insurgency or terrorism.

Marighella

Carlos Marighella is the most widely known of Brazil's urban guerrillas. Born in Bahia in 1911, he was the descendant of African slaves on his mother's side. He gave up plans to take an engineering degree at Salvador Polytechnic University to become a full-time Communist activist in São Paulo. During the 1930s, in imitation of the Stalin purges, he ruthlessly hunted out Brazilian Trotskyists. He successfully campaigned for a seat in Congress in 1946 and had become a member of the Communist Party Central Committee by 1952. He visited China, where he studied Maoist guerrilla methods. In the wake of the 1964 military coup, the leaders of the Brazilian Communist Party took the position that efforts at violent revolution would be premature.[21] Rejecting this stance, Marighella quit the party in 1965 and founded an urban-oriented guerrilla movement, the ALN (National Liberation Action).

In Marighella's conception, the functions of urban guerrilla warfare were to tie up the forces of order, attack the morale of those forces by assassination and elusiveness, show the population that the regime was vulnerable and even impotent, and commit calculated outrages that would provoke the regime to ferocious repression, which in turn would alienate the population. But in fact the repression destroyed Marighella's organization, as will be seen.

Marighella's principal writing is the *Minimanual of the Urban Guerrilla*, which has gone through various translations, titles, and publishers. In it, Marighella accepts the name of terrorist for his organization and strategy. In his scheme, urban guerrilla warfare was preparatory to guerrilla outbreaks in the countryside, which would eventually become the decisive theater (although the urban guerrillas would distract the forces of repression from concentrating against the rural insurgency). The urban guerrillas must also kill all "agents of North American Imperialism." For Marighella, the advantages of the urban guerrillas were knowledge of the terrain, intelligence, mobility, and surprise. They must avoid battle with government forces (and hence would not be true guerrillas, but merely terrorists). Marighella's vision was apocalyptic and utterly unconcerned with the suffering his campaign would seek to create: "The urban guerrilla is not afraid of *dismantling and destroying the present Brazilian economic, political and social system,* for his aim is to help the rural guerrilla and collaborate in the creation of a totally new and revolutionary social and political structure with the armed people in power" (my emphasis).

His followers, never numerous, were mainly upper-class youths. "They knew their Regis Debray [a foquista "theorist"] better than their Brazilian geography."[22] They robbed banks; bombed theaters, supermarkets, and government buildings; and assassinated a U.S. Army officer, Captain Charles Chandler.

In the urban environment, certain classic counterinsurgency techniques, such as dispersing long-range hunter-killer groups in known guerrilla areas, are inappropriate. But the value of intelligence gathering can not be overemphasized. Infiltrators, defectors, informants, and confessing prisoners were the fundament of the Brazilian counterinsurgent and counterterrorist campaign. In Brazil, as elsewhere, defectors were sometimes motivated by ideological disagreements and/or despair over the insurgency's lack of progress, but personality conflicts and jealousies were also numerous and produced much valuable information for the counterinsurgents. Surveillance was another pillar in the campaign: the security forces tapped phones and opened mail and watched the relatives, friends, and contacts of suspected guerrillas. Arrests, interrogations, and more arrests became the thrust of counterinsurgency in Brazil's urban setting. Then in June 1969 the police and military in São Paulo introduced the technique of the massive dragnet, detaining and questioning literally thousands of suspects or possible informants. The practice was soon imitated in other cities.

Kidnapping was of course a major insurgent weapon, mainly because it was so relatively easy. But the guerrillas fatally overplayed their hand when they snatched U.S. ambassador Burke Elbrick on September 4, 1969. They demanded that the government release imprisoned guerrillas. The government complied with the demands, and Elbrick in turn was freed unharmed. But the security forces carried out a truly massive crackdown: a great dragnet resulted in thirty-two thousand arrests. Information extracted from captured guerrillas in this operation revealed the whereabouts of Marighella himself, who was shot dead in the streets of São Paulo on November 4, 1969.[23]

During and after the suppression of the insurgency, allegations that the police (usually) and the military (sometimes) tortured known or suspected terrorists became widespread. Undoubtedly many of these allegations were well founded.[24] A distinguished student of Brazilian affairs writes that physical torture in interrogation was common in Brazil throughout the nineteenth century and during the Vargas regime (1930–1945), that indeed the use of police or judicial torture has, regrettably, been characteristic of most governments throughout history and was quite common in the twentieth century, not least in the Communist world.[25] During the 1920s the forces of the Irish Free State liberally employed physical persuasion against IRA prisoners, and the IRA used similar methods in Northern Ireland. Those who were aware of such practices in French Algeria seem to have been quite numerous and included persons in very high positions. (See the discussion of torture in Algeria, pp. 62–64.)

In any event, the death of Marighella in itself did not bring terrorism to a complete halt, in part because of the great fragmentation of urban guerrilla groups in Brazil. One of the larger of these splinter groups was the VPR (Vanguardia Popular Revolucionaria). Some VPR members had received training in Cuba; at least one of these persons became a valuable police informer.[26] In 1967 the VPR bombed the Peace Corps office in Rio de Janeiro. In March 1970 they kidnapped the Japanese consul-general in São Paulo, in June the German ambassador in Rio de Janeiro, and in December, also in Rio, the Swiss ambassador (killing his bodyguard). These kidnappings triggered massive roundups. By late 1970 the VPR had been reduced to about thirty militants.

At the same time (October 1970), police captured and killed Joaquim Camara Ferreira, close to eighty years old but nevertheless Marighella's designated successor. The last of the major guerrilla leaders, Carlos Lamarca of the VPR, was shot in Bahia in September 1971. His death for all practical purposes signaled the end of urban guerrilla warfare in Brazil.[27] Thus "by the beginning of 1972 the urban guerrillas had been defeated; most were dead; the rest were in prison or in exile."[28]

What, then, had the Brazilian urban guerrillas accomplished? The small and short-lived Symbionese Liberation Army in the United States of the early 1970s adopted the tactics set forth in Marighella's

Minimanual. So did terrorist groups in West Germany and Italy.[29] All these groups came to a bad end, with almost all of their small memberships shot or imprisoned—not exactly a resounding vindication for Marighella's ideas. "In the end, the [Brazilian] guerrillas' principal effect was to strengthen the hand of those arguing for greater repression."[30] Other revealing indicators of the effectiveness of the Brazilian episode: E. Bradford Burns, in his magisterial *History of Brazil,* a work of 450 pages, devotes exactly two paragraphs to the urban guerrillas, and Timothy Wickham-Crowley's 424-page study of Latin American guerrillas devotes less than three lines to Marighella.[31]

Uruguay

"The Tupamaros [of Uruguay] have been the most successful of all the Latin American urban guerrilla groups."[32] The definition of success can be wonderfully elastic.

Revolutionary movements seem to elicit an automatically sympathetic response from many quarters. "Put crudely, we tend to work on the assumption that there is no such thing as bad peoples, only bad governments, and the very occurrence of revolutionary violence establishes a prima facie judgment in our minds in favor of the rebels and against the authorities."[33] The belief that internal conflict "erupts spontaneously out of conditions grown socially and economically intolerable—and can only erupt out of such conditions—is a very important propaganda weapon in the hands of proponents of revolutionary warfare."[34] At any rate, the events in Uruguay in the early 1960s illustrate that a repressive regime is by no means a necessary condition for the appearance and development of an insurgency.

The Setting

During the first half of the twentieth century, Uruguay was a stable, prosperous society characterized by competitive elections, free labor unions, and a generous welfare system.[35] Its people enjoyed the highest literacy rate in Latin America, with free tuition at all educational levels. For decades the country's cattle-based export economy provided one of the highest living standards in Latin America. Many immigrants from Spain and Italy brought valuable skills, widening the middle class. The Church, the army, and the landed aristocracy did not exert the influence they did in most other Latin American countries. Two parties, the Blancos and the Colorados, dominated electoral politics, and loyalty to them was cultural and interclass, as in Colombia. By 1960, nearly half the population lived in or near the capital of Montevideo, where the middle class comprised almost two-thirds of the inhabitants.[36] Before 1973 the army, with no tradition of repression, numbered only nine thousand in a population of three million. A very long period of social peace had left the Uruguayan security forces unprepared to confront organized terrorism.[37]

The country's welfare system included early retirement on social security, with very generous pensions for members of the swollen state bureaucracy. But with the end of World War II came a sharp decline in the value of Uruguay's animal exports. By the 1960s, rising prices and growing unemployment were reinforcing one another.[38] In 1961, before the appearance of the Tupamaros, Philip B. Taylor, describing the Uruguayan method of administration as "compulsive inefficiency," wrote that "the extensive social commitments of the state, together with the obsolescent legal restraints on private enterprise, have made this country one of the highest-cost producers in Latin America. It therefore cannot compete for foreign markets for its manufactures. . . . The country is not attractive either to large new foreign or domestic investments, and it does not hold great appeal for the young university-trained specialist or professional who needs a job."[39]

More than half the workforce consisted of public service sector employees; only 28 percent worked in industry and 19 percent in agriculture.[40] In the decade after 1963 the cost of living rose by a factor of sixty. In 1967, when President Pacheco Areco took office, Uruguay had the lowest growth rate and highest inflation rate in South America. Cuts in benefits and late paydays for civil servants produced much bitterness, and alienated bank employees would help the Tupamaros pull off some spectacular robberies.[41] From July to September 1969, strikes by bank clerks shut down almost the entire national banking system. (Nevertheless, most unions were controlled by the Communists, who disapproved of Tupamaro violence.) Spectacular revelations by the Tupamaros of systematic peculation in banks and government ministries, along with President Pacheco's plans to seek an unconstitutional second term, compounded the political confusion and economic malaise.

The Tupamaro Worldview

The Tupamaros organized in late 1962–early 1963 under the leadership of veterans of sugar-beet strikes in northern Uruguay. They took their name from Tupac Amaru, an eighteenth-century Indian leader of an anti-Spanish revolt in distant Peru. (The profound disconnect between this symbolic name and the overwhelmingly Spanish and Italian population of Uruguay is very revealing.) Their emblem was the five-pointed red star of the Soviet empire. In 1965 they adopted the name Movimiento de Liberacion Nacional (Tupamaros).

Although their origins lay in the euphoria following Fidel Castro's victory, the Tupamaros generally understood that Uruguay was not a promising locale for a Maoist-type strategy. Hence their enthusiastic embrace of foquismo. In their estimation the Castro revolution had triumphed as a *foco,* and the Cuban success could be reproduced in almost any Latin American country. The Tupamaros bitterly criticized Latin American Communist parties for their inaction. Of course, the Communists (generally) eschewed insurgency because they believed that true revolutionary situations did not exist in most of Latin America. After all, Lenin had declared:

The fundamental law of revolution, which has been confirmed by all revolutions and especially by all three Russian revolutions in the twentieth century, is as follows: for a revolution to take place it is not enough for the exploited and oppressed masses to realize the impossibility of living in the old way, and demand changes; for a revolution to take place, it is essential that the exploiters should not be able to live and rule in the old way. It is only when the lower classes do not want to live in the old way *and the upper classes cannot carry on in the old way* that the revolution can triumph. This truth can be expressed in other words: revolution is impossible without a nation-wide crisis affecting both the exploiters and the exploited.[42]

That is, the Bolshevik coup d'état of October 1917 was possible only because the Russian army had disintegrated after three years of conventional war, and the Russian government was isolated from Allied assistance. Neither of these essential conditions prevailed in Uruguay (or Brazil either)—quite the contrary. Hence, all well-instructed Communists rejected foquismo as an anti-Leninist formula for disaster.

Events were to show that this Communist analysis (or at least their position) was correct, but the Tupamaros rejected it outright. "They [the Uruguayan Communists] do not understand that revolutionary situations are created by revolutionary actions."[43] Revolutionary deeds would provoke government reprisals, expose "the illusion of bourgeois democracy," and thus win a mass following for the Tupamaros.

The Tupamaros blamed most of Uruguay's problems on foreigners, especially the British and the Americans; these foreigners were exploiters by definition, because they made a profit on trade with and investment in Uruguay.[44] The solution to all ills would be Marxism-Leninism on the Soviet model. The Tupamaros saw the USSR, China, North Korea, North Vietnam, and Cuba as ready-made allies.[45] And they looked forward to provoking an invasion of Uruguay by Brazil or Argentina (or both) so that they could then assume the role of defenders of the nation.[46] Such a stunningly inadequate understanding of the realities and possibilities of their situation dramatically underlines how profoundly isolated from their society—from *any* society—the Tupamaros really were.

A Sampling of Tupamaro Analysis

The principal ideological guide and inspiration of the Tupamaros was Abraham Guillen. Born in 1913 in Guadalajara, Spain, he fought in the ranks of the Anarchists during the Spanish Civil War, and eventually settled in Argentina. Excerpts from several of his works have been published as *Philosophy of the Urban Guerrilla,* from which the following several quotations derive.[47] "In this planetary epoch," explains Guillen, "the North American proletariat will not liberate itself from Wall Street until it is assisted in its revolutionary struggle by the Latin American proletariat."[48] "During the second half of the twentieth century, a war between the two Americas [North and South] is likely to emerge from the historical and socioeconomic situation."[49] That is, Guillen foresees a united South America at war against the United States, which will also have to contend with an internal proletarian revolution. "The Americanization of Europe with the assistance of Eurodollars is the most disgraceful example of financial colonization the capitalist world has known."[50] World War II, of course, was just "an imperialist war," part of the "political game of power of Nazi fascism and Anglo-Saxon imperialism."[51] Writing of the riots in Europe of May 1968, Guillen rhapsodizes that "the students of France, Germany, Italy, Belgium, Spain and the United States are in a state of permanent rebellion [and thus are apparently immortal?]."[52] Indeed, "the Second French Revolution [the 1968 riots] was a sublime event: the urban combat of May 11 was worthy of the great classical battles with phalanxes and legions. Altogether 75 cars were set on fire . . . 72 policemen were wounded."[53]

Who Were the Tupamaros?

Many studies have identified the middle and upper class origins of revolutionary leaders all over Latin America, and the Tupamaros were no exception to this phenomenon.[54] Although the movement's membership contained some criminal elements both native and Argentinean, "in the case of the Tupamaros the commanding cadres and the greater part of the rank and file have come from the universities, the liberal professions, and the rebellious petty-bourgeois youth. . . . There are few workers or peasants in the columns of the Tupamaros."[55] Raul Sendic, founder and supreme leader of the Tupamaros, was born in 1925, the son of a landowner. He had attended the University of Montevideo and studied law. The average Tupamaro prisoner in the 1960s was between twenty-five and twenty-eight years old.[56] "Terrorists in democratic societies," writes Walter Laqueur, "tend to be elitists; they know better than the masses what is good for them."[57] Interviews with Tupamaro leaders showed them to be generally immature, narcissistic, and lacking sophistication, worldly experience, and analytical ability. Most active Tupamaros were actual or self-identified failures in society in various ways, including relations with the opposite sex, and assumed a pose of rejecting society instead of society having rejected them.[58]

Tupamaro Activities

The weaknesses of the police force allowed the Tupamaros time to get organized, and then to carry out some daring raids with impunity. They organized themselves into four- or five-man "firing groups," only the leaders of which knew members of any other squad. The first public act of the Tupamaros took place in 1963; they attacked

Montevideo's Swiss Rifle Club, escaping with many good weapons. In subsequent years they occasionally hijacked a food delivery truck and distributed the food in poor neighborhoods. They robbed banks, obtaining both the means to bribe police officers and jailers and evidence of corruption in certain banking and business sectors. They also kidnapped foreign diplomats, bombed the Brazilian embassy and the offices of the Colorado Party, firebombed the homes of government officials and army officers, and killed ordinary policemen who were riding buses on their way to work or walking their beats. The reaction of the security forces to these acts was very mild compared to what happened under similar provocations in Brazil and some other places.

On May 29, 1970, with inside help, a Tupamaro band took over the naval training barracks in Montevideo for several hours and carried away many rifles and explosives. Then on August 9 came the kidnapping of U.S. police adviser Dan Mitrione. The government refused to meet the insurgents' demands in exchange for Mitrione's release, while thousands of police and troops searched Montevideo sector by sector. The Tupamaros then murdered Mitrione, in a country that had long before abolished capital punishment. By this act, and the subsequent murder of other hostages, the Tupamaros lost their vague Robin Hood image and became a feared and unpopular group. The Mitrione killing led to truly massive searches; these uncovered Tupamaro "prisons" where kidnap victims were held, and resulted in the arrest of many insurgents, including key leaders. (Political hostage-takers should demand the publication of a manifesto in the press or the playing of an address over the radio; killing a hostage is almost always a costly mistake.) Nevertheless, the Tupamaros still had the means to pull off some spectacular coups. In January 1971 they kidnapped the British ambassador, Geoffrey Jackson, and held him for eight months. They also nabbed the Uruguayan attorney general the following March. But in that same month, after taking over a factory, a group of Tupamaros spent hours lecturing the assembled workers, giving the police plenty of time to surround the place and capture everybody involved.

Then in September, a mass prison break freed many Tupamaros and made the police look hopelessly incompetent. Prison conditions in Uruguay, even during this insurgency, were incredibly lenient; for

example, through visits from relatives and friends, Tupamaro prisoners kept themselves in contact with the organization outside.[59]

Prisons are schools in which revolutionaries make converts and learn much from professional criminals concerning secrecy, robbery, and kidnapping. Hence, locking up groups of revolutionaries can strengthen the insurgent cause.[60] In Uruguay, however, few things ever seemed to work out as predicted, and the prison escape turned out to be harmful to the insurgents. The Tupamaro organization had stressed the independence of individual activist cells and the consequent anonymity of Tupamaros to each other. But in prison many insurgents had gotten to know one another; hence, after the jailbreak, the arrest of one Tupamaro would lead to the apprehension of many others. Besides, reintegrating formerly imprisoned leaders back into the Tupamaro organization kindled jealousies and even betrayals.

The End

The Tupamaros seem to have received relatively little help from outside, even though they had made overtures to similar organizations in Latin America and elsewhere.[61] At least one authority, however, believes that they obtained some funds from China and Cuba and may have received a visit from Che Guevara in 1967.[62] (If such a visit actually took place, it would be interesting to know what Guevara said to the Tupamaros, since they were violating his fundamental warning about trying to make revolution against a democratic regime.)

Tupamaro efforts to expand their activities into the countryside in 1971 failed. Meanwhile, the Uruguayan government was increasing the pressure on the insurgents. In September 1971, in light of the disappointing efforts of the police, President Pacheco placed the army in charge of the anti-Tupamaro campaign (the army was not fully employed against them until 1972). He also imposed a news blackout concerning the Tupamaros, a serious blow to them, because publicity is "the lifeblood of the urban guerrilla."[63] In April 1972 his successor, President Bordaberry, asked the Congress to declare a state of internal war, greatly increasing the authority of the army.

The Uruguayan army was and remained a volunteer force. In the 1960s it was small, poorly trained, and meagerly equipped. In 1963, 1 percent of the national budget went to the army (versus 26 percent

by 1973).[64] It possessed no elite counterterror force, although in 1968 a special unit, the Metropolitan Guards, was created with help from Brazilian and U.S. advisers.

On the eve of the massive military campaign of 1972, a former police chief estimated that there were only three thousand active Tupamaros. But both the police and the army lacked good intelligence about the Tupamaro organization. Like the police, the army relied on massive and intrusive house-to-house searches, frightening and antagonizing many innocent civilians.[65] (A clear lesson from both Uruguay and Northern Ireland is that security forces must observe the strictest rectitude when searching civilian homes; only specially trained and supervised units should carry out this sort of activity.) In contrast, the Tupamaros had easily penetrated the civil service, the police, and even the army, and hence their members were frequently able to avoid being caught in big raids.[66] Captured Tupamaros, most of whom knew almost nothing about the organization and were acquainted with few other members, provided little information. Nor did anybody seem to make any serious efforts to attract defectors to the government side. Nevertheless, from time to time such persons appeared. The defection of a major leader in early 1972 produced valuable new information, and a great sweep of Montevideo in the spring of 1972 arrested hundreds of suspects, uncovered hiding places and equipment, and generally dealt a severe blow to the insurgent organization. Then in September 1972, the army captured the insurgents' supreme leader, Raul Sendic; with this blow, "the Tupamaros were effectively finished."[67] By mid-1973, the insurgency had ceased to be visible, just about the same time that the Brazilian urban guerrilla effort faded away.

Reflection

The experiences of urban guerrillas in Uruguay and Brazil expose certain structural impediments to this kind of revolutionary activity, especially but not exclusively in Latin America. In the first place, because of their disorganized social environment and well-founded fear of strangers, slum dwellers are not easy targets for insurgent organization.[68] Second, in most cases the legal or traditional left has already organized most of the organizable. Third, while the state

is often absent in rural areas, it will be heavily present in the cities, and especially in the capital; hence, guerrillas are vulnerable to mass arrests, information supplied to the authorities by captured or defecting members, and effective police work in general. And the visibility and equipment of a regular army, normally impediments in rural areas, turn into advantages in cities, where they give the government forces an appearance of unchallengeable power. Fourth, by establishing safe houses, "people's prisons," and other infrastructure, urban guerrillas can lose their mobility and make themselves vulnerable to neighborhood cordons and house-to-house searches. True guerrillas do not defend pieces of turf. Fifth, the geographical location of cities such as São Paulo and Montevideo negated any chance of establishing cross-border sanctuaries or receiving outside assistance. Sixth, because of these urban disadvantages, the insurgents must place tremendous emphasis on security and secrecy. They must be unseen, which serves to isolate them from society and each other. Their overt military organization cuts the insurgents off from their supposed constituency and reduces their ability to propagate those political issues intended to vivify the revolutionary movement. The recruitment of new members becomes dangerous. Communication between different units becomes difficult and often unidirectional. *Compartimentacion*—organizing and existing in small cells—makes large-scale operations perilous or impossible, not only because of poor communications but also because the participants do not know the members of other groups in their organization, or who is in charge. By definition, urban guerrillas must operate in secrecy, but "as a general rule, the greater the secrecy, the greater the inefficiency of the organization or operation."[69]

But in addition to structural impediments or the efforts of the forces of order, the failure of both rural and urban insurgencies in Latin America derived from the inadequacy of their strategies and tactics. The Tupamaros could rob banks and kidnap civilians in part because both the police and the army were small, inexperienced, and inefficient. But the insurgents never had the ability to deploy large formations and attack hard targets. Their analysis led them to expect that their violence would cause a mass popular uprising, but their elitism and their small numbers cut the Tupamaros off from the urban and rural populations.[70] Out of this isolation came the

Tupamaros' extraordinary proclamation in 1970 that "we believe we have won the support of the mass of the people."[71] Of course, if they had such support, then in democratic Uruguay they could have become a powerful, even victorious, political party. But in fact the Tupamaros "had not yet managed to provide themselves with a mass base."[72] Indeed, even the entire constitutional or nonviolent left obtained unimpressive vote totals; thus "there [was] no possible chance of the left gaining power through elections."[73] The Tupamaros' one big flirtation with electoral politics brought no success. In the presidential election of November 1971, they endorsed the leftist Frente Amplio (Broad Front). This highly diverse coalition, in which the Communists were the largest single component, received only 18.3 percent of the vote.[74] More than 80 percent of the ballots in that election went to the traditional Colorado and Blanco parties.

In essence, the most important reason the Tupamaros suffered final defeat was that they were completely unable to formulate a realistic plan to obtain popular support. They knew in the early 1960s that they could not pursue power through the ballot box because they lacked popular support; but in that case their turn to urban violence spelled their certain doom.

With the defeat of the Tupamaros, the leaders of the military increasingly pressured the government to implement reforms they saw as necessary to rescue the country from its problems. The conventional end of the traditional democratic system in Uruguay dates from the closing of the Congress by President Bordaberry in June 1973. Thus, by frightening the army and society at large and by publicizing corruption among elements of the political elite, the Tupamaros did achieve the distinction of bringing down Uruguay's decades-old democracy. Hence, some observers have warned that the Tupamaros showed the vulnerability of a democratic society to systematic violence.[75] However, one must be cautious in comparing Uruguay to other democracies; during the 1970s and 1980s, terrorists resoundingly failed in the United States, Italy, and West Germany. If terrorism could topple democratic governments, Israel would have fallen half a century ago. And anyway, Uruguay soon returned to normal political life; in the 1984 presidential election, the leftist coalition (whose elements were by no means all pro-Tupamaro) won only 21 percent of the vote.

As one distinguished student of urban guerrillas summarized the Uruguayan conflict, "Thus the failure of the Tupamaros (judged on their own aims) reinforces the view of most commentators—both radical and conservative—that a determined government can crush an urban guerrilla movement, particularly if that government takes care to give at least an appearance of adverting to popular grievances and legitimizes its stand through traditional devices such as elections."[76]

And, as the failure of those who sought to export their version of the Castro revolution suggested the path of urban guerrilla warfare, so the failure of urban guerrilla warfare helped produce the strategy of Peru's Sendero Luminoso Movement, actually a return to Mao's classic formulation of "encircling the cities from the countryside"—which also failed.

5

Saigon 1968

Named for the lunar month of Tet, the great offensive of January 1968 was the biggest operation ever launched by the Communist forces in South Vietnam and their North Vietnamese sponsors. It was the most spectacular event of the Vietnamese war. And it was the greatest defeat sustained by the Communists in that entire conflict.

The Genesis and Rationale of the Tet Offensive

By 1965, the United States had become heavily involved in what many Americans described as a "limited war." But there was certainly nothing limited about it on the Communist side; the state of North Vietnam was making an all-out effort. By spring 1967, Communist losses had reached horrendous levels. Hanoi was requiring its people to suffer casualty rates twice those of the Japanese in World War II. In 1969, General Vo Nguyen Giap, commander of the North Vietnamese army (NVA), told an interviewer that between 1965 and 1968, Communist losses amounted to six hundred thousand out of a total Vietnamese population of perhaps thirty-three million.[1] Morale among the Communist-led Viet Cong (VC) was becoming dangerously low.

In contrast, from 1960 to the summer of 1967, thirteen thousand Americans were killed in action in Vietnam, about the same number of Americans who died in that period by falling off the roofs of their houses, or one-fifth the number of Americans killed annually in the United States in highway accidents. World War II claimed fully 48 percent of the American GNP; the Korean conflict took 12 percent. But in 1967, only 9 percent of the American GNP was going to the military, of which one-third was for the war in Vietnam.[2] At its height in 1968, the number of U.S. military personnel in South Vietnam equaled about one-third of 1 percent of the total U.S. population. In summary, it is no great exaggeration to say that "in late 1967 the Allies *were* winning the war, and the Communists *were* losing it."[3]

Faced with its huge losses in personnel and morale caused by the tremendous firepower of the American troops, the Hanoi regime concluded that it had to do something radically different to reverse the course of the war: it decided to launch a vast surprise offensive, which would cause the collapse of the South Vietnamese army (ARVN) and simultaneously unleash a massive popular uprising against the Saigon regime and its U.S. allies. In January 1968, the plenum of the Communist Party Central Committee in Hanoi declared that the objective of the great offensive planned for the Tet holidays was to "annihilate and cause the total disintegration of the bulk of the puppet army, overthrow the puppet regime at all administrative levels, and place all government power in the hands of the people."[4]

There is not much serious evidence to support the later widespread belief that the Tet Offensive was consciously aimed at public opinion in the United States. "The primary objective of the Tet Offensive was to win the war by instigating a general uprising"; this concept of a general uprising "represents the major Vietnamese contribution to the [Maoist] theory of people's war."[5]

In essence, the decision to go for the Tet Offensive was nothing less than Hanoi's acknowledgment that its guerrilla campaign against the South had failed.

The Opposing Forces on the Eve of Tet

As the year 1967 drew to a close, there were about four hundred thousand Communist-led guerrillas of various classifications inside South Vietnam. "Main force" battalions deployed another hundred thousand men, of whom about half were NVA regulars.[6]

Opposing them were 409,000 U.S. soldiers and marines.[7] Almost all of these troops served in Vietnam for only one year. Consequently, just as U.S. military personnel had begun to acquire valuable knowledge of the country and their enemies, they were shipped home. Many have, therefore, said that instead of fighting a ten-year war, the Americans fought a one-year war ten times. This was a very serious weakness against an indigenous enemy who had been waging war in the country for more than two decades.

In addition to the Americans were scores of thousands of third-country troops, mainly South Koreans, but also Thais, Australians, and others. The U.S. and third-country forces were in South Vietnam to assist ARVN and the other armed forces of the Saigon government. ARVN was the descendant of the more than 300,000 Vietnamese who fought against the Communists from 1946 to 1954, either in French uniform or in the army of Emperor Bao Dai. In 1954, at the end of the first Vietnam war, those forces numerically equaled the troops under the command of General Giap.[8] As the Tet Offensive approached, the Saigon government counted 343,000 regulars in its army, navy, marines and air force. In addition to these were 70,000 men in the National Police, and about 300,000 in various poorly equipped and trained militia formations.[9]

ARVN had one of the most heavily degree-laden officer corps in the world. Five percent of its generals and 14 percent of its field-grade officers possessed doctorates. To become a lieutenant in ARVN required at least a secondary school diploma, a steep and expensive hurdle in the essentially peasant society of South Vietnam. As a consequence, the ARVN officer corps was heavily urban, and disproportionately of northern origin (25 percent in 1967) and Catholic (19 percent). Buddhists were 59 percent of the population of South Vietnam and 62 percent of the officer corps.[10] Led by men relatively unfamiliar with the mainly peasant society they were defending, ARVN required conscripted soldiers to serve in posts far from their homes, a grave burden for young peasant boys and a key to the sudden unraveling of ARVN in 1975. ARVN was too big to train properly, and it drained manpower away from the police and civil government. After the overthrow of President Diem in 1963, ARVN was the only cohesive national organization in the country. It thus had to assume more and more the burdens of governing as well as of fighting, with all the problems, including corruption, that such responsibility entails.

In the 1950s, U.S. Army instructors had built ARVN in the light of the perceived lessons of the Korean War. Hence, ARVN was a conventional force, road-bound, slow-moving, and dependent on artillery. It was heavily reliant on the United States for weapons and ammunition (as the NVA was on China and the USSR). Because it did not receive the American M-16 rifle in numbers until 1967 (and even then the supply was inadequate), ARVN was usually outgunned by both the NVA and the VC. This American-induced dependence on military supplies from the United States would one day spell ARVN's doom.

In spite of all these and other problems, some observers maintain that South Vietnam's Marine Division and Airborne Division had no equals in the NVA.[11] In the 1970s, the widely experienced Sir Robert Thompson actually ranked ARVN second only to the American and Israeli armies among free-world land forces.[12] From 1960 to 1974, the number of South Vietnamese in all military branches killed in action was 254,000; 48,800 of these deaths occurred between 1963 and 1967. During Tet ARVN casualties exceeded American casualties, as they had every year since 1961, and as they would continued to do until the end in 1975.[13]

Desertion rates in ARVN were high, as they were also among the Viet Cong. But gross desertion rates hide the fact that many ARVN deserters eventually returned to their original unit or joined the militia close to home (among whom casualty rates were high but desertion rates were low). While many deserted from ARVN, very few defected, that is, very few joined the Communist side. In contrast, between 1963 and 1972, over two hundred thousand enemy troops defected to South Vietnam, mainly Viet Cong but also some NVA.[14]

ARVN desertions need to be placed in context. Recall the battle of Gettysburg, the largest ever fought on the continent of North America. On the eve of that engagement, General Meade arrived to take command of the Army of the Potomac, the principal force defending the Union. He expected to command an army of 160,000 but found only 75,000 available, because 85,000 had deserted. In December 1863, the authorized strength of all Confederate armies was 465,000, but 187,000 soldiers were officially listed as absent without leave.[15]

Why Tet Was a Surprise

The allied forces (American, South Vietnamese, and third-country) were certainly not prepared for the size and scope of the Tet Offensive. But how could it have been possible to keep the preparations for such a huge enterprise secret? Actually, the historical record shows that strategic surprise is not uncommon. Consider the outbreak of the Russo-Japanese War in 1904, the Ardennes Offensive of 1940, Operation Barbarossa, Pearl Harbor, the Doolittle Raid, the 1943 invasion of Sicily (the largest Allied landing in World War II, next to Normandy), the Normandy invasion itself, the second Ardennes Offensive (the "Battle of the Bulge"), the North Korean attack of 1950, MacArthur's Inchon landing, the 1972 Yom Kippur War, and Iraq's invasion of Kuwait in 1990. All these undertakings involved successful deception on a massive scale. As will be seen, the Tet Offensive would entail great surprises not only for the allies but for Hanoi as well.

The principal problems the Communists faced in South Vietnam were the mobility and firepower of the Americans. Always outgunned, the Communists, as a rule, encountered American forces only when they wished to. But a great offensive would require that Communist forces abandon their guerrilla tactics and adopt conventional ones; they would come to the surface, exposing themselves, en masse and in fixed positions, to overwhelming U.S. and allied firepower. Besides, the South Vietnamese and Americans knew that there was no massive civilian upheaval in the cards; they believed (largely correctly) that all the Communist talk of a general uprising was just propaganda and/or wishful thinking. And without the aid of such a mass uprising, any conventional attack by the Viet Cong in the cities would be close to suicidal. That is exactly the fundamental reason why Tet took General Westmoreland and so many others by surprise: they just could not believe their enemy was on the verge of making such a catastrophic and irredeemable error.[16] In the words of one U.S. Army intelligence officer, "even if we had gotten the whole plan it would not have been believed. It wouldn't have been credible to us."[17] And a close student of the affair has concluded: "For the allies to predict the Tet Offensive they would have had to overcome probably the toughest problem that can confront intelligence analysts: they would have to recognize that the plan for the Tet offensive rested on a Communist mistake."[18]

This sort of intelligence problem was not new. Thucydides wrote that "in practice we always base our preparations against an enemy on the assumption that his plans are good. Indeed it is right not to rest our hopes on a belief in his blunders."[19] Machiavelli warned that "the commander of an army must always mistrust any manifest error which he sees the enemy commit, as it invariably conceals some stratagem."[20] And Clausewitz observed that "as a rule most men would rather believe bad news than good news."[21] In addition, the NVA siege of the Marine base at Khe Sanh (with its alarming pseudo-analogy to Dien Bien Phu) and the North Korean seizure of the USS *Pueblo* on January 23, severely distracted the Americans from preparing to counter an offensive in which they did not believe anyway.

Nevertheless, all kinds of intelligence, from prisoners of war, intercepted couriers, increased radio traffic, and reports from agents, was indicating that something big was about to happen. On December 18, 1967, General Earle Wheeler, chairman of the Joint Chiefs, delivered a speech to the Detroit Economic Club in which he spoke of a possible Vietnamese "Battle of the Bulge," but the news media ignored his warning.[22] General Westmoreland considered canceling the traditional Tet holiday truce, but Johnson administration officials dissuaded him. In retrospect, "the failure to cancel the cease-fire was by far the worst action taken by the Americans on the eve of the offensive."[23]

Still, General Fred Weyand, commander of U.S. forces in the Third Military Region, which contained Saigon, persuaded Westmoreland to move thirteen battalions of U.S. troops closer to or into Saigon in the week preceding the outbreak of the offensive. Consequently, there were twenty-seven U.S. battalions in greater Saigon just before the attack. This reinforcement almost certainly saved Ton Son Nhut air base, among other places, from capture by the Communists.[24] In the first hours of the attack, two ARVN airborne battalions were also in Saigon. By the fifth day of the offensive, ARVN had ten battalions in Saigon, not counting thousands of police officers.[25]

The greatest intelligence failure of the Tet Offensive, however, was on the part of Hanoi. The Politburo in North Vietnam gave the signal for the offensive on the proclaimed basis that ARVN would crumble and the mass of the civilian population would rise up against the Saigon regime. It took this position in the teeth of information from numerous and reliable sources inside South Vietnam that nothing like that was going to occur. In addition to this enormous and fundamental miscalculation, Hanoi changed the date for the opening of the offensive from January 30 to January 31. Quite predictably, many Communist units in South Vietnam failed to get the news about the change, and so they attacked on the originally set date. Such large-scale premature actions alerted the allied commanders that the enemy was indeed going to launch a major effort.

The Fighting in Saigon

In 1954, Saigon had a population of about 550,000. By 1967 that number had swollen to 2.2 million, with another million in the suburbs. On the eve of Tet, greater Saigon contained roughly one-sixth of the population of South Vietnam. The city was less than forty miles from the Cambodian border yet had not been the scene of serious fighting since the outbreak of the Franco–Viet Minh struggle in 1946.

This section will focus on the fighting in Saigon, but during the offensive, Communist forces simultaneously attacked 39 of 44 province capitals, 72 of 242 district capitals, the headquarters of all four ARVN military regions into which South Vietnam was divided, and the ancient capital city of Hue, which would become the scene of fierce conventional combat.[26] Since South Vietnam was no police state, allied forces were unable to prevent the entrance into Saigon of VC shock units and sappers (explosives teams) disguised as holiday makers. At the start, thirty-five Communist battalions—perhaps fourteen thousand men—had gathered in greater Saigon, with perhaps another four thousand sappers inside the city proper. Their main targets were predictable: the presidential palace, ARVN headquarters at Tan Son Nhut air base and the airfield itself, also Bien Hoa air base sixteen miles north of Saigon, naval headquarters, the Saigon radio station, the main Saigon prison, the Philippine embassy and the U.S. embassy (almost all other U.S. installations were left alone). Special units were assigned to assassinate President Thieu, the director of South Vietnam's Central Intelligence Agency, the chief of the National Police, the chief of the Saigon police, and U.S. ambassador Ellsworth Bunker. Many of the VC units active in Saigon were disguised as riot police or other security forces; the VC who attacked the presidential palace wore ARVN uniforms.

Practically nothing worked according to plan. The assassination units all failed to carry out their assignments. The attacking force sent to the main Saigon prison never reached it. A VC unit actually entered the radio station, prepared to play tapes announcing a general uprising and the imminent liberation of Saigon; but according to a prearranged emergency plan, the electric power to the station was shut off, and there was thus no broadcast. Three VC battalions attacked Ton Son Nhut air base but retired with heavy casualties.[27] A suicide squad penetrated the grounds of the U.S. embassy but was soon annihilated. (From the point of view of Saigon's defense, the embassy was the least important of the VC targets, but it was to get by far the greatest attention, much of it wildly inaccurate, from the U.S. media.)

Few of the guerrillas in Saigon had any familiarity at all with that city, or with any city. Unlike the insurgents of Warsaw, Budapest, Algiers, Montevideo, Belfast, or Grozny, they were trying to fight in territory that was not only strategically very disadvantageous but completely strange to them as well. Consequently, many units composed of young country boys easily became lost in Saigon's streets and avenues and thus failed to keep rendezvous, find their assigned targets, and locate or identify their potential supporters. (Many of the northerners taken prisoner were fourteen or even twelve years old, one of the first major appearances of the child-soldier phenomenon that would become so infamous later in Africa; these youngsters easily gave up valuable intelligence to their interrogators.) At the same time, Communist reserve units outside Saigon had been poised to come into the city, but they never arrived because on the second day of the offensive, General Westmoreland had blocked the roads and highways leading into Saigon.[28]

Repelled or expelled from their objectives, groups of guerrillas scattered, often taking shelter in random buildings in the city, where they were isolated and then wiped out. A number of VC sought refuge at the Phu To racetrack and were eventually destroyed there. The tenacity with which some of these groups tried to hold on to captured areas suggests their belief in the imminence of the often-proclaimed popular uprising, which never occurred.

Students of the Tet Offensive place the number of VC and NVA involved in the fighting all over South Vietnam at eighty-four thousand. Estimated deaths among these range upward from thirty thousand; one authority places the number of killed or captured at forty-five thousand.[29] Thousands of others were wounded. American combat deaths numbered four thousand, those of the South Vietnamese between four thousand and eight thousand. But however impressive this statistical asymmetry, it is less than half the story. Viet Cong losses not only were exceptionally heavy, but they "were concentrated in their political leadership cadres who had surfaced during the attack. In truth, the Tet Offensive for all practical purposes destroyed the Viet Cong."[30] In a word, "the Viet Cong lost the best of a generation of resistance fighters."[31]

Why the Viet Cong Failed in Saigon

Several key factors combined to produce the resounding defeat of the Tet Offensive. Among the most important—for the Saigon area, at any rate—was the redeployment of several battalions of U.S. troops into and around the city just a few days before the outbreak (as noted above). No less vital was the preventing of Communist units outside the city from coming in to reinforce the attack. But hardly less crucial were the complete nonoccurrence of the heralded civilian uprising, and the unexpectedly sturdy showing by ARVN. Absolutely counting on a popular uprising and an ARVN collapse, the VC had attacked in too many places and thus were sufficiently strong nowhere.

"The primary objective of the Tet offensive was to win the war by instigating a general uprising."[32] But that objective was far beyond possibility, either in Saigon or in the country as a whole, because by 1968 so much of the population was immune or even hostile to Communist appeals: Catholics; northern refugees; the Chinese minority; members of powerful indigenous religious sects; the urban business and professional classes; hundreds of thousands of officers, soldiers, militiamen, and policemen with their numerous relatives; employees of the South Vietnamese and U.S. governments; and the politically disengaged. Many of these groups were especially numerous in and around Saigon. (In contrast, according to a source very friendly to the Communist side, as late as 1974 there were in all of Saigon only five hundred Communist activists.)[33]

The absence of a popular rising stunned Hanoi.[34] Indeed, the lack of mass uprisings characterized not only Tet but also the Easter Offensive of 1972 and even the final conventional invasion in 1975, when it was clear to anyone who wished to see that all was lost.[35]

Regarding ARVN, General Westmoreland wrote later: "In the main, the Tet Offensive was a Vietnamese fight. To the ARVN, other members of the South Vietnamese armed forces, the militia, the National Police—to those belonged the major share of credit for turning back the offensive. Some individuals failed—an occasional commander proved incompetent; but overall, when put to the crucial test, no ARVN unit had broken or defected. The South Vietnamese had fully vindicated my trust."[36]

Apologists for the offensive sometimes try to explain away the absence of a popular uprising by pointing out that Saigon's regime was protected by ARVN. If that is true, why didn't anybody in Hanoi think of that beforehand? (Or perhaps they did?) Besides, ARVN was supposed to crack up at the first whiff of danger. In the supreme hour of crisis, the armies of Louis XVI, Nicholas II, and the Shah of Iran broke; so did the Communist-trained forces in Budapest in 1956 and in East Germany, Czechoslovakia, and Romania in 1989. ARVN did not break. On the contrary, "the professionalism and steadfastness of ARVN during the Tet Offensive surprised not only the enemy, but the Americans and themselves as well."[37] Indeed, ARVN "came of age during the 1968 fighting."[38] The performance of ARVN units varied widely under the attack, "but, overall, their stout resistance was an essential factor in Hanoi's military failure."[39] After Tet, the

United States began giving ARVN good M-16 rifles, a match for the Communist AK-47 and much superior to the vintage rifles ARVN had received before that.

The inability of Communist reserve units to enter Saigon to assist the insurgents within the city was by no means the least important element in the failure of the offensive. From this arises an important lesson for urban counterinsurgency:

Cities that are descending into chaos quickly must be isolated from the surrounding countryside. Whatever the main source of urban turmoil—insurrection, terrorist attacks, or simple anarchy—outside reinforcements, supplies, or sympathizers must be prevented from reaching the centers of urban disturbances. If reinforcements can be kept from urban centers, [enemy] units will eventually run out of ammunition, supplies and personnel as security forces systematically isolate and neutralize pockets of resistance.[40]

Afterward

For the Viet Cong, the consequences of the Tet Offensive were profound and permanent. Don Oberdorfer wrote that "among the Vietnamese people, the battles had created doubts about Communist military power. The Liberation Army had attacked in the middle of the Tet truce when the South Vietnamese Army was on leave, and even so it had been able to achieve only temporary inroads. If the Communists were unable to take the cities with a surprise attack in such circumstances, they would probably be unable to do better at any other time."[41] Samuel Popkin observed that "the perception of the craziness of what the Communists were doing was increased, and the idea that they were inevitable winners was so deflated that people changed very much how they felt."[42] Or, in Douglas Blaufarb's more succinct summary, after Tet "the population had abandoned the VC cause."[43] In acknowledgment of this change, following Tet President Thieu distributed hundreds of thousands of weapons to a greatly expanded militia. Desertions from the VC, and also NVA, reached a peak during the year after Tet.[44]

But more than an offensive had failed; so had an entire strategy of war-making. According to one source very sympathetic to the Viet Cong, "Never again was the Tet 1968 strategy repeated," because

"People's War, as a banner that had led the Party through a generation of trials, was finished."[45] The Tet Offensive of 1968 "was the end
of People's War, and essentially, of any strategy built on guerrilla
warfare and a politically inspired insurgency."[46] Consequently the
war became more and more a conventional conflict borne by the
regular North Vietnamese Army. And, in light of their undeniable
failure to rally popular support during Tet, both the VC and NVA
became notably unconcerned about causing civilian casualties among
the South Vietnamese.

U.S. ambassador Bunker had cabled President Johnson, "The
enemy has suffered a major military defeat."[47] Indeed, in light of
insurgent losses and the disastrous effects Tet had on public perception of Communist abilities and prospects, "the Tet Offensive was
the most disastrous defeat [the Communist side] suffered in the long
war."[48] It would be four years before the Communists felt recovered
enough to launch another offensive (the Easter Offensive of 1972, a
massive, conventional NVA attack, which also failed). So calamitous,
in fact, was the effect of Tet on the Viet Cong that it gave rise within
its ranks to widespread accusations that Hanoi had actually set up
the VC to be massacred, in order not to have any competitor for
power when, one day, Saigon finally fell.[49]

Yet hardly had the Tet explosion died down when elements of
the U.S. Congress began expressing the view that the offensive had
been in fact a disaster for the allied side and that the United States
must get out of the war. How was it possible for such a colossal di-
vergence to arise between reality in South Vietnam and perception
in the United States?

Getting the Story Wrong

In 1994, Senate Majority Leader George Mitchell (D-Maine) stated
that the U.S. news industry was "more destructive than constructive
than ever." Representative Barney Frank (D-Mass.) told a large group
of reporters: "You people celebrate failure and ignore success. *Nothing
about government is done as incompetently as the reporting of it.*"[50]

Assuming that these pronouncements by two experienced U.S.
politicians are not totally without merit, what do they mean? Do
they not mean that, in the minds of Mitchell and Frank (and perhaps

many others), U.S. journalists in the U.S. capital, where they know the language and culture and rules of the game, fail to inform the U.S. electorate correctly about national political events? And, if such statements are to be taken with any seriousness, is it impermissible to suspect that U.S. journalists in South Vietnam, unfamiliar with the history and cultures of Southeast Asia, unversed in Leninist strategy, unacquainted with guerrilla tactics, unable to speak Vietnamese or even French and thus dependent on English-speaking informants, including North Vietnamese agents[51]—is it impermissible to suspect that reporting by such persons might not always have been of the very highest quality, including reporting about the Tet Offensive? In fact, the performance of the U.S. news media during that episode, and indeed for much of the Vietnam War, has received searing criticism in subsequent years from professional journalists. Among these are Peter Braestrup, Saigon bureau chief for the *Washington Post* from 1968 to 1973; Don Oberdorfer of the *Washington Post;* ABC television news anchorman Howard K. Smith; and Robert Elegant, former editor of *Newsweek* and winner of three Overseas Press Club awards.

The difficulties American journalists had with reporting events in Vietnam go back at least as far as the administration of President Ngo Dinh Diem. Many American reporters in Saigon openly disliked Diem, blaming his perceived personal shortcomings for all the problems besetting South Vietnam. General Maxwell Taylor, chairman of the Joint Chiefs under President Kennedy and ambassador to South Vietnam under President Johnson, wrote of a "full-scale vendetta" by American journalists against Diem: "To me, it was a sobering spectacle of the power of a relatively few young and inexperienced newsmen [David Halberstam of the *New York Times* was twenty-nine years old during the Diem crisis] who, openly committed to 'getting' Diem . . . were not satisfied to report the events of foreign policy but undertook to shape them."[52] Assistant Secretary of State Manning complained to President Kennedy about "correspondents' hostility to the Diem government."[53] When some Buddhist monks began to immolate themselves in front of the presidential palace, many U.S. journalists insisted that Diem had to be removed from power. Readers of American newspapers would never suspect that the Buddhist suicides created much more stir in Washington than in South Vietnam and that such incidents had commonly occurred under French rule as well.[54] Indeed, these monkish immolations actually increased in frequency *after* Diem's assassination in November 1963, but the U.S. government and media eventually ignored them. In a terse summary of this entire disreputable episode, ambassador to South Vietnam Frederick Nolting informed President Kennedy, "I have no doubt that the American media played a major role in undermining U.S. confidence in the Diem government."[55]

South Vietnam was a country ravaged by both guerrilla insurgency and conventional invasion (via the Ho Chi Minh Trail).[56] Moreover, at their numerical peak U.S. forces in South Vietnam would be the equivalent of over nine million foreign troops in the United States of 2007. And these U.S. soldiers were very young and, to most Vietnamese, fabulously rich. All the consequent corruption, as well as cowardice and incompetence, in South Vietnam was visible to U.S. journalists; North Vietnam was not available for similar scrutiny, but nobody seemed to grasp the consequences of that stunning asymmetry.

The Tet Offensive in the Media

One often hears the observation that Vietnam was "the first television war." Television "increased the power and velocity of fragments of experience, with no increase in the power and velocity of reasoned judgment."[57] Consequently, according to Henry Kissinger, "a gap has opened up between information and knowledge, and, even beyond that, between knowledge and wisdom."[58] For one veteran *Washington Post* reporter, "Television recorded the high points of drama and tension, compressed them into two- or three-minute stories containing the most electrifying moments, transmitted them around the world, and broadcast them nationwide to the American public. It is probable that a regular viewer of the Cronkite or Huntley-Brinkley shows saw more infantry action over a longer span of days than most of the American troops who were in Vietnam during the Tet Offensive."[59] And the distinguished author of one of the first serious academic analyses of the Vietnam conflict concluded that television's "nightly portrayal of violence and gore and of American soldiers seemingly on the brink of disaster contributed significantly to disillusionment with the war."[60]

Although the failure of the South Vietnamese army to break apart was central to the defeat of Hanoi's aims in Tet, neither *Newsweek* nor *Time* published one single article on ARVN. Howard K. Smith, ABC television news anchorman, later wrote, "The Viet Cong casualties were one hundred times ours. But we never told the public that."[61] The only Pulitzer Prize in the entire war went to the photograph of the Saigon chief of police executing a captured Viet Cong in the street. Plastered all over the front pages of U.S. newspapers, this graphic illustration of conditions in Saigon naturally disturbed millions of Americans. Nobody bothered to explain that throughout the offensive, especially in Saigon, VC terrorists had deliberately attacked the wives and children of ARVN officers and that just before the picture was taken the police chief had seen the bodies of a family of six children massacred by the VC prisoner whom he would shoot in hot blood.[62]

Peter Braestrup, Saigon bureau chief for the *Washington Post* during and after the offensive, wrote that "*Newsweek* [made] an internal decision to take a formal stance against the war. The magazine did not separate, but closely welded, fact and opinion."[63] Given American journalists' "penchant for self-projection and instant analysis," they naturally "assumed average South Vietnamese reactions [to Tet] were those of American commentators."[64] Consequently, *Newsweek*'s "writers in New York, like journalists elsewhere, were seeking and offering instant explanation and measurement of disaster—telling the reader more than the writers themselves knew, or could know."[65]

During Tet, both the Associated Press and the UPI services reported that VC elements had taken over five floors of the U.S. embassy. When General Westmoreland and President Johnson denied these palpably false reports, much of the media reacted with contemptuous skepticism.[66] Robert Elegant, an editor of *Newsweek,* later wrote that "the press consistently magnified the Allies' deficiencies and displayed almost saintly tolerance for those misdeeds of Hanoi it could neither disregard nor deny."[67] The *Economist* accused U.S. reporters of accepting every claim made by the Viet Cong or Hanoi.[68] From Hanoi, the veteran journalist Harrison Salisbury sent the *New York Times* appalling stories of alleged U.S. bombing atrocities— stories handed to him directly by the government of North Vietnam.[69] And, for the pièce de résistance, the principal supplier of news and analysis about the war to *Time* magazine proved to be an officer in the North Vietnamese army.[70]

"Rarely," wrote Peter Braestrup, "has contemporary crisis-journalism turned out, in retrospect, to have veered so widely from reality. Essentially, the dominant themes in the words and film from Vietnam (rebroadcast in commentary, editorials, and much political rhetoric at home) added up to a portrait of defeat for the allies. Historians, on the contrary, have concluded that the Tet Offensive resulted in a severe military-political setback for Hanoi in the South. To have portrayed such a setback for one side as a defeat for the other—in a major crisis abroad—cannot be counted as a triumph for American journalism."[71]

In the face of all this confusion, President Johnson lacked the skill—or the will—to explain Tet, and the entire U.S. purpose, to the American people. Johnson was no Winston Churchill, no FDR, no Ronald Reagan, and failed to rally the American people. Thus, "the greatest casualty of the media's misreporting of Tet was the president himself."[72]

What if the attitudes and practices of the U.S. media in Vietnam had been in place during World War II? Would the complete surprise of Hitler's furious second Ardennes Offensive, called the Battle of the Bulge, have been cited as proof that President Roosevelt's assurances of Nazi Germany's approaching defeat were lies? Would the carnage inflicted upon U.S. ships and sailors by the first mass kamikaze attacks at Okinawa have been used to show that the war against Japan was unwinnable? During and after the costly battle on Guadalcanal, would the American people have been willing to fight on to ultimate victory in the face of the kind of news coverage that presented the Communist debacle of Tet as a disaster for the Americans and South Vietnamese?[73]

And Tet was not the only big story the major media got wrong that year. In the March 1968 New Hampshire Democratic presidential primary, Senator Eugene McCarthy of Minnesota campaigned as an opponent of President Lyndon Johnson and U.S. involvement in the Vietnam conflict. When the votes were counted, President Johnson had 49.6 percent, and McCarthy 41.9 percent. Immediately commentators declared that McCarthy had won a "moral" victory, because the number of his votes was "higher than expected." Soon the word "moral" was dropped and media people spoke and wrote simply of McCarthy's New Hampshire "victory": he had defeated an incumbent president of his own party by running as an antiwar candidate.

This interpretation persuaded Bobby Kennedy that it was politically safe for him to enter the presidential race on an anti-Vietnam platform. It also contributed to President Johnson's decision not to seek reelection. Thus McCarthy's New Hampshire "victory" changed history.

Very few tried to point out that only Senator McCarthy's name had appeared on the New Hampshire primary ballot; that is, President Johnson had *won the primary on a write-in vote,* an exceedingly unusual event in U.S. elections. Moreover, subsequent studies of the electorate revealed that many voters who described themselves as "against the war" meant that they opposed the apparently ineffective way President Johnson was waging the war in Vietnam. These persons outnumbered the true "peace" voters by about three to two. And a plurality of those who voted for McCarthy in the March Democratic primary voted for Alabama governor George Wallace in the November election.[74] Such was McCarthy's great antiwar victory.

Reflection

In any event, even though many Americans accepted the view that Tet had been a major calamity for the allied side, the South Vietnamese fought on for more than seven years—longer than the entire span of World War II—and all alone for the last two and a half years. "By 1972 the First, Marine and Airborne Divisions [of South Vietnam] were three of the best in the world."[75] In that year, South Vietnam defeated another Communist offensive, this time waged not by guerrillas but by the regular, Soviet- and Chinese-equipped North Vietnamese army. To finally capture Saigon, on April 30, 1975, the North Vietnamese army had to launch the largest conventional invasion seen on the Asian continent since the Chinese intervention in the Korean War, against a South Vietnam that had been abandoned by its American allies.

6

Northern Ireland 1970–1998

The Irish Republican Army is "the world's oldest, continually operating, unsuccessful revolutionary organization."[1] The most recent
effort of the IRA (not, of course, to be confused with the Army of
the Republic of Ireland) involved the partially successful hijacking
of a legitimate civil rights movement by the self-proclaimed revolutionaries of the breakaway Provisional Irish Republican Army—the
"Provos." The main theater of Provo activity was the urban centers of
Northern Ireland, especially Belfast, but their violence spread across
the border to the Irish Republic, to England itself, to the Continent,
and even to the United States.

A note about terminology: it was common practice in the U.S.
media to describe the contending parties in Northern Ireland as
"Protestant" and "Catholic." These terms were not always incor-
rect and will be employed herein where appropriate. But the recent
protracted conflict in that unhappy province was both much more
and much less than a strictly denominational one.[2]

A Tormented Land

Many of the problems of contemporary Northern Ireland have their
roots in the refusal of a large majority of the Irish people to accept
the English Reformation. To that fateful source one can trace English
absentee landlordism, the planting of Scottish Calvinist settlers in
the northern Irish counties, the abolition of the Irish parliament, and

the period of massive starvation and emigration of the 1840s some-times called the Great Famine. To alleviate this crushing burden of misery, a campaign for Irish Home Rule (*not* independence) gathered momentum in the nineteenth century, only to fail under Gladstone in the 1880s and again on the eve of World War I.[3]

By the beginning of that war, an organization had appeared in Ireland committed to national independence through armed revolution—the Irish Republican Army. The 1916 Easter Rebellion is the great icon of the IRA. In reality, that rising took place mainly in the streets of Dublin, with relatively little support across Ireland as a whole, or even from within the capital. But the harsh manner of its repression and the subsequent death penalties produced sympathy for the rebels and recruits for the IRA. Eamon De Valera, one of the captured leaders of the rising, narrowly escaped execution because of his U.S. birth.[4]

In 1900, the journalist Arthur Griffith, one day to become first president of the Irish Free State, founded the nationalist organiza-tion Sinn Fein ("We ourselves"). In the December 1918 elections for a new British House of Commons, there were 105 Irish constituencies, of which Sinn Fein won 73, with 46.9 percent of the total Irish vote. Refusing to take their seats in Westminster, the Sinn Fein MPs-elect instead gathered in Dublin and declared themselves the parliament of an independent Irish Republic, with De Valera as president. This revolutionary body nominally supervised the ensuing armed strug-gle, which lasted until late 1921. (During this conflict, the notorious British paramilitary organization known as the Black and Tans made its lamentable and still unforgotten record.)

In December 1921 the Anglo-Irish peace treaty partitioned Ire-land: twenty-six of Ireland's thirty-two counties would constitute a "free state" within the British Commonwealth, while six of the nine counties in the province of Ulster would continue to be united with Britain.[5] The new Irish Parliament, elected in 1921, approved the treaty after passionate debate by a vote of 64 to 57. The following June, Irish parliamentary elections returned fifty-eight pro-treaty Sinn Fein members, thirty-six anti-treaty Sinn Fein, and thirty-four others, all of the latter pro-treaty. Of 620,000 votes cast in that election, anti-Treaty Sinn Fein candidates won only 134,000.[6] But the election was the prelude to civil war.

Civil War 1922–1923

The De Valera followers in the IRA and Sinn Fein rejected the treaty that Michael Collins had negotiated and signed, and that two elected Irish parliaments had ratified.[7] In their eyes, the Protestant minority, comprising 20 percent of the population of Ireland, was not entitled to a veto over the desires of the remaining 80 percent for a united, independent republic. Their position was not without its merits. In addition, and equally important, De Valera's followers would not swear the oath of allegiance to the King of Great Britain required of all members of the Free State parliament. Instead of accepting the temporary necessity of the Free State as a stepping stone to a more acceptable settlement (Collins's position), the republican intransigents plunged the country into a civil war lasting from June 1922 to April 1923.

Though brief, the conflict was bloody and cruel. The armed forces of the Free State and the IRA rebels treated each other with impressive barbarity, not merely killing each other, but deliberately inflicting crippling wounds, and often castrating captives. The Free State forces killed more IRA men in 1922–1923 than the British had during the conflict of 1919–1921 and shot more IRA prisoners (around seventy-three) than the British had.[8] In all, approximately four thousand persons died in the 1922–1923 conflict, more than in the entire period from the Easter Rebellion to the 1921 treaty. Among the victims was Michael Collins, principal organizer of the anti-British resistance in 1916 and then commander of the Free State army, assassinated by IRA gunmen in August 1922. In addition, many priceless works of art were destroyed. "The irregulars' [IRA] campaign became one of guerrilla warfare, which generated acts of destruction and viciousness on both sides that the nation did not recover from for fifty years."[9]

During the civil war, the Catholic bishops of Ireland collectively and publicly condemned the members of the IRA who were fighting against the Free State and forbade priests to give such persons the sacraments. In 1931, the Irish episcopate collectively accused the IRA of wishing to impose a Soviet system on Ireland. Further collective denunciations by the bishops occurred in 1934 and 1935, and individual bishops reminded their congregants that simultaneous membership in the IRA and the Catholic Church was impermissible, a stance that persisted over the next fifty years.[10]

Elections for a new parliament closely followed the end of the civil war. Out of 153 seats, De Valera's intransigent partisans won but 44. (The two main parties of contemporary Ireland—Fianna Fail, founded by De Valera, and Fine Gael—are the direct descendants of the opposing sides during the civil war.)

Northern Ireland

Less than twenty miles across the North Channel from mainland Britain, Northern Ireland is considerably smaller than Aroostook County in Maine, and its population hardly equals that of Suffolk County in New York. Yet this small and proximate province became the scene of Britain's longest and most painful counterinsurgency conflict.

Predictably, the partition of Ireland relegated the large Catholic minority in Northern Ireland to the status of a permanent proletariat. During the 1920s, the new Northern state beat this Catholic minority into submission, but not into loyalty.[11] By the end of the 1960s, Northern Ireland was "a small, decayed, postindustrial slum with green fields on the margins of the continent," where the regime ruled with "authoritarian measures and sectarian purpose."[12] Elections there were not contests but rituals, reproducing a perpetual majority and a perpetual minority.[13] Northern Ireland was a "sectarian tyranny with a democratic face."[14] Politicians in London exhibited a profound indifference to this simmering cauldron; so did politicians in Dublin.

By the beginning of 1969, a powerful current was rising up within the Northern Catholic community, an unwillingness to submit anymore to blatant discrimination in jobs and schools or to gerrymandering and intimidation in elections. An emerging Belfast Catholic middle class, the example of changes sweeping across the United States and Western Europe, a not-unsympathetic Labour government in London—all these (and no doubt other, less obvious factors) combined to produce a burgeoning civil rights movement, committed to obtaining redress of grievances through peaceful means.[15] It is important to note that the civil rights programs of 1969 made no mention of reunification with the rest of Ireland, something elements within the Protestant majority had convinced themselves to fear above all things. The movement asked only for an end to the cruder and more provocative forms of political, economic, and social discrimination.[16]

This originally peaceful protest movement was confronted by Orange (i.e., militant Protestant) violence. In January 1969, a parade of about a hundred civil rights marchers in Derry (officially, Londonderry) was attacked by a Protestant mob armed with iron pipes and poles with protruding nails, while the Northern Ireland police—the Royal Ulster Constabulary (RUC)—stood about and watched.[17] Members of the RUC then randomly stopped and beat Catholics on the Derry streets—an authentic police riot.[18] Thus the Catholic community saw with unmistakable clarity that it would have to take charge of its own protection. With truly heroic stupidity, the Northern Ireland administration in Stormont allowed the deliberately provocative annual marches of Orange militants and bigots through Catholic neighborhoods to go forward, promising ferocious reprisals against anyone who tried to impede them. In the resulting carnage, ten persons died, nine hundred were injured, and hundreds of homes and factories were burned. From this preventable, disgraceful rampage would emerge the Provisional IRA, the Provos.[19] And incredibly, Stormont permitted the Orange parades to proceed the following year as well. "The failure to ban the 1970 Orange parades . . . was the last chance to avoid the catastrophe that has since engulfed Ulster."[20] Communal violence—beatings, burnings, shootings—raged at a level not seen in a generation.

On August 15, 1969, James Callaghan, home secretary in Harold Wilson's Labour cabinet, responded to the request from the Northern Ireland government to send in the British Army to restore order. It is important to note that British troops deployed to Belfast not to protect Catholics from violence but because the RUC, the main police organization, had been overwhelmed and exhausted by government-sanctioned communal violence.[21]

Enter the British Army

Classic British counterinsurgency theory is sophisticated. The British developed their counterinsurgency concepts and techniques mainly during the six decades preceding World War II: "Those techniques reflected three characteristics of the British Empire: first, its vast extent included peoples of many different races and religions, elements of which—from time to time, for diverse reasons, and in myriad circumstances—rose in armed rebellion against British control; second, the imperial power did not maintain a large standing military force; and third, Britain was in those decades transforming itself into a democratic polity."[22] The essence of British counterinsurgency theory was to combine emphasis on political initiatives with restraint on the use of naked force, decentralization of command at the tactical level, and heavy reliance on local police forces.[23]

Clearly, a viable strategy in this tradition for reestablishing order in Northern Ireland would have consisted of efforts to (1) concentrate on dividing and isolating the IRA, rather than shooting or arresting its suspected members or sympathizers; (2) make the collection and analysis of good intelligence the crux of the counterinsurgent effort; (3) redress at least some of the more glaring political and economic grievances of the Catholic population; (4) reassure the members of the Unionist (Protestant) community that there would be no change in the province's relationship to the United Kingdom against their will; and (5) keep the profile of the army as low as possible, especially in the matter of arrests and home searches.

Sir Robert Thompson, a celebrated authority on counterinsurgency, insisted that the breakup of the insurgent infrastructure—the civilians who actively support the guerrillas—will cause an insurgency to wither. In his view the best tool for disrupting the infrastructure of rebellion is the regular police establishment, because it has roots in the community, as opposed to troops, who are usually newcomers rotated in and out of an area; the police will be there long after the troops go away. Police will, or should, be the richest repository of intelligence. Thompson wrote that as a general rule the counterinsurgent side needed 2.5 policemen for every soldier.[24] Clearly, then, a basic precondition for the strategy sketched out above was the existence of a police force widely accepted as neutral with regard to the religiously designated communities. But such a police force did not exist, nor ever had existed, in Northern Ireland; most of the Catholic community saw the police, with much justification, as their enemy. Until the building of a proper police force, therefore, the British Army would have to maintain law and order in the province.

The British Army Falters

But, for a variety of reasons, the performance of the British troops that entered Northern Ireland in 1970 was very disappointing. There had always been—of course—a significant discrepancy between theory and practice in British counterinsurgency. It had acquired its experience in colonial wars, in which methods were used that could not be replicated in a British province such as Northern Ireland, at least not completely. "Curfews, bans, internment, collective punishments and reprisals, identity cards, compulsory resettlement, in-depth interrogation, a relaxed attitude toward the shooting of suspected insurgents, and capital punishment have either not been used [in Northern Ireland] or, when they have, quickly proved to be counter-productive."[25] During the suppression of the Malayan Emergency (1946–1954), thirty-four thousand civilians had been detained without trial, other thousands expelled from the country, and half a million resettled in new villages, more or less forcibly. "If South Armagh [a county in Northern Ireland] were a province in Malaya, many of its Catholic inhabitants would have had their homes burned down and have been either forcibly resettled in heavily-policed 'new villages' or deported across the border."[26] During the Falklands War of 1982, the British Army had proved itself to be a most potent force, one that could have easily overwhelmed Provo terrorists if it were granted carte blanche, but such a grant was absolutely impossible. What had been permissible, or at least possible, in Malaya or Kenya was not permissible in the British Isles.[27] Consequently, it appeared to some observers that "the British Army in Northern Ireland will continue to fight terrorism, but it is unlikely, within the context of a liberal democracy, to be able to defeat it entirely."[28]

In addition, while the post–World War II record of British

counterinsurgency certainly had its showpiece triumphs—notably Malaya—other episodes had ended with considerably less satisfaction. In 1948, the British withdrew in disarray from their violence-plagued Palestine mandate, leaving much of the Middle East a politico-military shambles. In Cyprus during its 1950s insurgency, the British had many troops, enjoyed the support of the large Turkish minority, and suffered comparatively light losses. Nevertheless, they could not bring terrorism and assassination under control on that island, considerably smaller than Northern Ireland. In 1967, some notable fighting with rebels in Aden led to a less-than-inspiring British withdrawal from that longtime outpost of empire. That these insurgencies took place in predominantly urban areas was not auspicious for British Army success in Northern Ireland.

Finally, most of the British soldiers who landed in Northern Ireland in 1969 and 1970 had little preparation for the task they faced. Many of them were initially sent to Ireland on four-month tours, an insuperable obstacle both to improving their operational skills and to collecting good intelligence. Now, intelligence is a key weapon, some would say the supreme weapon, in any effective counterinsurgency. Indeed, British testimony on this point is impressive. In his classic study of insurgency, C. E. Callwell wrote, "In no class of warfare is a well-organized and well-served intelligence department more essential than in that against guerrillas."[29] Field Marshal Sir Gerald Templer, "the tiger of Malaya," declared, "The [conflict in Malaya] will be won by our intelligence system."[30] And the experienced British theoretician-practitioner of counterinsurgency General Sir Frank Kitson believed, "If it is accepted that the problem of defeating the enemy consists very largely of finding him, it is easy to recognize the paramount importance of good information."[31] But short tours for British soldiers were inimical to acquiring familiarity with persons and places, a keystone of intelligence collection.

Yet another obstacle to acquiring useful intelligence was the view of many elements in the army that they could not perform their basic function in Northern Ireland without the support of at least one major section of the population. This was one reason the army displayed less hostility to armed Orange militants than to the IRA; another was religious and ethnic identification with the Protestant community among Scottish units. On too many occasions, the IRA was able to assume the role of defender of Catholic neighborhoods against raging Orange mobs because the army was nowhere to be seen. The disastrous intelligence situation was made worse, if such a thing were possible, by poor relations between the army and the Northern police.[32]

Certainly, all these shortcomings were correctable, or at least reducible—but not in any brief time period, and especially not in the absence of determined leadership equipped with clear ideas. Thus, predictably, the British Army in Northern Ireland eventually offended much of the population, without being able to establish real peace or even a semblance of order.

Searches

One instructive example of how inadequate preparation for the task at hand combined with a lack of good intelligence to produce very bad effects emerged in the practice of army searches. The army sought to gather intelligence by foot patrols and "contact," which meant stopping and inspecting countless automobiles (in 1972 sometimes five thousand auto stops *per day*) as well as searching tens of thousands of homes—thirty-six thousand in 1972, seventy-five thousand in 1973–1974.[33] Most Catholic homes were searched at least once, many as often as ten times. Beatings, thefts, and smashing of religious images not infrequently accompanied these intrusions. In July 1970, house searches in Lower Falls (Belfast) left five Catholic civilians dead and many houses looted and destroyed. "Until the spring of 1970, most Catholics regarded the troops as their protectors. The Lower Falls operation changed everything."[34] Several soldiers were convicted of murder between 1969 and 1984, "all for criminal acts unconnected with their official duties."[35] Those who cannot acquire intelligence in one way will eventually turn to another; torture, in varying degrees, of IRA suspects by the army produced little intelligence of value but damaged the army's image and its morale (as in Algeria).[36]

Worse—if possible—British soldiers were being sent into private homes "in [this part of] the United Kingdom on a shoddy mission and in full view of an unsympathetic media."[37] In this conflict, journalists "eager for the latest photogenic outrage" busily sensationalized tragedy or misbehavior on British soil.[38] The media made army misconduct the issue, rather than analyzing what the struggle was about.

Thus, bad behavior by some army elements toward the Catholic minority, especially its working-class components, created sympathy for the IRA, hurt recruitment into the army itself, and further reduced its already quite inadequate intelligence-gathering capacities, because Catholics mistrusted soldiers and Protestants knew next to nothing useful about the IRA.[39]

Internment

In August 1971, as a response to IRA threats against juries and trial witnesses, the government of Northern Ireland introduced internment—preventive detention without trial—of IRA suspects. This practice was unusual on neither side of the border. Nevertheless, internment proved to be "probably the single most disastrous measure introduced during the recent troubles."[40] That was because "internment was demonstrably sectarian," imposed with violence and accompanied by torture, meant to intimidate the Catholics and reassure the Protestants.[41]

Internment threw nonviolent people into jail with committed Provos; thus the prisons became schools for violence and recruiting grounds for the IRA. "Internment was a political disaster, nor was it particularly effective in military terms."[42] In return for this political disaster, internment netted very few authentic IRA members, because police intelligence regarding the Provos was so poor. Besides, by the time the practice came to an end in December 1975, internment had jailed fewer than two thousand men and women, a tiny percentage of the Catholic population of well over half a million. But aside from internment, a very high proportion of the Catholic male population was arrested between 1972 and 1977, most of them quite uninvolved with the Provos.

If the purpose of internment had been to reduce violence, it was a colossal failure. In the two years prior to the introduction of internment, 66 people, including 11 British soldiers, had been killed; in the seventeen months following internment, 610 people were killed, including 146 British soldiers.[43]

Contrary to expectation and myth, the first serious attack on the British Army came from elements in the Protestant community. The fall of 1969 saw "savage Protestant riots during which [British] troops came under fire."[44] In October 1969, drunken Orange gunmen in Belfast wounded thirteen British soldiers and killed and wounded numerous civilians.[45] But the first British soldier to die in Ireland in fifty years was killed by the IRA in February 1971. Violence escalated: IRA gasoline bombs ignited armored cars on Belfast streets; small groups of soldiers were attacked with acid bombs, nail grenades, and flaming gasoline.[46]

Then came Bloody Sunday, January 30, 1972. In Derry, Catholic women had served tea and cakes to arriving British soldiers, imagining that the troops had come there to protect them.[47] But on that Sunday, British paratroopers fired on a civil rights march of several thousand persons, killing thirteen. Two weeks later the British embassy in Dublin went up in flames, while the police watched. (How the people involved in that event imagined that they would intimidate the British government by burning down a beautiful old building in Dublin is not clear.) In March 1972, the British cabinet suspended the provincial government at Stormont and assumed direct administration of Northern Ireland. It was a very late move: in December 1970 active Provo gunmen numbered perhaps eight hundred; before the end of 1972 that figure would swell to fifteen hundred.[48]

By any measure, 1972 would prove the worst year of the entire conflict. The number of British troops in the province peaked at thirty thousand, roughly one soldier for every fifty inhabitants. Nevertheless, violent death claimed 474 persons: the IRA killed 255 of these, Protestant terrorists 103, the security forces another 74, with the remainder unclassified but probably most by the IRA. The total figure includes 103 regular British soldiers and at least 95 Provos.[49] (The following year, British army fatalities fell to 58.)

In summary, "the British behaved like an army of occupation in what was supposed to be a British province, and achieved the complete alienation of the Catholic population."[50] Here was the origin of a mass base for a greatly expanded IRA: not just intimidation, but capitalizing on the mistakes of the authorities. Perhaps John Newsinger was not exaggerating very much when he wrote, "There can be little doubt that if Catholics had been the majority community, the British would have been forced to withdraw in a repeat of the Aden debacle."[51]

The Provos

Although the IRA had always claimed to be nonsectarian, "the Protestants interpret[ed] the killing of the RUC and UDR [Ulster Defence Regiment] as deliberate acts of sectarian genocide."[52] In any event, the IRA never had significant support outside the Catholic community. Thus, the base for the IRA, and later its provisional faction, was limited to the minority population in Northern Ireland. But a most significant aspect of this post-1969 conflict is that, despite all the discrimination, harassment, and humiliation to which the Catholics in that province had been subjected every day for generations, the Provos were never able to gather the active sympathy of anything approaching a majority of that community.

The IRA had split into Official and Provisional factions during December 1969 and January 1970. The main, formal issue between them was this: Should the IRA "recognize" the governments in London, Stormont, and Dublin? The Provos took the negative. In practical (if that is the word) terms, the question was whether IRA candidates occasionally elected to the respective legislatures of those governments should actually take their seats. But underlying this dispute was a real difference in general strategies between the two factions: the Officials wanted to plan and work for a Bolshevik-style revolution in Northern Ireland, uniting the entire working class, both Protestant and Catholic; the Provos wanted to use classic guerrilla insurgency (as they understood the term) to drive the British from the island and establish a "progressive" regime.[53]

The typical Provo was a young, unemployed Catholic male who might have become a simple criminal if not for the IRA. The most influential factor in joining that organization was family connection.[54] "The Provisional IRA was a working class movement . . . almost all young men . . . an army without special skills, often without any skills, school-leavers or the habitually unemployed of the Catholic North and their Southern counterparts."[55] The leadership was not much more impressive. At the First Provisional Council in December 1969, the leaders showed themselves "well beyond youth, rumpled, inelegant, unsophisticated, poorly read, without funds or trained minds, unknown but to the police."[56]

Time would illustrate clearly that the ranks of the Provos contained quite a liberal proportion of riffraff and sociopaths. But there had always been precious few jobs for Catholics in Northern Ireland, and nothing like neighborhood playing fields to occupy the unemployed or the young men. The IRA's continued existence owed a great deal to the deliberate failure of Stormont to pursue its own interests by working to ameliorate poverty and discontent among those it claimed to govern. In any event, for fifty years the Stormont regime treated the minority population with alternating repression and neglect. All that, reinforced by the scandalous hostility of the RUC toward the Catholic minority, and then inflamed by mistakes and even crimes by elements of the at-first-welcomed British Army, made bloodshed predictable, even inevitable. Indeed, the failure of the army to protect Catholic neighborhoods from Orange mobs, and shameful behavior in those same neighborhoods by too many soldiers, provided the first real stimulus to the growth of the Provos. Of course Bloody Sunday was an incalculable boon to them. In addition, the Provos became the de facto police in Catholic areas, because the uniformed police were perceived, correctly in most cases, as the willing agents of a sectarian, malevolent Stormont regime. Thus the Provos hijacked the civil rights movement of 1969 into a nationalist insurgency because of decades of inexcusable mistreatment of the minority population with the indifference or permission of the government in London.

Provo Money

Terrorists need money. Provo robberies on both sides of the border (at least 587 in Northern Ireland alone) provided a fairly steady source of income.[57] Additionally, the IRA obtained funds by extortion from the Catholic community in the North.[58] Consequently, "to the outside observer, the insurgents look more like an American crime family than a national liberation movement."[59]

Help came from overseas. The Royal Canadian Mounted Police

broke up a flourishing arms-shipment ring in 1975. Five U.S. citizens were arrested in Philadelphia in December 1977 for illegally shipping rifles to Ireland. Others stole guns from a National Guard armory near Boston in 1976 and from U.S. military bases.[60] The IRA was behind the famous 1993 Brinks armored van robbery in New York City. Contributions made to various "northern aid" societies in the United States purchased weapons for the Provos, despite the reiterated pleas from the embassy of the Irish Republic in Washington and prominent Irish American politicians that Americans not give money to Noraid and similar organizations that collected money to "help Catholics" in Northern Ireland. The Provos also established relations with the PLO, the Colombian FARC, the Qaddaffi regime in Libya, and the Basque terrorist ETA.[61]

Notably, the Provos received very little sympathy from the Irish diaspora in England. But balancing this was the ironic twist whereby jobless IRA men living in England receive unemployment compensation; thus the British welfare state duly made its contribution to terrorism.

Provo Methods

The major public controversy that followed and aggravated the splitting of the IRA into Provos and Officials was the role of violence. From the beginning, many in the IRA had as their main objective not military victory—certainly not in their lifetimes—but rather fidelity to a republican ideal, a tradition of violent uprisings, stretching from those of the United Irishmen in 1798 and Young Ireland in 1848 through the Fenians of 1867 and the sacred Easter Rebellion of 1916. Fidelity to this tradition, purity of commitment, demanded not victory but combat. The IRA was and is about violence: hence the civil war of 1922, divisions within the IRA that led to internecine murders before World War II, the emergence of the Provos themselves, and the repeated splinterings in the 1990s and after. Thus, in the Provo mind, even if a clear majority of Irishmen did not support IRA violence, *even if a clear majority opposed it*, it must go on. Violence would open the eyes and steel the hearts of the passive or cowardly majority. Violence linked the precarious present to the glorious past.[62]

Beatings and robberies were standard practices. Arson became an IRA specialty; the Provos would set a building on fire and shoot at the arriving firemen. One of their particular triumphs was the burning down of the Belfast Opera. They tossed bombs into pubs and restaurants and firebombs into stores, first in Northern Ireland, then in England. They forced drivers to deliver truck bombs by threatening their families.[63] (An impressive number of Provo bomb-makers blew themselves or their comrades up through incompetence.) They ambushed small groups of soldiers and fired mortars at border police posts. They assassinated magistrates, including Catholic judges, as well as businessmen. They targeted for death or injury the families of British soldiers in Northern Ireland. And as early as 1971, Provos were killing members of the Official IRA on the streets, often torturing them first. (The Officials also killed, but through incompetence and against their own interest, innocent persons such as cleaning women and priests.)[64] The Provos often murdered their victims in the presence of their families, and, in at least one instance, they shot their victim on the steps of St. Patrick's Cathedral in Armagh. By 1992, the Provos were killing more of their own members (accused of being informers) than they were British soldiers.[65]

Provo Activities beyond the North

In 1974 the Provos began attacking targets outside Northern Ireland. Letter bombs, already used in Northern Ireland, now went also to England (e.g., to the London Stock Exchange and to civil servants) and to Washington, D.C. Many secretaries received terrible wounds from these devices. Provo bombings became a regular occurrence in England, often killing or maiming very young children; the Birmingham bomb outrage of November 1974 killed at least twenty-one persons. (The FLN in Algeria had never carried out a bombing on this scale.) The Provos struck Harrod's department store in 1983 (among the victims were American tourists) and executed mortar attacks against Heathrow Airport in March 1994.

Most of their operations killed innocent bystanders, but sometimes the Provos aimed quite deliberately at selected individuals. They tried to kill Elizabeth II, narrowly missed Prime Minister Margaret Thatcher in 1984, threw a bomb into the private home of former prime minister Edward Heath, and tried to blow up Prime Minister

John Major inside 10 Downing Street.[66] In July 1976, they assassinated the British ambassador to Ireland, in Dublin. They also killed the British ambassador to the Netherlands in 1979. Their attempt on the life of the British ambassador to NATO failed, killing Belgian civilians instead.[67] They did succeed in murdering the eighty-year-old World War II hero Lord Mountbatten, not for anything he had done but because he was the uncle of Prince Philip; slain along with him were his fourteen-year-old grandson and a fourteen-year-old local boy. British servicemen in England and Europe also became targets: the Provos killed 3 Royal Air Force enlisted men in the Netherlands in 1988 and an RAF corporal and his six-month-old daughter in Germany in 1989. They also murdered Irishmen serving in the British Army. But with all this, in Ireland, England, and Europe, the Provos succeeded in killing 96 British soldiers during the entire decade of the 1980s, compared to 103 in 1972 alone.

Orange Terror

Of course, criminal terrorism was not a monopoly of the IRA. If it is true that people hate and fear those they have injured, then the fear and hatred Orangemen felt for the minority population of Northern Ireland is no mystery. To oppression, discrimination, and simple cruelty, some Orangemen now added organized terrorism. Orange terror groups included the Ulster Volunteer Force, the Ulster Freedom Fighters, and the Ulster Defence Association. During the 1970s Orange terrorists killed civilians on both sides of the border.[68] The police were notably ineffective against Orange violence; "The failure to respond effectively to the threat posed by the Protestant paramilitaries has been one of the most serious of the security forces' failures in Northern Ireland."[69] Loyalists committed 20 percent of communal murders during the 1980s; the figure rose to 52 percent by 1992.[70] Most of the victims of Orange violence appear to have been randomly chosen, unlucky Catholic men.[71]

The Price of Provo Violence

Some in the United States, both critics and supporters of the IRA, see that group as the quintessential manifestation of the Catholic population of Ireland. This view is far from correct. In the first place, among the Provo leadership were convinced Leninists, and everybody, including bishops of the Catholic Church, knew it. But it was the IRA's belief that exemplary violence would mobilize Catholic opinion that proved both ill-founded and costly.[72] Learning to avoid hard targets, the Provos aimed their terror at soft ones, such as bars and parades, thereby necessarily killing civilians. By 1972 the Provos' manifest lack of concern over civilian casualties had generated increasing revulsion among Northern Catholics, especially women, who would begin organizing marches against violence (that is, against the Provos).[73] That year, even the Official wing of the IRA condemned Provo violence against civilians.[74] "The constant din of the Troubles shamed the nation."[75] Consequently, by early 1978 the number of active Provo fighters may have fallen to a low of 250. In September 1979, at Drogheda, thirty miles south of the border, John Paul II declared to an audience of 250,000: "On my knees I beg you to turn away from the paths of violence."

While violence continued at a diminishing level, the politicians were busy. In November 1985 came the Anglo-Irish Agreement, signed by Prime Ministers Thatcher and Fitzgerald, in which the government of the Irish Republic agreed that the status of Northern Ireland could be changed only by a majority vote of its inhabitants. In addition, the Irish government prevented public broadcasts or interviews by "revolutionary groups" (restrictions on such activity already existed in Britain). This prohibition had the effect of limiting most IRA messages and propaganda to its own membership. In 1987, in the town of Enniskillen, not far from the border, the Provos bombed a memorial service for the 1918 Armistice, killing eleven and wounding fifty-five, many of whom were children. In reaction to this outrage, the Irish Republic signed an extradition treaty with the United Kingdom. Dublin had previously increased the penalty for mere membership in any "illegal organization" (that is, the IRA) to seven years, and ordered its police and army to increase security along the 123-mile border.

The IRA continued to lose public support. In the early 1980s, polls reported that only 46 percent of Northern Catholics agreed that "the IRA are basically patriots."[76] Sinn Fein, the public face of the IRA, never replaced the SDLP (Social Democratic and Labour Party) as the principal Catholic party in the North. In House of Commons elections, Sinn Fein polled 13.4 percent of the total Northern vote in 1983, 11.4 percent in 1987, and a mere 10 percent in 1992, compared to the SDLP's 23.5 percent. In that election Gerry Adams, principal spokesman for Sinn Fein, lost his West Belfast seat in the House of Commons.[77]

In the Irish Republic, Sinn Fein's vote increased, from 1.9 percent in 1987 to 2.6 percent in 1997—*after* Sinn Fein had publicly renounced violence. (In June 1997, the single successful Sinn Fein candidate for the Irish Parliament actually took his seat there, the first time Sinn Fein officially recognized the legitimacy of that Republic.)

As public support for the Provos on both sides of the border receded, British Army intelligence improved. The army would often publicly state that the arrest of a certain individual had been the result of a betrayal inside the IRA. It would also inflate the declared amount of money taken in a robbery. Actions of this kind touched off deadly fighting within the Provo ranks, not a terribly hard thing to do in any case.[78]

The police, for their part, were getting better at using surveillance, interrogation, agents, and informers. For instance, a vulnerable suspect would be offered leniency and some money to help him move away, in return for testimony.[79] Careful observation, along with raids on known Provo gathering places and arrests of known members, produced an increasing supply of information. Computerization of army and police intelligence greatly aided in correlating previously separate data.

Other changes were also going forward. "Ulsterization" aimed to decrease the number and visibility of British troops in the province, increase reliance on the police and the civil courts, and offer basic concessions to the minority community. More attention went to raising the numbers and professionalism of the RUC. Nevertheless, that organization continued to be composed predominantly of Protestants (with apparently only 11 percent of its membership Catholic), partly because the Provos went out of their way to kill Catholic members of the RUC.[80]

In April 1998 multiparty peace talks produced agreement on disarmament of paramilitary forces, a renewed pledge from the Irish Republic that reunification could only follow a majority vote in favor, structural changes in Northern Ireland governance to require intercommunity agreement on legislation, and a rapid reduction of the number of British troops in the province.

Casualties

Estimates of the death toll in the long Northern Ireland insurgency of course vary, but not very widely. Between 1968 and 1998, possibly 3,600 persons died as a result of the violence in Northern Ireland. That averages out to 120 per year, or 2.3 per week—less than the traffic death toll (149) in Northern Ireland in 1992.[81] According to Prime Minister Thatcher, by the end of 1979, 1,152 civilians and 543 security personnel had been killed by terrorists.[82] One authority estimates that 330 insurgents were killed between 1969 and 1988.[83] Approximately 500 British soldiers died in Northern Ireland between 1969 and 1994. The worst year was 1972, when 103 British regulars were killed; the figure dropped in the following year to 58, in 1974 to 28, and in 1975 to 14.[84] Even including 1972, the average is 20 military deaths per year, fewer than 2 per month. (During 2006, there were approximately 400 homicides in Philadelphia, Pennsylvania, whose population is smaller than that of Northern Ireland.)[85]

Reflection

Communal violence and hatred in Northern Ireland is a long and disedifying story. Clearly, responsibility for what occurred beginning in 1969 is not equally distributed among all parties, but certainly all parties have their measure of guilt.

The fundamental cause of the fighting in Northern Ireland was not the presence of British troops. It was rather the unwillingness of the majority community in that province either to be reunified with the rest of Ireland or to grant the minority community those political and social rights considered the norm in Western Europe for generations. In such circumstances, no London government was ever willing enough or clever enough to offer both sufficient reassurance to the uneasy majority and sufficient relief to the exasperated minority.

Eventually, British strategy in Northern Ireland evolved from seeking military victory over the IRA to achieving its containment.[86] That strategy worked well enough. Consequently, it is not too much of an exaggeration to state that Northern Ireland ultimately witnessed "a successful counterinsurgency strategy that moved the Provisional Irish Republican Army from a tradition of employing terror and military force to a willingness to adopt a purely political solution to the perceived problems."[87]

What success this British strategy was able to achieve owed less to its brilliance or timeliness than to fundamental weaknesses in the position of the Provisional IRA. "The history of the IRA has been marked [by] a tradition of poor strategic analysis which has often caused the movement to overestimate the ability of its means to overcome far more powerful adversaries."[88] The Provos' strategy was not to seek reform in Northern Ireland but to wage a protracted war against British authority there. They expected that such a conflict would both unite the Catholic population behind them and exhaust the British into abandoning the province, as they had abandoned the scene of other postimperial conflicts. Then, rather than face IRA guerrilla warfare all alone, the Protestant majority would acquiesce in a federal union with the Republic.

This Provo strategy suffered from multiple and profound miscalculations. In the first place, it is close to certain that a total British withdrawal from Northern Ireland between 1969 and 1972 would have produced a unilaterally independent Northern state both willing and able to expel great numbers of its Catholic inhabitants into the Irish Republic. The IRA, having thus been driven out of the North, would then almost certainly have turned in fury against the Dublin regime.

But those calamitous events did not occur, because clearly no such withdrawal was ever politically possible. The British could afford to grow tired of fighting antiterrorist conflicts in Palestine, Kenya, Aden, and Cyprus because they were far from home and among people who were not and could never be British. "Neither the British nor the Americans seem willing to hazard the lives of even volunteers in conflicts that do not clearly affect their national interests."[89] But abandoning Northern Ireland, an integral part of the kingdom, just a few miles away from the mainland and inhabited by a vociferously loyalist majority, was never a real political option. And not least, a British cabinet appearing to give in to IRA terror in England would undoubtedly have encouraged other groups, domestic and foreign, to pressure any future British government with similar tactics.[90]

That fact by itself—no British withdrawal under fire, no matter how long the distasteful conflict lasted—was primary and decisive, dooming the strategy of the Provos. But they carried additional, and quite serious, burdens. The most important of these was an inadequate base of popular support. Clearly, the British Army could antagonize the minority population but could not subdue it—the worst of two worlds. When the army lost the confidence of the Catholics, space appeared for the Provos to find something like a mass following (if such a term is appropriate in the context of Northern Ireland's limited population and constricted territory, which were also factors operating against the Provos). But the IRA's targeted base of support, the Northern Ireland Catholic community, was by everybody's definition a minority of the population. Even more importantly, the IRA spoke for *only a minority of that minority*, as election returns and opinion polls repeatedly showed. Indeed, the Provos did not encompass even the whole of the IRA. Beginning with World War II and continuing into the 1980s, fewer and fewer persons on either side of the border were willing to actively support an armed struggle to unify Ireland.[91] In fact, Provo violence caused increasing dismay among the Catholic community even as it strengthened militancy among Protestant loyalists. For years the Provos had ignored both the government in Dublin and the hierarchy of the Catholic Church. They ignored Guevara's dictum—and all the empirical evidence supporting it—about trying to make revolution against a democratic, or even pseudo-democratic, state. "They ignored the qualms of their own Northern people, ignored civilized standards, ignored all restraints. They were intent on imposing their own will on the whole island and on Ulster first."[92] But they never possessed the strength, nor the means to obtain the strength, to accomplish these aims. The very violence that the Provos believed to be the proof of their might was in fact the testament of their impotence.

Northern Ireland's demographic data are not on the side of the majority community. If the trends of the past three decades continue across the next two, a not unlikely scenario, they will produce a "Catholic" majority in Northern Ireland, and that in turn may produce a large emigration—a return, in a sense—of Northern Ireland Protestants to Scotland and England.

7

Grozny 1994–1996

The "Disgraceful Failure"

Only six years after their disastrous experience in Afghanistan, the Russians found themselves fighting another traditional, mountain-warrior Islamic people, the Chechens. With an area of six thousand square miles, Chechnya is one-fortieth the size of Afghanistan, and significantly smaller than El Salvador (eighty-two hundred square miles), Wales (eight thousand) or New Jersey (seventy-eight hundred). The resident Chechen population in 1992 numbered only three-quarters of a million, about half that of Northern Ireland, or Clark County, Nevada.

Russia's seemingly endless entanglement in the Chechnya conflict had its first and most dramatic act in an assault on the capital city, Grozny (which in Russian means "menacing"). Before the Russian attack, Grozny had an area of one hundred square miles and a population of four hundred thousand, less than today's Edinburgh or Sacramento. The Russian attack on Grozny was one of the largest urban operations since World War II. It also turned out to be a catastrophic humiliation for the Russians, worse than that in Afghanistan in the 1980s, worse than that in Finland in 1940.

Arguably, the Russian army had more experience with urban fighting than any other modern force. Soviet troops conquered a hundred cities during World War II. After that, they carried out ultimately successful operations in East Berlin (1953), Budapest (1956), Prague (1968), and Kabul (1979). But all this experience did the Russians no good in Chechnya: "By September of 1996 the Russian Army was mired in one of the most disastrous situations it had ever experienced" and ultimately suffered "an unparalleled defeat."[1] The campaign had hardly begun before it became painfully clear that "the Russian army was simply in no shape to fight a war."[2]

How can one explain "the disgraceful failure of the Russian army of the 1990s in Chechnya"?[3] This question is of much more than merely academic interest, because, for one thing, "the enemies that U.S. forces will face in the future are far more likely to resemble the Chechen rebels than the Russian Army, and the battlefield will very likely look more like Grozny than Central Europe."[4]

Who Are the Chechens?

The Chechens are a Muslim people, but the conversion of the country was not complete until well into the nineteenth century. Lying in the North Caucasus region, Chechnya is a rugged land, with a long history of resistance to foreign intrusion. Beginning in the late eighteenth century, successive Russian invasions destroyed many of the forests which traditionally sheltered Chechen guerrillas.[5] The conquest of the North Caucasus area, including Chechnya, took the Russians most of the first half of the nineteenth century.

Tsarist Russian methods for defeating guerrillas included deploying large numbers of troops into the affected territory, isolating it from the outside world, establishing control in the major towns first and extending domination outward from them, constructing lines of forts to confine the enemy's movements to an ever-diminishing area, and drying up the wellsprings of resistance by destroying settlements, livestock, crops, and orchards.[6] To these methods the Soviets added assassination of resistance leaders, exemplary massacres of local civilians, hostage-taking from heads of families, and mass deportations. Tsarist aggression and repression were the principal instruments in forming Chechen national and religious self-identification. Indeed, Chechnya was the scene of one of longest guerrilla insurgencies of the nineteenth century, out of which arose Shamil Basayev, "one of the great guerrilla commanders of his age."[7] The Chechens' experiences of the past two hundred years have "made them in fact one of the great martial peoples of modern history."[8] Every teenaged boy, for example, is expected to know how to handle weapons.

After the 1917 Bolshevik coup in Petrograd, the Chechens declared their independence. Betrayed by Bolshevik duplicity, they waged guerrilla war against tremendous odds well into the 1930s. But worse was to come: during and after World War II, the Stalinists deported Chechens and other groups from their traditional homelands. Close to six hundred thousand Chechens—men, women, old people, infants—were packed into overcrowded railroad cars, without heat, water, or sanitation. Many developed typhus. At stopping points, local people were forbidden to give the Chechens water. Half the inmates in some railroad cars perished. Those who survived these journeys were generally dumped into desolate areas devoid of shelter or food. As many as one-third of the deportees perished.[9] Along with the deportations, the Stalinists were busy burning Chechen books, destroying mosques, and changing Chechen place names to Russian. Stalin said the reason for the deportations was that the Chechens collaborated with the German occupation, but this was mainly propaganda.[10] Stalin and the head of his secret police, Lavrenty Beria, were both men of the Caucasus. They knew and feared the rebellious potential of the Chechens. Stalin went to great expense and trouble to deport them, diverting many resources to that task even while the struggle against the Nazis was at its height.[11] Russian and Communist efforts to "denationalize" the Chechens had only the opposite effects. Like the Armenians and the Jews, the Chechens have a common recollection of attempted genocide: "The memory of the deportation became the central defining event in modern Chechen history."[12]

Eventually, surviving Chechens began to return to their homeland. They found that many Russians had moved into the depopulated districts. By the end of the 1980s unemployment in Chechnya was widespread, levels of medical care and education were among the very lowest in the USSR, mortality from infectious diseases and parasites was very high, and most of its important offices were held by Russians. In view of the experiences the Chechens had undergone at the hands of the Russians for two hundred years—wars, massacres, confiscations, collectivization, purges, deportations, attempted genocide—it was no surprise that with the breakup of the Soviet Union they saw their chance to take back control of their own country. Increasing agitation resulted in the Chechen parliament declaring full independence in November 1991. Russian president Boris Yeltsin rejected that declaration and dispatched six hundred Interior Ministry troops to Chechnya. At the airports crowds of civilians surrounded and confined these soldiers. Consequently all Russian forces were withdrawn from Chechnya by June 1992.

Nevertheless, several influences helped shape the Russian decision to mount a serious invasion of Chechnya. The most immediate cause, or excuse, was the hijacking of Russian buses by Chechen bandits. Political rivalries among politicians in Moscow, poor intelligence about the real situation inside Chechnya, and Russian fears of growing Turkish influence in the Caucasus region were other factors.[13] The insulting and inflammatory rhetoric of Chechen president Dzhokhar Dudayev made him particularly loathed in Moscow. (Dudayev had been born in exile in 1944, a survivor of Stalin's anti-Chechen genocide.) But "the most important" cause of the invasion was Dudayev's refusal to sign any treaty of union with Russia: "In the end, only an issue as critical as Russian territorial integrity could have brought on an actual invasion of Chechnya."[14] Chechen opponents of Dudayev, supported by Moscow, attacked Grozny in mid-October 1994 and again in late November. Both efforts were easily repulsed. Russian involvement in these episodes became publicly known, permitting Dudayev to assume the mantle of defender of a free Chechnya.[15] Thus the die was cast.

In any full-scale trial of arms between Chechnya and Russia, all the advantages seemed to lie with the latter. According to a 1989 census, the Chechnya-Ingush Autonomous Republic had a population of 1.29 million, of whom 735,000 were Chechens and 304,000 Russians. There was also a Chechen diaspora of about 300,000 in the former Soviet Union. The area of Chechnya proper was quite small, only a few thousand square miles. Except for the second battle of Grozny in August 1996 (see below), active Chechen fighters probably never exceeded 3,000 at any one time, while estimates of the number of Russian troops of various types in Chechnya range (revealingly: nobody really knows) from 30,000 to 55,000.[16] The Russians enjoyed uncontested air superiority. Chechnya was easily accessible by land. And the Chechens would fight alone. During 1992 and 1993, President Dudayev visited many countries in the Middle East as well as Britain, France, and the United States, but none of these would recognize Chechen independence. No neighboring states offered shelter or easy access routes for supplies, nor would the Americans send Stinger missiles, as they had done in Afghanistan. The other Caucasian states feared Russian reprisals involving their internal economic and ethnic problems; and besides, centuries of slave and cattle raiding by Chechens had not endeared them to their neighbors in the region. In time, Turkey would protest the Russian invasion, and Saudi Arabia would appeal to other Muslim states to complain to the Russians, but there was little else. Yet in fact the relative strength of the opposing forces was radically different from what these circumstances might suggest.

General Condition of the Russian Army

"The army, in tandem with the party, *was* the Soviet Union." Consequently, "with the exception of the Communist Party, no institution suffered more from the dissolution of the USSR than the Soviet armed forces."[17] In the 1990s, the exhaustion, malaise, and general disruption of Russian society were reaching alarming proportions. The population was falling; indeed Russia had entered the early stages of a veritable demographic crisis. In 1999 the Russian national budget was smaller than that of Illinois.[18]

The Russians went into Chechnya only a half dozen years after their debacle in Afghanistan. The Soviet military weaknesses made manifest in that unhappy country had not been seriously addressed, indeed had been allowed to grow worse. Even after Afghanistan, the Russian army made little preparation for counterinsurgency, especially in cities. With the exception of elite Spetsnaz units, "by the 1980s, urban combat was no longer the focus of in-depth exercises, and military textbooks ignored the issue almost entirely."[19] Most Russian soldiers received fewer than six hours of training for urban warfare.[20] The last remaining Russian army unit specializing in urban fighting had been handed over to the Ministry of the Interior in

February 1994, whereupon most of its officers resigned.[21] The army had shut down its sniper schools long before.

Like the Soviet army before it, the Russian army continued to train (to the extent that it did any training) for the Big War against NATO, not urban fighting. And then in the early 1990s the Russian withdrawal from Eastern Europe and the western USSR was followed by massive and ill-planned budget cuts. Even payment of basic army salaries seemed beyond the interests or capabilities of the politicians: in 1996, a majority of Russian officers held part-time jobs. On several occasions, the wives of army officers blocked landing fields to dramatize their desperate need for their husbands' back pay.[22]

Urban combat requires a good deal of initiative from junior officers, a quality notably lacking in those of both the Soviet and post-Soviet armies. In light of Russian experience fighting in cities from Sevastopol and Stalingrad to Berlin and Budapest, this absence of initiative underlines one more price the Russians have paid for seventy years of Communist rigidity.

The brutality the Russians were about to display in Chechnya reflected the brutality inside the Soviet and Russian army. Beatings, rape, and murder of young conscripts were common. About 2,000 conscripts died every year, from nervous and physical breakdown or from suicide. In 1997, 487 Russian soldiers were officially recorded as having taken their own lives. In 1996, nearly 1,100 soldiers were murdered, mostly by fellow soldiers. Without doubt these figures are too low.[23] How could the all-important esprit de corps exist in a world of savage cruelty practiced not only against young private soldiers but even against sergeants?[24]

Beyond that, close to 85 percent of Russian youths were exempted or deferred from the draft. In addition, in 1992–1994, draft dodging in some cities reached 75 percent.[25] Those actually conscripted often did not show up for induction, or were found to be unable to serve because of medical problems or lack of education. Hence, the army had to take soldiers who were physically and mentally handicapped and criminals as well; the latter group comprised about one-third of actual inductees, a fact that goes far to explain this army's conduct toward civilians in Chechnya.[26] To meet minimum needs, the army had to employ contract soldiers, mercenaries who had no interest in the war in Chechnya.[27] In 1996, to fill the ranks of junior officers, the military academies began graduating students before they had completed their preparation.[28] According to one authority, units of the army were so understrength that the seventy thousand troops that were supposed to move into Chechnya in 1994 probably numbered no more than fifteen thousand.[29] Moreover, according to a U.S. Marine study of the conflict, "some [Russian] soldiers actually entered combat without weapons or ammunition."[30]

The results of years of cutbacks in training were devastating. Most battalions engaged in field training only once a year.[31] "Some [Russian] servicemen did not know how to dig a foxhole, lay mines, prepare sandbagged positions, or fire a machine gun, let alone conduct urban operations."[32] Most of the soldiers were completely unfamiliar with fighting at night, the favorite time of the insurgents in Grozny. Often conditions even in elite units were not much better. "What serious elite force anywhere in the world," demands one student of the war, "makes an eighteen-year-old conscript with six months service into a sergeant?"[33] Russians who were taken prisoner in Chechnya often did not know where they were or who the enemy was supposed to be.[34] Of course, Russian logistics were awful. The shortage of food was scandalous: soldiers in Grozny eventually killed and ate street dogs.[35] Worse, "logistics units were often unable to provide fresh drinking water, which caused Russian troops to consume contaminated water that resulted in [additional] health problems."[36]

No one seemed to know how to take care of the "undernourished and untrained teenage conscripts who perished in Chechnya."[37] Their condition provoked pity even from Chechen mountain women: "You almost have to feel sorry for these Russian conscripts, they are so hungry and miserable."[38] According to General Valery Vostrotin, all over Chechnya great numbers of both officers and men were drunk all the time.[39] Those who were sober often accepted bribes to let Chechens pass through their lines. And suppose the Russians actually had cut all the supply corridors into Chechnya? No matter; many Russian soldiers willingly sold weapons to Chechen insurgents: "As long as Ivan is here, there will always be guns for us to shoot at him."[40]

Understandably lacking confidence in the abilities of their conscript troops, Russian officers relied on aerial bombing and artillery to blast the rebels out of their positions.[41] This practice had a number of seriously negative effects. A bombed city can provide good positions for its defenders; the guerrillas simply dug in to ruined buildings and waited, often making use of tunnels and bunkers. The ruins of Grozny became a sort of forest for guerrillas.

Even worse, overreliance on artillery and airpower produced many casualties from friendly fire. "Fratricide was a serious and continuing problem throughout the campaign. Poorly trained units, operating in a confused and uncertain battle environment, often unable to tell friend from foe, and lacking quality leadership and interunit coordination, were often as dangerous to themselves as they were to the Chechens."[42] Russian aircraft were responsible for as much as 60 percent of Russian troop fatalities in the first battle of Grozny, even though planes did not begin supporting ground forces in the city until January 3.[43] Russian pilots flew too high because they were afraid of antiaircraft fire. Besides, they were of course poorly trained: Russian combat pilots had 25 hours of flying time per year, compared to 250–300 hours for NATO pilots. The numerous casualties inflicted on Russian ground troops by their own aircraft simply devastated morale.[44] In addition, soldiers believed their losses were several times as high as official reports. Soviet propaganda always told lies (especially in Afghanistan), and everybody always knew it; hence nobody now believed Russian army bulletins.[45] Besides, this was Russia's first television war, and that fact undermined belief in official casualty reports as well.[46] Thus, "the Russian Army was mired in one of the most disastrous situations it had ever experienced."[47]

Russian Intelligence

As they prepared for their 1994 invasion of Chechnya, "the Russian military—and evidently the Russian government as well—had contracted a case of historical amnesia, and this amnesia, in turn, constituted an intelligence failure of immense proportions."[48] Quite aside from what they didn't remember about the Chechens' past or had never known about it, Russian intelligence services completely underestimated the reality of the Chechens' nationalism, seeing them as merely a collection of clans.[49] But the author of a major work on the Chechen wars found nationalism (and certainly *not* Islamic fundamentalism) to be the motivating Chechen ideology.[50] The Russians wished to believe their Chechnya operation would be like those in Budapest and Czechoslovakia: they would close off the borders, sweep through the territory, take the capital city, seize the rebel leadership, set up a puppet regime, withdraw the army, and hand responsibility over to Ministry of the Interior forces. "Victory would be achieved through awe."[51] Because of incredibly poor intelligence and reconnaissance failures, Russian military planners had not realized that the Chechens had been preparing for months to defend Grozny, that indeed they had tanks, rocket launchers, and antiaircraft units and were ready to put up a furious fight. This astounding failure of intelligence stemmed in part from the fact that most Russian information regarding Chechnya came from pro-Russian elements there and in Moscow. Besides, the Russians were not eager to face a major battle in urban terrain.[52] So they ignored any evidence that Grozny was well defended and grossly underestimated the strength and determination of its defenders. Clearly, "the December 1994 Russian military invasion of Chechnya was the result of a massive intelligence failure."[53] To make things worse, if possible, Russian maps of the area were inadequate and of the wrong scale.[54] And when operations began, the Russian troops failed to complete the encirclement of the city for weeks, allowing insurgent reinforcements and supplies to enter almost at will.[55]

The Invasion

Small numbers of Russian aircraft began bombing Grozny early in December 1994. On December 11, Russian ground forces, possibly numbering around forty thousand, entered Chechnya. Soon protesting civilian crowds surrounded most of their columns, and the soldiers did not know what to do. Civilians also stopped another unit approaching Chechnya through neighboring Dagestan. In Ingushetia, soldiers in yet another blocked detachment began shooting. The confrontation resulted in several civilian deaths and the burning of some army trucks.[56] Chechen fighters in the neighboring hills, who were impervious to daily air attack, mined or shot up Russian vehicles on their way to Grozny. The operation was called off.

The real assault on Grozny came on December 31, 1994. Six thousand Russian troops attacked the capital. The Russians later claimed that at least fifteen thousand Chechen fighters were in Grozny, a figure possibly three times the actual number.[57] In tanks, the Russian advantage was 1.6 to 1, in artillery 1.8 to 1.[58] But Russian doctrine from World War II maintained that in urban operations the attacker needed a ratio of 6 to 1 to offset the natural advantages of the defense.[59] Leadership of the Russian forces was disorganized and even dysfunctional. "In the initial organization for the operation, the assault units were divided along separate axes which complicated unity of command. The overall headquarters did not have an ongoing staff-planning relationship with these separate units. Command and control of the operation was spread among several different ministers [in Moscow]. A direct chain of command did not exist. The North Caucasus Military District Command Structure (the district which included Chechnya) was bypassed and decisions for the operation were made by the Russian Defense Minister, General Grachev."[60] Thus the scene was prepared: "What transpired on New Year's Day in the small republic of Chechnya was Russia's greatest military disaster since World War II."[61]

As a general rule, the best procedure for taking control of a defended city is to close it off completely, occupy large buildings such as government offices and factories on the outskirts, and then move toward the center, methodically establishing control, district by district. But the Russian assault on Grozny came from two sides only, mainly because of a lack of sufficient troops. Indeed, the Russians failed to encircle Grozny through the whole month of January, allowing Dudayev to reinforce its defenses.[62] In mid-February Dudayev would use the still-open southern side to carry out an orderly retreat to the mountains. Having failed to block important routes into and out of the city, the Russians committed another grievous error by going straight into downtown Grozny, moving along parallel avenues lined with substantial buildings, so that their tank columns—unsupported by infantry—were not able to assist one another. The results were predictably disastrous.

How the Chechens Fought

For the Russians to win, they had either to disperse the Chechen forces or bring them to battle and defeat them. For the Chechens to win, they had only to undermine the Russian will to fight. The Chechen aim was to inflict sufficient casualties on the Russian forces to turn opinion within Russia against the conflict. The battle of Grozny was a good laboratory for this strategy. In cities, "the defender has all the advantages," partly because fighting in urban areas reduces the importance of technology (usually the attacker's most important advantage) and also entails heavy casualties, both military and civilian.[63]

The defenders of Grozny were inferior in what many consider the essentials of modern war: heavy artillery, armor, airpower, and electronic intelligence. But they were certainly not unarmed. The whole area was awash in weapons after the disintegration of the USSR. When the Russian troops pulled out in 1992, they sold many of their heavy weapons to the Chechens or simply left them behind.[64] During the siege of Grozny, the Chechens smuggled arms through Dagestan, and bought yet more from Russians. (By having opened Chechnya to illegal business ventures, Dudayev had obtained lots of cash for arms purchases.)[65] The Chechen diaspora, from Moscow to the United Arab Emirates, was another source of aid. And for the modern equipment that was in short supply, the Chechens substituted solidarity, a complete belief in the justice of their cause, and a conviction of their superiority to the enemy.[66] In the words of one Chechen military commander: "This isn't an army. It's the whole Chechen people that is fighting."[67]

The first period of the battle for Grozny was not a true example of urban guerrilla warfare, because most of the Chechen defenders of the city relied primarily on conventional tactics. When the assault on Grozny came, the Chechens, who had prepared for months to defend the city, were settled into well-made strongpoints and fortifications erected by men who had served in the regular Russian army.[68] The fighting Chechens in the capital possessed dozens of artillery pieces, 150 antiaircraft guns, thirty rocket artillery units, and as many as thirty-five tanks and forty armored infantry vehicles.[69]

(The Russians later claimed to have destroyed twenty-six Chechen tanks and 150 aircraft.)[70]

Many of the insurgents spoke Russian. This was of crucial importance, because, especially in the January fighting, much Russian radio traffic was broadcast uncoded. Russian soldiers wanted to avoid sending coded messages (which often take considerably longer to transmit than plain speech) because when Russian forward air controllers broadcast their coordinates to aircraft, Chechen artillery would have time to target and hit them.[71] The insurgents also gave the Russians misleading information over Russian radio channels; on the other hand, Chechen communications were relatively safe because few Russians spoke Chechen.

Substantial numbers of the Chechens defending Grozny had a keen understanding of Russian tactics because they had undergone Russian military training. President Dudayev himself had once been a general in the Soviet air force; another outstanding Chechen leader, Aslan Maskhadov, was a former Russian artillery colonel.[72] Many of the insurgents had received their training in the days when the Russian government was trying to put pressure on neighboring Georgia.[73] The hard core of Grozny's defense was the five-hundred-member Chechen national guard, composed of men mostly in their twenties who were veterans of the Soviet and/or Russian armies.[74] Hence the Chechen forces could anticipate Russian moves even if they had not had the tremendous advantage of listening in on Russian radio transmissions. The Chechens had set up three defensive rings around the presidential palace. They held it until the Russians bombed and shelled it down to the ground, a process that took a full month and killed countless civilians. The raising of the Russian flag over the ruins of the palace on January 20 is generally viewed as the end of the battle, or at least of that phase of it.

During and after the siege of the presidential palace, the Chechens increasingly employed classic guerrilla tactics. As the battle progressed, they relied on light equipment, including portable anti-tank weapons; they also used automobiles as platforms for mortar ambushes.[75] Civilians often guided Russian soldiers through Grozny streets into these ambushes, at which the Chechens excelled. They struck small or exposed enemy positions and then scattered, melting into the civilian population, or ambushed Russian columns coming to the rescue. Surrounded Chechen units escaped by dispersing in small groups during the night. But their mobility also enabled them to concentrate quickly several fighting groups for big attacks, even regimental-sized ones. The insurgents usually sought out the enemy, even when outnumbered. In contrast, Russian units tried to avoid battle.[76] Chechen fighters would "hug" Russian forces, staying close to them to neutralize Russian artillery and airpower. The Chechens sent out fast-moving hunter groups to attack tanks and planted antitank mines everywhere. Poor Russian communications made these tactics easy. Russian troops wanted to stop fighting after dark and hunker into their positions, but the Chechens liked to fight at night.[77] The Chechens' taste for night fighting and the deadliness of their snipers filled Russian soldiers with constant dread.

The insurgents were on home ground; they knew Grozny. They enhanced their mobility and communications routes by breaking through the basement walls of entire city blocks. They used networks of underground passageways to evacuate their wounded and bring in reinforcements and supplies. Like the Polish Home Army in Warsaw, they made good use of the sewer system. Russian airpower ruled the skies over Grozny, but the Chechens' subterranean communication systems limited its effectiveness. Besides, "the Russians found their helicopters to be far too vulnerable to rooftop snipers and ambushes in the urban setting."[78] All these dangers swirled around the Russian troops, who unsuccessfully sought safety inside their vehicles.[79]

Insurgents versus Tanks

During the first battle of Grozny, Russian tank losses were heavier than was necessary, as they had been in Budapest.

Russian unit commanders were totally unfamiliar with Grozny and did not have good maps, so they became lost in a city twice the area of Pittsburgh. Russian armored units had to divide into narrow columns to approach the city center, down long streets lined with multilevel buildings, and thus were easy targets for ambush. According to the U.S. Marines, "armored vehicles cannot operate in cities without extensive dismounted infantry support."[80] But Russian tanks in Grozny did not have infantry support. Thus they could easily be attacked from the second or third story of a building or from basements, places toward which the cannons of the tanks could not point. The Russian tendency was to stay inside their vehicles during ambushes, giving the insurgents the opportunity to drop hand grenades on them from balconies. Hence, in Grozny "the majority of lethal hits [on tanks] came from above, easily penetrating turrets and engine decks, and from the rear."[81] (The reader may wish to return to the passage from Thucydides found on the first page of this book's introduction.)

The Chechens excelled at the classic tank ambush: they allowed a tank column to advance down avenues deep into the city, then disabled the first and last tanks, and threw explosives and gasoline down from upper stories or rooftops at those caught in the middle. It is both fascinating and dismaying to discover that "as had happened fifty years before in Berlin, entire tank columns were effectively paralyzed by the immobilization of the lead and tail vehicles."[82] The crews of disabled tanks were easy targets as they emerged from their vehicles. The rocket-propelled grenade launcher (RPG), very effective against tanks, was the insurgents' weapon of choice. It was relatively cheap and required only a single operator. Tank crew casualties were very high. As in the Warsaw uprising half a century before, the best tank killers were almost always teenagers.[83]

Thus, the insurgents negated to a serious degree the Russian advantage in heavy equipment. The vulnerability of tanks on city streets eventually forced the Russians to employ infantry in substantial numbers, which they had been reluctant to do. The Russians learned to mount wire-mesh protection several inches from the body of a tank; they also put undefended vehicles in advance of a moving column to provoke an ambush. Even with these improved tactics, the Russians lost more than half the armored vehicles sent into Grozny. "If the comparative relationship between the attacking and defending forces is taken into account, the conclusion must be drawn that, percentage-wise, the [Russian] armored equipment losses in Grozny street battles had been even more severe than in Berlin [in 1945]."[84] But without doubt, those who paid the highest price of all for the battle of Grozny were its civilian inhabitants.

The Russian Army versus Civilians

The Russian forces that attacked Grozny in January 1995 "were simply not capable of conducting complex military operations, especially one that required discriminate use of fire and avoidance of collateral injuries and damage."[85] But more than collateral damage was in store: the invasion of Chechnya became "a war against all Chechens, both those who wanted to stay in Russia and those who did not."[86] Many villages wished to keep out of the war and would have made accommodations with the Russian forces, but were prevented from doing so by the indiscriminate brutality of the invaders.[87] In the eyes of Russian soldiers, Chechens were not and could not be Russians, but were an alien, dangerous, and hateful people. A report by the organization Médecins sans Frontières (Doctors without Borders) stated that Russian troops put women and children on tanks to serve as human shields and also used them as cover to enter houses and loot them.[88]

The Russians dropped tons of explosives on Grozny to eliminate snipers. This practice, of course, alienated both Chechen and Russian civilians and made recruits for the insurgents.[89] After their initial setbacks, the Russians began using artillery as a substitute for maneuvers on the ground; the intensity of artillery fire reached the level of World War II battles. Concerns about resulting civilian casualties disappeared, a sure indicator of deteriorating morale and discipline.[90] "The Russians captured Grozny primarily through the use of excessive, overwhelming firepower, and at great cost to themselves and to the local Chechen population."[91] Indeed, "Russian military actions displayed an almost complete indifference toward casualties. The remains of Russian soldiers, Chechen rebels, and innocent civilians were left to rot on the streets for weeks."[92] The Russians believed the destruction of Grozny and other centers was a good thing, because it would eliminate potential Chechen fighting positions and make it impossible for the insurgents to hide among civilians, who would have either fled or died.[93]

The Russian army did not know or did not care that a majority of Grozny's inhabitants were not Chechens but Russians. Most of the latter lived in large apartment blocks reserved for Russians in the city center, where most of the fighting took place. Those who could flee the battle area had done so, leaving behind mainly old people with no place to go. Thus Russian civilian casualties were very high; indeed it appears that most of the civilians killed by Russian bombing and artillery fire in Grozny were Russian.[94]

The Russian provisions to bring drinking water to the devastated city were inadequate, so that civilians who survived all the explosions still suffered terribly, and hepatitis and cholera spread among civilians and Russian soldiers alike.[95] But it was not just the effects of normal war-fighting, however fierce, that afflicted the civilians of Grozny. In this war "against the entire population of Chechnya,"[96] Russian soldiers committed random atrocities upon persons, property, and animals; looting, beatings, rape, arson, even murder—against Chechen and Russian alike—went on openly.[97] (During World War II, the Red Army had behaved in the same manner in "liberated" eastern Germany, and even in "allied" countries. Stalin explained to President Benes of Czechoslovakia that the Red Army "was not composed of angels."[98] Surely no one doubted him.)

Casualties

It is very difficult to know for certain how many Chechen fighters died in this battle for Grozny. In fact, one cannot be sure how many fighting Chechens there were altogether. Some Russian sources claim that fifteen thousand Chechen insurgents were killed; one American source puts the figure between one thousand and four thousand.[99] Upwards of twelve hundred Russian troops were killed in action.[100] For the entire war up to the end of 1997, Russian sources indicate roughly three thousand Russian troops killed, thirteen thousand wounded, eight hundred taken prisoner or missing.[101] Estimates of civilian deaths in the Grozny fighting run from four thousand to twenty-seven thousand; the smaller the number, the larger the proportion of these deaths that was made up of ethnic Russians.[102] For comparison, during the ten-year war in Afghanistan, between thirteen thousand and fifteen thousand Russian soldiers perished. The first Chechen conflict also cost the Russians two trillion rubles worth of combat equipment, enough money to support the entire Russian army for a half year.[103]

The Second Battle for Grozny

In the spring of 1996, Chechen forces launched a major effort to expel the Russians from Grozny. This second battle for Grozny would be the biggest Chechen offensive operation of the 1994–1996 war. The Chechens intended to inflict sufficient costs and casualties on the Russians to show them that the war was stalemated, so that they would tire of the whole conflict. Their aims were successful: the effect of the recapture of Grozny on public opinion in Russia would be roughly comparable to the effect of the 1968 Tet Offensive on public opinion in the United States.[104] Many of the Russian soldiers who had participated in the first battle for Grozny had been rotated back to Russia; thus the city was now held largely by inexperienced troops, a fact that would greatly facilitate the aims of the Chechens.

The first Chechen attack on Russian-occupied Grozny was essentially a raid, carried out between March 6 and 19, 1996. Several hundred Chechen fighters actually rode into the Grozny railway station on a train, completely surprising the Russian garrison. They caused tremendous panic and damage until they withdrew, taking many hostages with them.

Not long thereafter the Russians scored their only real success in the entire war: a rocket attack killed President Dudayev on April 22. The Russians probably hated Dudayev more than any other Chechen alive or dead, and consequently his death would make it easier for them to conclude a peace agreement later on.

The Chechens mounted their main attack on Grozny and some other key towns on August 6. They had shown in their March raid how easily they could come into Grozny, but even so, the Russians had not improved the defenses of the city. The Chechens had also been circulating flyers urging Russian soldiers to defect and civilians to leave town. Nevertheless, the attack was yet another huge surprise for the Russians.

On August 6, 1996, about fifteen hundred Chechen fighters, many of whom had previously entered Grozny on foot, attacked its Russian garrison of twelve thousand soldiers and two hundred armored vehicles.[105] More Chechens came in, eventually numbering between three thousand and four thousand.[106] The overall plan was to capture the most important government buildings in the city, attack rescue columns coming into Grozny, and pin down Russian troops in other areas of Chechnya to prevent them from going to the city.[107]

The Chechens sealed off the main avenues of approach to the city and penetrated to the center, inflicting numerous casualties on the confused Russians. Soon they had most of the Russian units blockaded in the city center. By August 16 the fighting had died down. On August 18, former Russian presidential candidate Alexander Lebed, now in charge of security, agreed to a cease-fire. Under its terms, the city would be temporarily under dual control, until Russian troops evacuated it; the question of Chechnya's exact relations with Russia was to be postponed for five years, until 2001. The Russians began pulling out of the city toward the end of August. On January 4, 1997, the last Russian military units withdrew from Chechnya. It was the end (at least for a while) of a Russian military presence centuries old. Total Russian casualties in the second battle for Grozny reached five hundred dead and fourteen hundred wounded and missing. Eighteen Russian tanks and sixty-nine other armored vehicles had been destroyed.[108] The fall of Grozny in August 1996 was Russia's "worst military defeat since the disasters of [the Nazi invasion in] 1941."[109]

The Roots of the Russian Debacle

According to numerous professional observers and analysts, "the intervention [in Chechnya, December 1994] violated just about every rule of modern warfare."[110] Indeed, "the assault on Grozny raised the level of [Russian army] mistakes to new heights of stupidity. The assault violated every basic conventional doctrine and common sense."[111]

Russian analysts tend to view the costliness of the 1995 campaign as the result of three main factors: failure to seal off the city of Grozny, the absence of public support for the war, and poor coordination of forces, especially between the army and the Ministry of Internal Affairs.[112] This last factor—coordination—has attracted the attention of Western analysts as well. For example, "the single, overriding cause behind the Russian defeat in Chechnya was the dissension among the various levels and branches of command."[113] There is much merit in this view: certainly, Russian troops lacked a clear chain of command. Different high-ranking commanders often gave contradictory orders to the same subordinates. The identity of those holding the highest levels of command in Chechnya would change with notable frequency. In addition, all note that the force that invaded Chechnya in 1994 had been slapped together from disparate elements, "a rag-tag collection of various units," with no time to learn to operate together.[114] Lack of cohesion was indisputably a major Russian weakness.

Yet to some others, "it was clear that Russia's problems were more fundamental than force coordination. Rather, they were rooted in an overall low quality of troop training and competence."[115] Still other commentators identify the disastrous morale level of many Russian soldiers in Chechnya as the "greatest single reason for the Russian defeat."[116] Low Russian morale had of course multiple causes. Probably few Russians, either in the armed forces or the general public, really wished to lose the *territory* of Chechnya. Even fewer, however, looked upon the Chechens as true Russians; most despised them as a foreign, Islamic, treacherous, criminal people, "the most hated national group in Russia."[117] There had been much open and strenuous opposition by high-ranking Russian officers against intervention.[118] Five hundred and forty generals, other officers and NCOs resigned from the army rather than go to Chechnya.[119] The feeling among Russian soldiers that Chechnya was not truly part of the Russian homeland "was of the most critical importance in determining the level of their fighting spirit."[120] On the civilian home front, the government failed to mobilize public opinion behind clear aims.

Of perhaps equal importance, Russia had nothing—Russia had never had anything—to offer the peoples of Asia except force: no attractive ideology, no enviable success, no viable order, no prosperity, no justice.[121] Hence in dealing with colonial and/or subordinated peoples, Russian soldiers and administrators never felt that they could take the superiority of their civilization for granted, the way the French, the British, and the Americans did.

The campaigns in Chechnya exposed the "demoralization, corruption, and rampant inefficiency of the Russian military."[122] Before the war the Russian political elites, bent on self-enrichment at any cost, had presided over the humiliation of the Russian officer corps, failure to replace or maintain aging equipment, and cutbacks in training to an army lacking esprit de corps or even simple pride as a result of shocking brutality against young conscripts and noncommissioned officers. In short, "The Russian army was simply in no shape to fight a war."[123]

But that is only a part of the story of the Russian failure. Two distinguished students of the Soviet Union wrote, "It is hard to believe that the Russian Army has found it so difficult to overwhelm and defeat the Chechen rebels."[124] But *why* was it so hard to believe? The Russian army suffered from multiple pathologies, many of which had surfaced in Afghanistan years before. But these became so prominent, so fatally visible, in Chechnya in large part because the Russians were fighting a formidable foe. It is an error of the greatest magnitude and the profoundest peril to assume automatically that the armed forces of any "modern" society or "great power" will simply romp over the resistance of any "traditional" or "primitive" people. The Chechens saw themselves as a proud warrior race who had been savagely and systematically maltreated. They were fighting in their own land, for independence from the hated historical oppressor. The assurance of belonging to the true religion presumably reduced the fear of death, at least for some. They had plenty of weapons and employed tactics learned from generations of hit-and-run battles. They were fighting against enemies most of whom would have been happy to abandon the country, just as they had happily abandoned Afghanistan only a few years before. To win, the Chechens had only not to lose.

And so it came to pass that "the victory of the Chechen separatist forces over Russia has been one of the greatest epics of colonial resistance of the past century."[125]

Conclusion: Looking Back and Ahead

We should now review the most essential aspects of the eight urban insurgencies examined in this volume, to see what common salient features they display and what lessons they suggest.

Warsaw

Five years of Nazi savagery made the uprising in Warsaw inevitable. But in addition, its leaders had high expectations of outside help. Soviet armies were fast approaching from the east, and the Polish resistance hoped that Allied airpower would help overcome their woeful shortage of arms and munitions. The rising might well have succeeded if either of these expectations had been fulfilled. But Stalin halted his forces within clear sight of burning Warsaw, and Allied planes found the flight to the city too dangerous without permission to refuel or at least land on Soviet-occupied territory. Besides, in the eyes of the Western powers, Warsaw was remote from the decisive battlefield of Normandy. Nevertheless, the fighting in the isolated city went on for months, during which hundreds of German tanks were destroyed. But in the end, betrayed by the Soviets and overwhelmed by the Nazis, Warsaw—capital of the first state to resist Hitler—perished in blood and fire.

Budapest

In 1956, provoked by a decade of repression, incompetence, and mendacity, massive but orderly protest demonstrations of students and workers confronted the Hungarian Stalinist party-state in its capital city. Indiscriminate firing on these crowds by the hated political police brought the regime to its crisis; the siding of the army with the demonstrators brought it to its doom, as in the Petrograd of 1917. But after some hesitation, leaders in the Kremlin decided that the overthrow, however bloodless, of a dependent Communist satrapy right across the Soviet border, in a part of the world tacitly recognized as within its sphere of influence, was unacceptable. Moscow sent in overwhelming force, isolating Budapest from the rest of the country and Hungary itself from the rest of Europe. Most of the invading soldiers could understand neither the language nor the culture of the Hungarians and were uninhibited by outside observers. As in Warsaw a dozen years before, tank losses by the invading army were as impressive as they were unexpected. Again as in Warsaw, the outside world did not respond to increasingly desperate cries for help. Inevitably, therefore, sheer force suffocated the revolt of Budapest.

Algiers

The origin of the insurgency in the city of Algiers lay in the failure of the insurgency in the rural areas. Like almost all wars of decolonization of the 1950s and after, the Algerian rebellion against French rule was a civil war, in which substantial elements of the Muslim population took the side of the French. Hence, the French were able to construct an effective intelligence and operational network from among Muslim ex-servicemen and local enemies of the FLN. The systematic and near-hermetic isolation of the Casbah, followed by thorough, painstaking, and repeated searches, soon allowed the French to capture most of the leaders and sub-leaders of the FLN organization in Algiers.

In Algeria, as in Vietnam a decade later, the insurgents, including (especially) the urban guerrillas, were defeated, but their political masters nevertheless succeeded in eventually obtaining control of their societies. French counterinsurgency methods in Algeria were successful, but the FLN was victorious in *France* and on the world stage. "Here was the basic contrast: France was strong militarily in

Algeria, but weak politically at home; the FLN was weak militarily at home, but strong politically abroad."[1]

The true key to the doom of French Algeria was the Gaullist vision of France's proper role in Europe. Nevertheless, the controversies that swirled around the use of torture by elements of the military divided the French army from much of public opinion and within itself, and the whole issue has contentiously resurfaced in recent years.

Latin America

During the 1960s, the governments of Uruguay and Brazil found themselves confronted by would-be urban guerrilla movements whose activities were usually hard to distinguish from those of mere terrorist gangs. The Uruguayan government was neither foreign nor repressive. The military regime in neighboring Brazil, on the other hand, while not foreign, was indeed repressive; but it also had the support or acquiescence of major strata of the civilian population. Accordingly Brazilians participated in regular elections for state and congressional offices. Thus, in both Uruguay and Brazil the insurgents acted in defiance of Ernesto Guevara's warning about the impossibility of making revolution against a democratic or even a quasi-democratic state. But quite aside from this perhaps controvertible judgment of Guevara (which he himself violated in his fatal attempt to begin a rural insurgency in Bolivia), the Brazilian and Uruguayan insurgent efforts suffered from the most severe structural weaknesses. First, in both countries the secrecy and elitism of the rebels interfered with propaganda, recruitment, and even basic operations. Second, in some Latin American states, Peru and Colombia for example, the government has historically been absent from large areas of the countryside, leaving an opening for the organization of insurgent groups. But all governments concentrate resources in key cities, especially the capital. For this reason alone, the insurgents' choice of São Paulo and Montevideo as the loci of conflict were strategic errors of the most serious type. Third, urban guerrillas, like their more traditional rural counterparts, need some kind of popular base to sustain them. At first glance, the natural base of such groups would seem to consist of left-wing political parties and labor unions.

But in neither Uruguay nor Brazil was the organized left very strong, and—more importantly—in both countries the left for the most part opposed urban guerrilla warfare and especially terrorism.

Last, and perhaps most important, neither the Brazilian terrorists nor the Tupamaros came close to developing a realistic strategy to take power, because, like the Irish Republican Army, *they proved utterly incapable of any serious analysis of the political situation in their countries*. The ideological extremism of the Latin American urban terrorists trying to masquerade as guerrillas, and especially their notion that by wrecking the infrastructure of urban life they would win popular support, both reflected and reinforced their isolation from normal society. Indeed the Tupamaros—middle-class, inexperienced, immature—combined arrogance, incompetence, and naiveté to such a degree that one might almost be tempted to feel sorry for them.

Saigon

The guerrilla fighting that flared in Saigon and other cities of South Vietnam during the Tet Offensive of 1968 flowed from expectations, or at least hopes, that the sudden appearance of numerous and well-armed guerrillas in the cities would both cause the South Vietnamese army to crumble and unleash a massive anti-regime uprising among the presumably seething civilian population. Neither of these hopes proved realistic; on the contrary, ARVN for the most part fought well, and the much-touted popular uprising turned out to be a pipe dream. These two factors alone doomed the Saigon guerrilla insurgency of 1968. Indeed, reliance on a mass uprising in the cities, especially in Saigon, was the greatest Communist error of the entire conflict.

But in addition, the fighting in Saigon was not a true urban insurgency, certainly not in the sense that Warsaw or Budapest or Grozny—or even Algiers or Belfast—was. In the main, the Viet Cong guerrillas in the capital were outsiders, strangers, an armed force moving from the countryside to the city, familiar with neither Saigon's population nor its geographical layout. (That the VC had to *come into* Saigon is very revealing of what they were.) Hence the failure of the mass uprising to occur was truly disastrous for the guerrillas. And on the second day of the uprising General Westmoreland blocked off all access into Saigon, preventing reinforcement of the insurgents and thus giving them the coup de grâce. The fighting inside Saigon culminated in a disaster for the Viet Cong. After Tet, South Vietnam fought on for another seven years—a longer period than World War II—in an increasingly conventional struggle, and in the end fell not to guerrillas but to the regular North Vietnamese army.

Northern Ireland

The ill treatment of the minority elements in Northern Ireland over several generations finally produced a civil rights protest movement that soon experienced violent attacks. Because the police were unable to subdue and unwilling to protect the Catholic community, units of the British Army were dispatched to restore order. The Catholic population at first welcomed these soldiers. But unprepared for this kind of operation, and with some of its members sympathetic to Orange extremists, the army soon appeared to be merely a new part of the apparatus of repression. Thus the road to widespread public support within the minority community opened to the IRA's Provisional wing, despite the fact that the organization was historically and ideologically estranged from the Catholic Church.

Despite the grave resentment of injustice among the Catholic population on which it capitalized, the IRA suffered from fundamental and irredeemable political weaknesses. The essence of its strategy—bombing the British out of Northern Ireland—was totally misconceived: no British government could abandon the British province of Ulster, especially as a response to criminal violence. But other factors also doomed the insurgents to futility. The small area and population of Northern Ireland and its capital, Belfast, and the limited numbers of the pro-IRA elements in those places were key advantages to the counterinsurgent side. Within that constricted space, British troops were operating close to their bases (for comparison, Washington, D.C., is closer to the South Pole than to Saigon), among an English-speaking population the majority of which was sympathetic to them, and in support of a political and legal system that presented at least the real possibility of reform. Indiscriminate or incompetent IRA violence soon repelled many Catholics, with the result that the insurgency represented considerably less than half of a community that was itself a minority of the population. Electoral support for Sinn Fein, the political arm of the IRA, remained far below what a united Catholic community could have delivered. Thus IRA violence was a sign not of its strength but of its weakness.

The insurgencies in Warsaw and Budapest rallied very wide popular support and still were overcome. In Northern Ireland, the Irish Republican Army's guerrilla campaign, based within only a segment of a small population, had no chance at all. Strategically, the conflict in Northern Ireland bore some notable similarities to that in Malaya after World War II: Malaya's location and size made it easy to isolate, and the majority of its civilian population was hostile to the insurgents. But even with those and other advantages, the counterinsurgent forces required decades to bring the Northern Ireland campaign to a conclusion.

Grozny

The 1994 battle against insurgents in Grozny is often called Russia's greatest military disaster since World War II, and not without reason. The Russian state and army (which half a decade earlier had been the vaunted Soviet state and army) were in terrible shape. The army's logistical system, at least in Chechnya, was so grotesquely inadequate that many Russian soldiers became sick from drinking dirty water from puddles in the streets. In addition, the fifty thousand troops the Russians committed to the battle proved inadequate to isolate the city (which was certainly not one of the great world metropolises). Consequently, reinforcements for the insurgents constantly came into Grozny, and then, having decided to abandon the battle, the insurgents were able to escape and continue the war in the nearby mountains.

On the guerrilla side of the ledger, most Chechens nursed a long history of hatred for Russians in general. Several of the commanders of the Chechen guerrillas in Grozny had held high rank in the Soviet army or air force; hence they not only knew how to make war, they could anticipate how the Russian invaders would make war. Many Chechens spoke and understood Russian, but very few Russian soldiers understood Chechen. The Chechens had many good weapons, with the Russian advantage in tanks and artillery amounting to a mere two to one. The guerrillas could neutralize Russian airpower and aerial reconnaissance by underground communications networks and by "hugging" tactics—fighting very close to the enemy, as the Viet Cong had done. Moreover, "the Russians found their helicopters to be far too vulnerable to rooftop snipers and ambushes in the urban setting."[2] Russian armor also fell victim to classic, World War II–type tank ambushes. In fact, in proportional terms more Russian tanks were lost in Grozny in 1994 than in Berlin in 1945. In Grozny, "the majority of lethal hits [on tanks] came from above, easily penetrating turrets and engine decks, and from the rear." The fighting in Grozny, as in Warsaw and Budapest, strongly suggests that "armored vehicles cannot operate in cities without extensive dismounted infantry support."[3]

Nevertheless, with all their shortcomings, the Russians eventually subdued Grozny—even if, through their own fault, they were unable to hold it.

Some Lessons Learned

Nowhere in the twentieth century has urban guerrilla warfare achieved an unambiguous success. To the contrary, from truly popular and even heroic upheavals in Warsaw, Budapest, and Grozny to elitist outbreaks in Algiers, Montevideo, São Paulo, and Belfast, the record of urban guerrilla warfare is one of complete and sometimes tragic defeat.[4] Indeed, in Brazil and Uruguay the insurgents disappeared with hardly a trace. True, the troubles in Northern Ireland lasted for far too long, but the British constitutional system did not collapse, Britain did not abandon Ulster, and Sinn Fein did not come to power, either North or South. So unpromising, indeed, is the record of urban guerrilla war, especially in recent decades, that the leaders of Peru's notorious Sendero Luminoso insurgency, which emerged in the 1980s, apparently never even contemplated any other strategy but that of classic Maoism, at least as they conceived it.[5]

The weaknesses of urban guerrillas persist into the twenty-first century, illustrated by the battle of Fallujah in November 2004. The attack on that insurgent-dominated city forty miles west of Baghdad involved six thousand U.S. troops, drawn from the Marines, army, special forces, and other units—"the best since World War II"

—supported by two thousand Iraqi allies.[6] Opposing them was a well-entrenched enemy force estimated at three thousand of various types.[7] A majority—perhaps most—of Fallujah's three hundred thousand residents left the city before the fighting. The assault began on November 8 and ended on November 20, with the flight of the surviving insurgents, at a cost of fifty-one American and twelve hundred guerrilla fatalities. In one journalist's summary, "The battle of Fallujah will go down in history as a textbook example of urban warfare. The U.S. military used the most advanced technology and the best street-fighting tactics to hunt down the entrenched insurgents while keeping civilian casualties to a minimum."[8] Perhaps; in any event, the insurgents lost the city.

This continuing unhappy record of urban guerrillas can be no surprise if we reflect that urban insurgents deviate almost completely from the fundamental principles of guerrilla warfare laid down by Clausewitz, Mao Tse-tung, and others. According to their teachings, guerrillas need to operate in mountainous, jungle, or otherwise inaccessible regions that negate the power of conventional forces, and preferably close to an international border that can provide a sanctuary or become a source of outside assistance. But, in dramatic contrast, urban guerrillas wage their fight in the limited space of cities possessing transportation grids, sometimes quite well developed, that facilitate the rapid movement of the forces that any regime will pour into a threatened city, especially a capital.[9] In addition, all urban guerrilla efforts are vulnerable to encirclement and ultimate annihilation.[10] Nobody has been able to develop a strategy for overcoming these structural impediments to urban guerrilla warfare, nor is it easy to foresee changes that will seriously reduce their decisive gravity.

All this is true even for widely popular upheavals such as those in Warsaw, Budapest, and Grozny. But those insurgencies that received the support of only a minority of the urban inhabitants—sometimes a quite exiguous minority—as in Montevideo, São Paulo, and Belfast, are burdened with even graver handicaps, including the necessity for strictest secrecy and absolute anonymity. But beyond that, the Tupamaros, the followers of Carlos Marighella, and the Irish Republican Army demonstrably suffered from serious and obvious analytical debilities, psychological peculiarities, and fratricidal proclivities. The consequences of these weaknesses have been presented in such compelling terms by the distinguished student of insurgency J. Bowyer Bell that they deserve quotation at some length. Urban guerrillas "find few charms but rather enormous penalties in the covert, a myriad of obstacles to action, and obstacles always increasing. Their life is consumed by the cost of merely maintaining, much less escalating, the armed struggle." Moreover, the underground "is always inherently inefficient, a flawed, usually fatally flawed, world created in desperation by those who have made it a last refuge before despair." Consequently, "the [guerrilla] does not really anticipate winning, but rather that the regime will lose. Thus, the primary goal is not the armed struggle, is not efficiency, but persistence." But in fact "most gunmen end in the gutter or the prison."[11] One authority calculated that the average life of an urban guerrilla in Brazil was one year.[12]

The United States and Urban Military Operations

Nevertheless, even though the record strongly suggests that urban guerrilla conflicts must invariably end in the total defeat of the insurgents, the United States needs to contemplate committing its troops to such battles with extreme reluctance, for several good reasons. For one, although the counterinsurgent forces eventually emerged victorious in all the cases we have studied, victory had its costs. "U.S. planners [need to] recognize that a resident insurgency force enjoys significant advantages over even a technically superior foreign aggressor," at least in the short term.[13] Cities contain innumerable soft targets, including electric power plants, water and telecommunications systems, bridges, banks, and the offices and homes of government and business leaders, and so on. Even a premodern city can prove to be very complex; extensive slums, sometimes mushrooming overnight, prevent easy control or even access by security forces and enable insurgents to establish their dominance over significant areas and populations. Indeed, the city of Karachi alone is large enough to swallow up the entire U.S. Army.[14]

Other aspects of the urban environment also favor the defender. Among these aspects: most combat takes place at close range; sewer systems and underground tunnels for mass transit offer guerrillas relatively safe passage from one quarter to another and add a very complicating third dimension to the battle; and city buildings can degrade an army's wireless communications.[15] Moreover, urban combat almost always requires an abundance of infantry, a commodity with which the contemporary U.S. Army is not overly supplied.[16]

Consequently, even if badly armed, a determined or fanaticized opponent could inflict serious casualties on the most well-equipped and well-trained U.S. troops. And it is a certainty that in the future urban guerrillas will acquire more powerful weapons and sometimes more effective tactics. Even if that were not to happen, high casualty rates—a term constantly defined downward in American public discourse—and the media penchant for sensational pictures will almost certainly erode public support sooner rather than later. This erosion is most likely when the fighting occurs in a place many Americans do not view as vital to U.S. national interests or of which few of them have ever heard, such as Mogadishu or Fallujah.[17] This distaste for fighting in remote locales will increase dramatically when some, and perhaps more than a few, American casualties result from fratricide—friendly fire—a phenomenon that profoundly and understandably dismays great strata of the American public. Much of the time, "given the prospects for global news coverage, urban operations will have widespread and immediate political ramifications."[18] The contemporary media tend to present any number of American and/or civilian casualties as horrendous and any battle as catastrophic. Enemies of the United States are quite aware of these weaknesses and will continue to manipulate them.

Finally, many observers have enumerated the "characteristics that history has shown to be most effective in counterinsurgency [which include] perseverance, restrained use of force, and emphasis on intelligence, law enforcement, and political action."[19] These are definitely not characteristics commonly associated with the American method of making war. On the contrary, "the exercise of maximum violence for swift results has been the American way."[20] Indeed, "in American strategic culture, two dominant characteristics stand out: the preference for massing a vast army of men and machines, and the predilection for direct and violent assault."[21] As a consequence, "the larger and more violent the effort, the more effectively the United States is likely to perform."[22]

These American combat proclivities are not promising foundations for urban counterinsurgency, at least not for one waged by a media-dominated democracy. The American preference for massive firepower may well save American lives, and failure to employ it might prove very costly. But massive firepower in urban areas can cause much suffering to innocent civilians. Very few Americans would wish to see their homes or neighborhoods "liberated" in the manner U.S. forces often employed in Vietnam or Korea. That constitutes a serious ethical and moral problem in itself, but the trouble will be magnified because urban battles will be watched in real time by American and foreign news media. Even when American forces practice restraint to a heroic degree, it will not be enough to silence their critics, even (or especially) in the common situation where the insurgents themselves deliberately seek to create great numbers of civilian casualties. If it is true that "winning and losing in such a war are largely a matter of perception," U.S. forces will be at a great disadvantage in these combats.[23]

The best solution—or at least the best response—to these and other troubling questions may be for the United States *to adopt a settled policy against committing U.S. forces to counterinsurgency operations in cities.* There is no lack of commentators, contemporary and historical, who offer advice along those lines. One authority has recently urged that American "military operations in urban areas should be avoided to the extent possible."[24] In the early months of World War II, preparing for the blitzkrieg into Western Europe, Adolph Hitler warned his generals that tank divisions "are not to be lost among the maze of endless houses in Belgian towns. It is not necessary to attack towns at all."[25] And more than two millennia ago, Sun Tzu wrote: "The worst policy is to attack cities. Attack cities only when there is no alternative."[26] And there are always alternatives.

For the United States, the most dreadful scenario, to be avoided at absolutely any cost, would be to commit American military personnel against an urban insurgency that clearly enjoys the support of the majority of the local population.

If, nevertheless, a future U.S. administration determines that it has no real choice but to employ American forces against urban insurgents, it needs to be clear about what the desired outcome is, what price it is willing to pay for that outcome, and what regional or other allies will be available. It will also need to think clearly about the news media's proper role in the combat area; one Tet Offensive in a century is enough. (Recall that during the invasion of Panama in the administration of the first President Bush, journalists were not given access to infantrymen or the wounded until after operations were over; but this may not be an action some future U.S. administration will feel confident enough to choose.)

Once American troops have been committed to an urban counterinsurgent mission, keys to success will be isolation, intelligence, and political preemption.

Isolation. Preventing reinforcements and matériel from reaching the guerrillas is the supreme military necessity: "No single factor is more important to the attacker's success than isolation of the urban area."[27] The Soviets cut Budapest off from the world, but the Russians failed to do the same in Grozny, to their great cost. The French not only isolated the Casbah of Algiers but actually closed off the whole country of Algeria from assistance to the guerrillas coming from Morocco and Tunisia; the famous Morice Line, an elaborate barrier stretching for hundreds of miles along the Tunisian border, not only interdicted supplies to the guerrillas but also demonstrated French determination and power.[28]

Intelligence. Recall Callwell's observation that "in no class of warfare is a well-organized and well-served intelligence department more essential than in that against guerrillas."[29] Successful counterinsurgents require a good portrait of the population among whom they will be operating. They need real knowledge of the opponents: who they are, how many they are, what weapons they have. But equally important is knowledge of the opponents' state of mind: why they are prepared to fight Americans and what they believe the outcome of such a clash will be. The Russians knew hardly anything of their enemy when they attacked Grozny in 1994 and thus incurred the predictable penalties. Nor is it clear that the United States can, or really wishes to, develop effective human-intelligence capabilities in underdeveloped countries, the locale of most, if not all, future urban insurgencies. But the results of numerous interviews with former Viet Cong are on record, and the American military can enrich its understanding about who participates in insurgency, why, and how, by carrying out extensive and detailed noncoercive interviews with former insurgents from Bosnia, Chechnya, Colombia, Kashmir, and a dozen other societies.[30]

Political Preemption. An effective political program designed to assist U.S. forces about to undertake an urban counterinsurgency is indispensable. Essential elements of such a program include co-opting planks from the insurgent program that have widespread popularity, offering amnesty to all insurgents who surrender promptly, and sincerely promising to create or restore a peaceful method of pursuing change. This latter undertaking would probably not be effective with most of the leaders of the insurgency but almost certainly would exert a positive influence on their more marginal supporters, uncommitted civilians, and—most importantly—public opinion in the United States. The ballot box has rightly been called the coffin of insurgency. Enlisting military help, however token in fact, from countries in the region of the counterinsurgency effort may also be of great benefit, unless the ethnic or religious makeup of their troops would inflame rather than discourage the insurgents.

But by far the most important component of any U.S. political strategy is rectitude, that is, lawful conduct on the part of American troops toward prisoners, defectors, amnesty seekers, and civilians. One sometimes hears the criticism that U.S. forces are not ruthless enough or are not permitted to be ruthless enough, especially when facing a cruel and cowardly foe. Such a view is easily understandable but extremely dangerous. It may be true, in a limited tactical sense, that "a distinct advantage accrues to the side with less concern for the safety of the civilian population."[31] Nevertheless, callousness—or worse—on the part of counterinsurgent forces toward prisoners and civilians will exact its price, often sooner rather than later. Nazi savagery prolonged the Warsaw Rising. The indifference on the part of Russian troops to even Russian civilian deaths in Grozny brought them no lasting benefit; to the contrary, bad behavior by Russian troops steeled the determination and increased the numbers of their enemies, and hence their own casualties. Harsh treatment of prisoners in the Algerian conflict undermined the French cause and eventually the solidarity of the French army itself. (The rule holds true for insurgents as well: for example, Viet Cong excesses against civilians in Saigon and especially in Hue during the Tet Offensive repelled great numbers of South Vietnamese.) Quite true, the insurgents in Warsaw, Grozny, Budapest, and Algiers were defeated, but the principal reason for their defeat in each of these cases lay not in the ruthlessness of the counterinsurgents but in their overwhelming military superiority.

Right conduct by U.S. counterinsurgent forces—conduct in accord with the best traditions, teachings, legal norms, and instincts of the American armed services—has direct payoffs, most notably in the quantity of intelligence the counterinsurgents receive and in the numbers of the enemy who surrender or defect. More fundamentally, rectitude on the part of American fighting forces is essential both to their own discipline and morale and to the way they wish and need to be perceived by American society. To paraphrase Frederick Douglass: Right conduct is the ship; all else is the sea.

The more deplorable the circumstances in which American troops find themselves, the more important their adherence to high standards becomes. For a specific example: in years to come, U.S. military personnel engaged in counterinsurgency will capture known or suspected terrorists, often of the most horrific stripe—Walter Laqueur's "enemy of humankind, outside the law"—and will thus confront the nearly irresistible temptation to use whatever means necessary to make these prisoners give up information that could save many innocent lives.[32] To place American soldiers directly in the path of such temptations and then punish them for succumbing to them is unjust, as well as self-defeating. The U.S. government, therefore, must make every effort to ensure that, as soon as possible, traditional methods of interrogation are replaced or at least augmented by more sophisticated and medically legitimate lie-detecting instruments, "truth drugs," and brain scan techniques.[33]

In the end, bad conduct creates more insurgents; right conduct saves counterinsurgent lives. Especially in urban guerrilla warfare, rectitude is worth many battalions.

Notes

Introduction

1. *The Landmark Thucydides,* ed. Robert B. Strassler (New York: Free Press, 1996), p. 90.

2. Jennifer Morrison and Bruce Hoffman, "The Urbanisation of Insurgency: Potential Challenges to U.S. Army Operations," *Small Wars and Insurgencies,* vol. 6 (Spring 1995), p. 68.

3. Sharon Camp, *Cities: Life in the World's Largest Metropolitan Areas* (Washington, DC: Population Crisis Committee, 1990).

4. See two remarkable essays by Ralph Peters: "The New Warrior Class," *Parameters,* vol. 24 (Summer 1994); and "Our Soldiers, Their Cities," *Parameters,* vol. 26 (Spring 1996). And see Max G. Manwaring, *Street Gangs: The New Urban Insurgency* (Carlisle, PA: Strategic Studies Institute, 2005).

5. Steven Metz and Raymond Millen, *Insurgency and Counterinsurgency in the Twenty-first Century: Reconceptualizing Threat and Response* (Carlisle, PA: Strategic Studies Institute, 2004), p, 12.

6. Olga Oliker, *Russia's Chechen Wars, 1994–2000: Lessons for Urban Combat* (Santa Monica, CA: RAND, 2001), p. xv. Of course, counterinsurgent troops face the same difficulty in traditional guerrilla wars.

7. Anthony James Joes, *Resisting Rebellion: The History and Politics of Counterinsurgency* (Lexington: University Press of Kentucky, 2004), p. 10.

8. Mao Tse-tung, *Basic Tactics,* trans. Stuart Schram (New York: Praeger, 1966), p. 102.

9. Sun Tzu, *The Art of War,* trans. Samuel B. Griffith (London: Oxford University Press, 1963), p. 98.

10. Mao, *Basic Tactics,* p. 86.

11. Basil Liddell Hart, *The Real War 1914–1918* (Boston: Little, Brown, 1930), p. 324.

12. Mao, *Basic Tactics*, p. 73.

13. John S. Mosby, *Memoirs of Colonel John S. Mosby* (New York: Kraus Reprint Company, 1969), p. 285. Mosby also advised that "if you are going to fight, then be the attacker." Jeffrey D. Wert, *Mosby's Rangers* (New York: Simon and Schuster, 1990), p. 83.

14. Machiavelli wrote, "When once the people have taken up arms against you, there will never be lacking foreigners to assist them." *The Prince*, ed. W. K. Marriott (New York: Everyman's Library, 1992 [orig. 1515]), p. 100.

15. Carl von Clausewitz, *On War*, ed. and trans. Michael Howard and Peter Paret (Princeton, NJ: Princeton University Press, 1976), p. 480.

16. Mao Tse-tung, *Selected Military Writings* (Peking: Foreign Languages Press, 1963), p. 171.

17. One distinguished scholar has defined terrorism as "the threat or use of physical coercion, primarily against noncombatants, especially civilians, to create fear in order to achieve various political objectives." Bard E. O'Neill, *Insurgency and Terrorism: From Revolution to Apocalypse*, 2d ed. (Washington, DC: Potomac Books, 2005), p. 33. See also Jane's *World Insurgency and Terrorism* (May–August 2002).

18. See, for example, V. I. Lenin, *Collected Works*, vol. 6 (Moscow: Progress Publishers, 1960).

1. Warsaw 1944

1. Norman Davies, *Rising '44: The Battle for Warsaw* (New York: Viking, 2003), p. 618.

2. At Tours in A.D. 732, Charles Martel (Charles the Hammer), grandfather of Charlemagne, halted the Muslim invasion of Europe.

3. William Henry Chamberlin, *The Russian Revolution, 1917–1921* (New York: Macmillan, 1935), vol. 2, p. 306.

4. Norman Davies, *White Eagle, Red Star: The Polish-Soviet War 1919–1920* (New York: St. Martin's, 1972), p. 197. See Thomas Fiddick, *Russia's Retreat from Poland, 1920* (New York: St. Martin's, 1990); Waclaw Jedrzejewicz, *Pilsudski: A Life for Poland*, introduction by Zbigniew Brzezinski (New York: Hippocrene, 1982); Alexandra Pilsudska, *Pilsudski: A Biography by His Wife* (New York: Dodd, Mead, 1941); Jozef Pilsudski, *Memories of a Polish Revolutionary and Soldier* (London: Faber and Faber, 1931); Jozef Pilsudski, *Year 1920 and Its Climax: Battle of Warsaw during the Polish-Soviet War* (New York: Pilsudski Institute of America, 1972).

5. Maxime Weygand, *Memoirs* (Paris: Flammarion, 1950–57), vol. 2, p. 166.

6. J. F. C. Fuller, *A Military History of the Western World* (New York: Da Capo, 1987 [orig. 1954–57]), vol. 3, p. 360.

7. Fuller, *Military History*, vol. 3, p. 360.

8. Fuller, *Military History*, vol. 3, p. 361.

9. Edgar Vincent, Viscount D'Abernon, *The Eighteenth Decisive Battle of World History: Warsaw 1920* (London: Hodder and Stoughton, 1931), p. 172.

10. Fuller, *Military History*, vol. 3, p. 361; my emphasis.

11. E. H. Carr, *The Bolshevik Revolution, 1917–1923* (New York: Macmillan, 1961), vol. 3, p. 218.

12. Antony Polonsky, *Politics in Independent Poland 1921–1939: The Crisis of Constitutional Government* (Oxford, England: Clarendon Press, 1972), p. 463.

13. Polonsky, *Politics in Independent Poland*, pp. 35–45, 470.

14. See Ernest R. May, *Strange Victory: Hitler's Conquest of France* (New York: Hill and Wang, 200), p. 277.

15. See Robert M. Kennedy, *The German Campaign in Poland 1939* (Washington, DC: Zenger, 1980). Short accounts appear in Basil Liddell Hart, *History of the Second World War* (New York: Da Capo, 1999 [orig. 1970]); Len Deighton, *Blitzkrieg: From the Rise of Hitler to the Fall of Dunkirk* (Edison, NJ: Castle Books, 1979); and Hanson Baldwin, *Battles Lost and Won: Great Campaigns of World War II* (New York: Harper and Row, 1966).

16. Jan T. Gross, *Polish Society under German Occupation* (Princeton, NJ: Princeton University Press, 1979), p. 304.

17. Davies, *Rising '44*, p. 95.

18. Timothy Garton Ash, *The Uses of Adversity: Essays on the Fate of Central Europe* (New York: Vintage, 1990), p. 134.

19. Tadeusz Komorowski [Bor], *The Secret Army* (New York: Macmillan, 1951), p. 39. "General Bor" was his nom de guerre, and he will hereafter be referred to in these notes by that name.

20. Nuremberg Document 2325, in Joanna K. M. Hanson, *The Civilian Population and the Warsaw Uprising of 1944* (Cambridge, England: Cambridge University Press, 1982), p. 13.

21. J. K. Zawodny, *Nothing but Honor* (Stanford, CA: Hoover Institution, 1978), p. 167.

22. Stefan Korbonski, *Fighting Warsaw: The Story of the Polish Underground State* (London: Allen and Unwin, 1956), p. 31. Vidkun Quisling was the head of the puppet regime in Nazi-occupied Norway. His name became a synonym for "traitor."

23. Bor, *Secret Army*, p. 30.

24. Richard Lukas, *Forgotten Holocaust: The Poles under German Occupation, 1939–1945* (Lexington: University Press of Kentucky, 1986), p. 13.

25. Bor, *Secret Army*, p. 28.

26. Josef Garlinski, "The Polish Underground State, 1939–1945," *Journal of Contemporary History*, vol. 10 (1975), p. 227; Bor, *Secret Army*, p. 142.

27. Stanislaw Mikolajczyk, *The Rape of Poland* (New York: McGraw-Hill, 1948), p. 7.

28. Bor, *Secret Army*, p. 39.

29. F. H. Hinsley et al., *British Intelligence in the Second World War*, 5 vols. (London: Her Majesty's Stationery Office, 1979–90), vol. 1: *Its Influence on Strategy and Operations*, pp. 487–95; Davies, *Rising '44*, p. 38.

30. William Casey, *The Secret War against Hitler* (Washington, DC: Regnery Gateway, 1988), p. 43.

31. Bor, *Secret Army*, p. 151.

32. Garlinski, "Polish Underground State," p. 229; Davies, *Rising '44*, p. 201, 216–18; Hinsley et al., *British Intelligence*, vol. 3: *Its Influence on Strategy and Operations*, pt. 1, pp. 437ff.

33. Korbonski, *Fighting Warsaw*.

34. Korbonski, *Fighting Warsaw*, p. 237 and passim.

35. Bor, *Secret Army*, pp. 152–53.

36. Korbonski, *Fighting Warsaw*, p. 219. The resistance would take two pigs from a farm but give the farmer a receipt for six. Thus the farmer could kill four pigs for consumption, and the Germans could not object (p. 216).

37. Korbonski, *Fighting Warsaw*, p. 127.

38. Bor, *Secret Army*, p. 156; Lukas, *Forgotten Holocaust*, pp. 91–92.

39. Jan Karski [Jan Kozielewski], *Story of a Secret State* (Boston: Houghton Mifflin, 1944), pp. 272–73. This poignant, beautiful book was written during the war by a youthful member of the Polish resistance.

40. Bor, *Secret Army*, p. 144.

41. Lukas, *Forgotten Holocaust*, p. 93.

42. John Keegan, *Six Armies in Normandy: From D-Day to the Liberation of Paris* (New York: Viking, 1982), p. 262.

43. See Lynne Olson and Stanley Cloud, *A Question of Honor: The Kosciuszko Squadron; Forgotten Heroes of World War II* (New York: Knopf, 2003); Adam Zamoyski, *The Forgotten Few: The Polish Air Force in World War II* (Barnsley, England: Pen and Sword, 2004).

44. Wladyslaw Anders, *An Army in Exile* (London: Macmillan, 1949), chapter 10.

45. Keegan, *Six Armies*, p. 262.

46. Keegan, *Six Armies*, chapter 7.

47. Zawodny, *Nothing but Honor*, p. 118.

48. See Allen Paul, *Katyn: The Untold Story of Stalin's Polish Massacre* (New York: Scribner's, 1991).

49. See document 5, appendix D in Zawodny, *Nothing but Honor*, p. 233.

50. Winston Churchill, *The Second World War*: vol. 4, *The Hinge of Fate* (Boston: Houghton Mifflin, 1952), p. 761. George Kennan said that one reason Stalin wanted a Communist regime in Poland was to prevent any revelations about Katyn, deportations of Polish soldiers and civilians, etc. (Zawodny, *Nothing but Honor*, p. 220).

51. *New York Times*, April 13 and 14, 1990. See Paul, *Katyn*.

52. See the letter from Zbigniew Brzezinski in *Commentary*, December 1990, p. 2.

53. Israel Gutman, *Resistance: The Warsaw Ghetto Uprising* (New York: Houghton Mifflin, 1994), p. xx.

54. Dan Kurzman, *The Bravest Battle: The Twenty-eight Days of the Warsaw Ghetto Uprising* (New York: Da Capo, 1993 [orig. 1978]), p. 17.

55. Gutman, *Resistance*, pp. 14ff., 24.

56. Gutman, *Resistance*, p. 67.

57. Gutman, *Resistance*, p. 87 and passim.

58. Gutman, *Resistance*, p. 62.

59. Gutman, *Resistance*, p. 74.

60. Gutman, *Resistance*, p. 183. See also Israel Gutman, *The Jews of Warsaw: Ghetto, Underground, Revolt* (Bloomington: Indiana University Press, 1982).

61. Shmuel Krakowski, *The War of the Doomed: Jewish Armed Resistance in Poland 1942–1944* (New York: Holmes and Meier, 1984), p. 165.

62. Krakowski, *War of the Doomed*, chapter 10.

63. Gutman, *Resistance*, p. xvii.

64. Gutman, *Resistance*, p. 204.

65. Gutman, *Resistance*, p. 153.

66. Leonard Tushnet, *To Die with Honor: The Uprising of the Jews in the Warsaw Ghetto* (New York: Citadel, 1965), pp. 98, 103.

67. Gutman, *Resistance*, p. 220. See also Gutman, *The Jews of Warsaw*.

68. Gutman, *Resistance*, p. 231.

69. Gutman, *Resistance*, pp. 175ff.

70. Krakowski, *War of the Doomed*, p. 302.

71. Lukas, *Forgotten Holocaust*, p. 127.

72. Bor, *Secret Army*, p. 103. Nechama Tec, *When Light Pierced the Darkness: Righteous Christians and the Polish Jews* (New York: Oxford University Press, 1988) reproduces a German poster announcing the execution on one day in December 1943 of eight Poles for the crime of "sheltering Jews."

73. Krakowski, *War of the Doomed*, chapter 13; Tushnet, *To Die with Honor*, p. 121.

74. Tushnet, *To Die with Honor*, p. 121.

75. Anders, *Army in Exile*, p. 201; Jan M. Ciechanowski, *The Warsaw Rising of 1944* (Cambridge, England: Cambridge University Press, 1974), p. 262.

76. Zawodny, *Nothing but Honor*, pp. 102ff.

77. See Ciechanowski, *Warsaw Rising*, pp. 260, 314, and passim.

78. Ciechanowski, *Warsaw Rising*, pp. 261, 256.

79. Ciechanowski, *Warsaw Rising*, p. 258.

80. John Erickson, *The Road to Berlin: Stalin's War with Germany* (New Haven, CT: Yale University Press, 1999), p. 281.

81. Anders, *Army in Exile*, p. 16.

82. Bor, *Secret Army*, p. 195.

83. Bor, *Secret Army*, p. 196.

84. Bor, *Secret Army*, p. 48.

85. Lukas, *Forgotten Holocaust*, p. 183.

86. Korbonski, *Fighting Warsaw.*

87. Garlinski, "The Polish Underground State," p. 247.

88. Hanson, *Civilian Population*, p. 87.

89. Bor, *Secret Army*, p. 216.

90. Garlinski says there were 50,000 AK, but his figures are unusually high ("The Polish Underground State," p. 248).

91. Hanson, *Civilian Population*, p. 77.

92. Korbonski, *Fighting Warsaw*, p. 183; Garlinski, "The Polish Underground State," pp. 227, 244.

93. Zawodny, *Nothing but Honor*, p. 45.

94. Erickson, *Road to Berlin*, p. 286.

95. Hanson, *Civilian Population*, p. 84.

96. Hanson, *Civilian Population*, p. 85.

97. Korbonski, *Fighting Warsaw*, p. 374.

98. Hanson, *Civilian Population*, p. 91; Bor, *Secret Army*, p. 232.

99. Davies, *Rising '44*, p. 279.

100. Hanson, *Civilian Population.*

101. Bor, *Secret Army*, p. 171.

102. Hanson, *Civilian Population*, pp. 96–97, 111.

103. Erickson, *Road to Berlin*, p. 274.

104. Hanson, *Civilian Population*, p. 46.

105. Bor, *Secret Army*, pp. 357–58.

106. Zawodny, *Nothing but Honor*, p. 137.

107. Zawodny, *Nothing but Honor*, pp. 166–68.

108. Lukas, *Forgotten Holocaust*, p. 219.

109. Bor, *Secret Army*, p. 378.

110. Erickson, *Road to Berlin*, p. 273.

111. Erickson, *Road to Berlin*, p. 246.

112. Erickson, *Road to Berlin*, p. 273.

113. Davies, *Rising '44*, p. 433.

114. Davies, *Rising '44*, especially appendix 31.

115. Bor, *Secret Army*, p. 46.

116. Davies, *Rising '44*, p. 96; Hanson, *Civilian Population*, p. 54.

117. Winston Churchill, *The Second World War*: vol. 3, *The Grand Alliance* (Boston: Houghton Mifflin, 1950), p. 368.

118. Hart, *History of the Second World War*, p. 171.

119. Erikson, *Road to Berlin*, p. 259.

120. Zawodny, *Nothing but Honor*, p. 181.

121. Krystyna Kersten, *The Establishment of Communist Rule in Poland, 1943–1948* (Berkeley: University of California Press, 1991); Edward J. Rozek, *Allied Wartime Diplomacy: A Pattern in Poland* (New York: Wiley, 1958). See as well Jan Karski [Jan Kozielewski], *The Great Powers and Poland: From Versailles to Yalta* (Lanham, MD: University Press of America, 1985); and John Lewis Gaddis, *The United States and the Origins of the Cold War, 1841–1947* (New York: Columbia University Press, 1972).

122. Mikolajczyk, *Rape of Poland*, p. 76. Mikolajczyk was prime minister of the PGE from July 1943 to November 1944.

123. Zawodny, *Nothing but Honor*, p. 74.

124. Bor, *Secret Army*, pp. 257–58; Zawodny, *Nothing but Honor*, p. 191.

125. Davies, *Rising '44*, pp. 318–19.

126. Korbonski, *Fighting Warsaw*, pp. 274–75.

127. Erickson, *Road to Berlin*, p. 285.

128. Erickson, *Road to Berlin*, p. 236.

129. Winston Churchill, *The Second World War*, vol. 6, *Triumph and Tragedy* (Boston: Houghton Mifflin, 1953), p. 142. Marshal Zhukov, conqueror of Berlin, wrote, "Churchill wants the Soviet Union to barter with a bourgeois Poland, alien to us, while we cannot allow this to happen." Giorgi Zhukov, *Memoirs of Marshal Zhukov* (New York: Delacorte, 1971), p. 583.

130. Korbonski, *Fighting Warsaw*, p. 388.

131. Churchill, *Triumph and Tragedy*, p. 144.

132. Erickson, *Road to Berlin*, p. 289.

133. Zawodny, *Nothing but Honor*, p. 115; Davies, *Rising '44*, p. 328.

134. Sir John Slessor, *The Central Blue* (London: Cassell, 1956), p. 612.

135. Korbonski, *Fighting Warsaw*, p. 388.

136. Davies, *Rising '44*, p. 321.

137. Hanson, *Civilian Population*, p. 263.

138. Bor, *Secret Army*, p. 385.

139. Hanson, *Civilian Population*, p. 152.

140. Hanson, *Civilian Population*, p. 53.

141. Anders, *Army in Exile*, pp. 250–52, 256. This conversation does not appear in Churchill's history of World War II.

142. Robert E. Sherwood, *Roosevelt and Hopkins: An Intimate History* (New York: Harper and Brothers, 1948), pp. 910, 907.

143. Zawodny, *Nothing but Honor*, p. 226.

144. Zawodny, *Nothing but Honor*, p. 227.

145. Davies, *Rising '44*, p. 458.

146. Anders, *Army in Exile*, p. 299.

147. Korbonski, *Fighting Warsaw*.

2. Budapest 1956

1. Robert A. Kahn, *A History of the Habsburg Empire, 1526–1918* (Berkeley: University of California Press, 1974), p. 605; A. J. P. Taylor, *The Struggle for Mastery in Europe, 1848–1918* (Oxford, England: Clarendon Press, 1965), p. xxv.

2. A. J. P. Taylor, *The Habsburg Monarchy, 1809–1918* (Chicago: University of Chicago Press, 1976); Kahn, *History of the Habsburg Empire*.

3. Friedrich Engels, *The German Revolutions: The Peasant War in Germany*, ed. Leonard Krieger (Chicago: University of Chicago Press, 1967), pp. 103–4,

4. Rudolph Tokes, *Bela Kun and the Hungarian Soviet Republic* (New York: Praeger, 1967), pp. 199–203.

5. Frank Eckelt, "The Internal Policies of the Hungarian Soviet Republic," in *Hungary in Revolution, 1918–1919*, ed. Ivan Volgyes (Lincoln: University of Nebraska Press, 1971); Gabor Vermes, "The October Revolution in Hungary: From Karolyi to Kun," in *Hungary in Revolution*, ed. Volgyes.

6. Stephen Borsody, *The Triumph of Tyranny: The Nazi and Soviet Conquest of Central Europe* (London: Cape, 1960).

7. See Miklos [Nicholas] Horthy, *Memoirs* (London: Hutchinson, 1956).

8. C. A. Macartney, *A History of Hungary, 1929–1945*, 2 vols. (New York: Praeger, 1957).

9. Ferenc A. Vali, *Rift and Revolution in Hungary* (Cambridge, MA: Harvard University Press, 1961), p. 29.

10. Jorg K. Hoensch, *A History of Modern Hungary, 1876–1986* (London: Longman, 1988), p. 195.

11. Hugh Seton-Watson, *The East European Revolution* (Boulder, CO: Westview, 1985).

12. Sandor Kopacsi, *In the Name of the Working Class* (London: Fontana/Collins, 1989).

13. George [Gyorgy] Mikes, *The Hungarian Revolution* (London: A. Deutsch, 1957), p. 115. See his *A Study in Infamy: The Operations of the Hungarian Secret Police* (London: A. Deutsch, 1959).

14. David Pryce-Jones, *The Hungarian Revolution* (New York: Horizon, 1970), p. 67. See United Nations, *Report of the Special Commission on the Problem of Hungary*. UN General Assembly Eleventh Session, Supplement no. 18 (New York: United Nations, 1957).

15. Vali, *Rift and Revolution*, p. 269.

16. Vali, *Rift and Revolution*, p. 270; Kopacsi, *In the Name of the Working Class*, p. 124.

17. Vali, *Rift and Revolution*, pp. 264, 271.

18. Pryce-Jones, *The Hungarian Revolution*, p. 77; Vali, *Rift and Revolution*, p. 271.

19. Mikes, *The Hungarian Revolution*, p. 111.

20. Pryce-Jones, *The Hungarian Revolution*, p. 83. See Peter Fryer's book *The Hungarian Tragedy* (London: D. Donson, 1957).

21. Mikes, *The Hungarian Revolution*, pp. 110ff.

22. Pryce-Jones, *The Hungarian Revolution*, p. 71.

23. Pryce-Jones, *The Hungarian Revolution*, p. 94.

24. Vali, *Rift and Revolution*, p. 275.

25. Andropov (1914–1984) would become head of the KGB in 1967 and premier of the Soviet Union in 1982.

26. Kopacsi, *In the Name of the Working Class*, p. 120.

27. Mikes, *The Hungarian Revolution*, p. 89; see also Kopacsi, *In the Name of the Working Class*.

28. Pryce-Jones, *The Hungarian Revolution*, p. 64.

29. Tibor Meray, *Thirteen Days That Shook the Kremlin* (London: Thames and Hudson, 1958), p. 101. The author writes from a Marxist but anti-Stalinist viewpoint.

30. Vali, *Rift and Revolution*, pp. 314–15.

31. Pryce-Jones, *The Hungarian Revolution*, p. 107.

32. Mikes, *The Hungarian Revolution*, p. 155.

33. Mikes, *The Hungarian Revolution*.

34. Kopacsi, *In the Name of the Working Class*, p. 121.

35. Michael Orr, "Hungary in Revolt," in *War in Peace: Conventional and Guerrilla Warfare since 1945*, ed. Sir Robert Thompson (New York: Harmony, 1982), p. 140.

36. Mikes, *The Hungarian Revolution*, pp. 126, 154. In Russian, *Pravda* means "truth."

37. Kopacsi, *In the Name of the Working Class*, pp. 144–45.

38. Pryce-Jones, *The Hungarian Revolution*, p. 99.

39. Meray, *Thirteen Days*, p. 167; Kopacsi, *In the Name of the Working Class*, p. 169.

40. Vali, *Rift and Revolution*, p. 279.

41. See the comments of the Yugoslav Communist dissident Milovan Djilas in the *New Leader,* November 19, 1956.

42. Mikes, *The Hungarian Revolution,* p. 141.

43. Bela Kiraly says that they began entering Hungary on the 28th; "Hungary's Army: Its Part in the Revolt," *East Europe,* vol. 7 (June 1958).

44. Mikes, *The Hungarian Revolution,* p. 153.

45. Pryce-Jones, *The Hungarian Revolution,* p. 110.

46. Pryce-Jones, *The Hungarian Revolution,* p. 109.

47. Mikes, *The Hungarian Revolution,* p. 154; Pryce-Jones, *The Hungarian Revolution,* p. 107.

48. Mikes, *The Hungarian Revolution,* p. 149.

49. Mikes, *The Hungarian Revolution,* pp. 156 and passim.

50. Kopacsi, *In the Name of the Working Class,* pp. 171–72.

51. Vali, *Rift and Revolution,* p. 365.

52. Mikes, *The Hungarian Revolution,* pp. 139–49.

53. See Pryce-Jones, *The Hungarian Revolution,* p. 95; George G. Heltai, "International Aspects," in *The Hungarian Revolution of 1956 in Retrospect,* ed. Bela Kiraly and Paul Jonas (Boulder, CO: East European Quarterly, 1978); Hoensch, *History of Modern Hungary;* Gyorgy Litvan, *The Hungarian Revolution of 1956: Reform, Revolt, and Repression, 1953–1963* (London: Longman, 1996).

54. Charles Gati, *Hungary and the Soviet Bloc* (Durham, NC: Duke University Press, 1986), p. 154.

55. Mark Kramer, "The Soviet Union and the 1956 Crises in Poland and Hungary: Reassessments and New Findings," *Journal of Contemporary History,* vol. 3 (1998). Figures vary among authors, and I believe Kramer's figures for Hungarian dead are too low.

56. See a moving account of this exodus in James Michener, *The Bridge at Andau* (New York: Random House, 1957).

57. Pryce-Jones, *The Hungarian Revolution,* p. 110.

58. For further reference: Francois Fejto, *Behind the Rape of Hungary* (New York: McKay 1957); Reg Gadney, *Cry Hungary! Uprising 1956* (New York: Atheneum, 1986); Eva Haraszti-Taylor, *The Hungarian Revolution of 1956: A Collection of Documents from the British Foreign Office* (Nottingham, England: Astra, 1995); Andor Heller, *No More Comrades* (Chicago: Regnery, 1957); David J. C. Irving, *Uprising* (London: Hodder and Stoughton, 1981); Imre Kovacs, *Facts about Hungary* (New York: The Hungarian Committee, 1959); Melvin J. Lasky, *The Hungarian Revolution: A White Book* (New York: Praeger, 1957); Miklos Molnar, *Budapest 1956: A History of the Hungarian Revolution* (London: Allen and Unwin, 1971); G. R. Urban, *The Nineteen Days* (London: Heinemann, 1957).

59. Mikes, *The Hungarian Revolution,* pp. 129–31; for a portrait of the Hungarian Communist leadership, see Paul E. Zinner, *Revolution in Hungary* (Freeport,

NY: Books for Libraries Press, 1962); another study, brief but invaluable, is Paul Kecskemeti, *The Unexpected Revolution: Social Forces in the Hungarian Uprising* (Stanford, CA: Stanford University Press, 1961).

60. Chalmers Johnson, *Revolutionary Change* (Boston: Little, Brown, 1966), p. 99.

61. Katherine Chorley, *Armies and the Art of Revolution* (Boston: Beacon, 1973), p. 23. See also Hannah Arendt, *On Revolution* (New York: Viking, 1963); and Anthony James Joes, *From the Barrel of a Gun: Armies and Revolution* (Washington, DC: Pergamon-Brassey's, 1986).

62. See Joes, *From the Barrel of a Gun.*

63. Pryce-Jones, *The Hungarian Revolution,* p. 109.

64. Dwight D. Eisenhower, *The White House Years,* vol. 2: *Waging Peace* (Garden City, NY: Doubleday, 1965), pp. 88–89.

3. Algiers 1957

1. Martin S. Alexander, Martin Evans and J. F. V. Keiger, "'The War without a Name,' the French Army, and the Algerians: Recovering Experiences, Images, and Testimonies," in *The Algerian War and the French Army, 1954–1962: Experiences, Images, Testimonies,* ed. Martin S. Alexander, Martin Evans, and J. F. V. Keiger (New York: Palgrave Macmillan, 2002), p. 2.

2. Paul-Marie de la Gorce, *The French Army: A Military-Political History* (New York: George Braziller, 1963), p. 447.

3. Michael Carver, *War since 1945* (New York: Putnam's, 1981), p. 120.

4. Mohammed Harbi, *Aux origines du FLN* (Paris: C. Bourgeois, 1975), and *1954: La guerre commence en Algérie* (Brussels: Éditions Complexe, 1954). The military arm of the FLN was the Armée de Libération National (ALN), but in this chapter both groups will be referred to as the FLN.

5. See Hugh Thomas, *The Suez Affair* (London: Weidenfeld and Nicholson, 1967); Anthony Nutting, *No End of a Lesson: The Story of Suez* (London: Constable, 1967); A. J. Barker, *Suez: The Seven Day War* (New York: Praeger, 1965); André Beaufre, *The Suez Expedition 1956* (New York: Praeger, 1969); *Suez 1956: The Crisis and Its Consequences,* ed. William Roger Louis and Roger Owen (Oxford, England: Clarendon Press, 1989).

6. "It was because of these promises that thousands of Vietnamese [and others] joined the fight against the Viet Minh." Alexander J. Zervoudakis, "From Indochina to Algeria: Counterinsurgency Lessons," in *The Algerian War and the French Army,* ed. Martin S. Alexander, Martin Evans, and J. F. V. Keiger, p. 55. More than three hundred thousand Vietnamese were serving either under French colors or in the French-equipped army of Emperor Bao Dai, a number at least equal to the forces of the Viet Minh.

7. George Kelly, *Lost Soldiers, The French Army and Empire in Crisis* (Cambridge, MA: MIT Press, 1965), p. 145. See Alistair Horne, *The French Army and Politics, 1870–1970* (London: Macmillan, 1984).

8. Alexander, Evans, and Keiger, "'War without a Name,'" p. 23.

9. The French had learned a good deal from their bitter experiences in Vietnam; see Marie-Catherine Villatoux and Paul Villatoux, "Aerial Intelligence during the Algerian War," in *France and the Algerian War, 1954–1962: Strategy, Operations and Diplomacy,* ed. Martin S. Alexander and J. F. V. Keiger (Portland, OR: Frank Cass, 2002).

10. See Anthony James Joes, *Resisting Rebellion: The History and Politics of Counterinsurgency* (Lexington: University Press of Kentucky, 2004), pp. 94–104.

11. See John Pimlott, "The French Army: From Indochina to Chad, 1946–1984," in *Armed Forces and Modern Counter-Insurgency,* ed. Ian F. W. Beckett and John Pimlott (New York: St. Martin's, 1985); Claude Curré, "Aspects opérationnels du conflit Algérien, 1954–1960," *Revue Historique des Armées* (March 1987); Jean-Jacques Servan-Schreiber, *Lieutenant en Algérie* (London: Faber, 1958); Jean Lartéguy, *Les centurions* (Paris: Presses de la Cité, 1959).

12. For example, see Carver in *War since 1945.*

13. John Talbott, *The War without a Name: France in Algeria 1954–1962* (New York: Knopf, 1980), p. 84; Edgar O'Ballance, *The Algerian Insurrection* (Hamden, CT: Archon, 1967), p. 9 and passim; Alistair Horne, *A Savage War of Peace: Algeria, 1954–1962,* rev. ed. (New York: Penguin, 1987), pp.134–35.

14. Martha Crenshaw Hutchinson, *Revolutionary Terrorism: The FLN in Algeria 1954–1962* (Stanford, CA: Hoover Institution, 1978), p. 143.

15. Hutchinson, *Revolutionary Terrorism,* p. 135; see also Abder-Rahmane Derradji, *The Algerian Guerrilla Campaign: Strategy and Tactics* (Lewiston, NY: Edwin Mellen, 1997).

16. Serge Bromberger says only three hundred thousand of Algiers' seven hundred thousand people were Europeans. *Les rebelles Algériens* (Paris: Plon, 1958), p. 157.

17. Kelly, *Lost Soldiers,* p. 192; Bromberger, *Les rebelles Algériens,* p. 157.

18. Horne, *Savage War of Peace,* p. 187.

19. Talbott, *War without a Name,* p. 80. Naturally, numbers concerning FLN membership, the terrorist network, and the real activists vary.

20. Horne, *Savage War of Peace,* p. 187.

21. Talbott, *War without a Name,* p. 82.

22. Horne, *Savage War of Peace,* pp. 183–84.

23. Hutchinson, *Revolutionary Terrorism,* p. 140.

24. Talbott, *War without a Name,* p. 79.

25. Alexander, Evans, and Keiger, "'War without a Name,'" p. 25.

26. Eric Wolf, *Peasant Wars of the Twentieth Century* (New York: Harper and Row, 1969), p. 239.

27. Horne, *Savage War of Peace,* p. 191.

28. See Horne, *Savage War of Peace;* and Hutchinson, *Revolutionary Terrorism,* p. 118.

29. Talbott, *War without a Name,* p. 44. For Muslim-on-Muslim terrorism, see Michael K. Clark, *Algeria in Turmoil: A History of the Rebellion* (New York: Praeger, 1959), David C. Gordon, *The Passing of French Algeria* (New York: Oxford University Press, 1966), chapter 3; and O'Ballance, *Algerian Insurrection.* During the anti-French conflict, the FLN simultaneously fought a bloody struggle with the rival Algerian National Movement (MNA).

30. O'Ballance, *Algerian Insurrection,* pp. 80ff.

31. Horne, *Savage War of Peace,* p. 199.

32. Talbott, *War without a Name,* p. 85; Jacques Massu, *La vraie bataille d'Alger* (Paris: Plon, 1971), pp. 126–28. Massu wrote five volumes of memoirs. See also the work of Colonel Yves Godard, chief of staff of the Tenth Paratroops and an architect of the antiterror campaign, *Les paras dans la ville* (Paris: Fayard, 1972).

33. Alexander S. Martin and J. F. V. Keiger, "France and the Algerian War: Strategy, Operations, and Diplomacy," *Journal of Strategic Studies,* vol. 25 (2002), p. 7.

34. Kelly, *Lost Soldiers,* p. 194.

35. Talbott, *War without a Name,* p. 87.

36. Clark, *Algeria in Turmoil,* p. 328.

37. Hutchinson, *Revolutionary Terrorism.*

38. Massu, *La vraie bataille,* p. 170.

39. Trinquier, another veteran of Vietnam, wrote several notable books, of which perhaps the most well-known is *Modern Warfare: A French View of Counterinsurgency,* trans. Daniel Lee, with an introduction by Bernard Fall (London: Pall Mall Press, 1964 [orig. 1961]). See also André Beaufre, *La guerre révolutionnaire: Les formes nouvelles de la guerre* (Paris: Fayard, 1972); and Claude Delmas, *La Guerre révolutionnaire,* 3d ed. (Paris: Presses universitaires de France, 1972 [orig. 1959]).

40. Paul Aussaresses, *Battle of the Casbah: Terrorism and Counterterrorism in Algiers, 1955–1957* (New York: Enigma, 2002), p. 128. He also writes: "The executions of prisoners [under my control] were often listed as aborted escape attempts" (p. 122).

41. Massu, *La vraie bataille,* pp. 165ff.

42. Aussaresses, *Battle of the Casbah,* p. 128.

43. Aussaresses, *Battle of the Casbah*, p. 18.

44. Kelly, *Lost Soldiers*, p. 204; O'Ballance, *Algerian Insurrection*.

45. Hutchinson, *Revolutionary Terrorism*, p. 122. In *The Wretched of the Earth* (1961), a book that became a bible for third-world intellectuals, Franz Fanon wrote, "Violence is a cleansing force."

46. Aussaresses, *Battle of the Casbah*.

47. Kelly, *Lost Soldiers*, p. 202.

48. Kelly, *Lost Soldiers*, p. 201.

49. Kelly, *Lost Soldiers*, pp. 200–201.

50. Godard, *Les paras dans la ville*.

51. Edward Behr, *The Algerian Problem* (London: Hodder and Stoughton, 1961). See also Ted Morgan, *My Battle of Algiers* (New York: Collins, 2006).

52. In his later years, General Massu expressed this same view. See the discussion in Horne, *Savage War of Peace*, pp. 198–207.

53. The discussion of the issue in contemporary France is also linked to the decades-old practice of torture by the regime and its enemies in today's Algerian Republic. Neil MacMaster, "The Torture Controversy 1998–2002: Toward a 'New History' of the Algerian War?" *Modern and Contemporary France*, vol. 10 (2002).

54. Carver, *War since 1945*, p. 128; my emphasis.

55. Horne, *Savage War of Peace*, p. 98.

56. Talbott, *War without a Name*, p. 61.

57. Danièlle Joly, *The French Communist Party and the Algerian War* (Basingstoke, England: Macmillan, 1991).

58. Talbott, *War without a Name*, p. 89; my emphasis. The special powers "were to make General Massu the master of Algiers." Philip M. Williams, *Crisis and Compromise: Politics in the Fourth Republic* (London: Longman, 1964), p. 75.

59. Pierre Vidal-Naquet, *Torture: Cancer of Democracy* (Harmondsworth, England: Penguin, 1963).

60. In the spring of 1968, antigovernment riots engulfed France. President de Gaulle went to Germany, to assure himself of General Massu's support in case the internal disorders escalated. Alistair Horne believes that Massu's price for support was an amnesty for the officers involved in the 1961 failed putsch, which de Gaulle delivered. See Horne, *Savage War of Peace*, p. 551.

61. See, for example, Bruce Hoffman, "A Nasty Business," *Atlantic Monthly*, January 2002.

62. Walter Laqueur, *The New Terrorism: Fanaticism and the Arms of Mass Destruction* (New York: Oxford University Press, 1999), p. 281. My emphasis.

63. Kelly, *Lost Soldiers*, p. 238.

64. John Talbott, "French Public Opinion and the Algerian War," *French Historical Studies,* vol. 9 (1975); Williams, *Crisis and Compromise,* chapter 4.

65. Between January 1946 and June 1958 there would be no fewer than twenty-four different cabinets in office.

67. Alfred Grosser, *French Foreign Policy under de Gaulle* (Boston: Little, Brown, 1967). To continue to hold Algeria "would be to keep France politically, militarily and financially bogged down in a bottomless quagmire when, in fact, she needed her hands free to bring about the domestic transformation necessitated by the twentieth century and to exercise her influence abroad unencumbered. At the same time it would condemn our forces to a futile and interminable task of colonial repression, when the future of the country demanded an Army *geared to the exigencies of modern power.*" Charles de Gaulle, *Memoirs of Hope: Renewal and Endeavor* (New York: Simon and Schuster, 1971), p. 45. My emphasis.

68. Pierre Boyer de Latour, *De l'Indochine á l'Algérie: Le martyre de l'Armée française* (Paris: Presses du mail, 1962).

69. See Geoffrey Bocca, *The Secret Army* (Englewood Cliffs, NJ: Prentice-Hall, 1968); Rémi Kauffer, *Histoire de la guerre franco-française* (Paris: Seuil, 2002); Paul Henissart, *Wolves in the City: The Death of French Algeria* (New York: Simon and Schuster, 1970).

70. Two and a half million men served with the British Army in India, the largest volunteer force in history. More than a third of Portugal's troops waging counterinsurgencies in Africa during the 1960s were indigenous. In Indonesia, the Ambonese served in the Royal Dutch Army until the bitter end; many chose to live in the Netherlands after Indonesia became independent. See Joes, *Resisting Rebellion,* pp. 125–34.

71. Martin Evans, "The Harkis: The Experience and Memory of France's Muslim Auxiliaries," in *The Algerian War and the French Army,* ed. Alexander, Evans, and Keiger, p. 120.

72. Evans, "The Harkis," p. 124.

73. Peter Paret, *French Revolutionary Warfare from Indochina to Algeria: An Analysis of a Political and Military Doctrine* (New York: Praeger, 1964), p. 41.

74. Evans, "The Harkis," p. 123. See also Horne, *Savage War of Peace,* p. 255.

75. Paret, *French Revolutionary Warfare,* p. 41. See also Alf Andrew Heggoy, *Insurgency and Counterinsurgency in Algeria* (Bloomington: Indiana University Press, 1972).

76. Talbott, *War without a Name,* p. 49.

77. See François-Marie Gougeon, "The Challe Plan: Vain Yet Indispensable Victory," *Small Wars and Insurgencies,* vol. 16 (December 2005); Carver, *War since 1945,* p. 145.

78. Evans, "The Harkis," p. 127; Carver, *War since 1945*, p. 147; Horne, *Savage War of Peace*, p. 538.

79. Evans, "The Harkis," p. 127; Alexander, Evans, and Keiger, "'War without a Name,'" pp. 24–25, give the number as one hundred thousand.

80. Evans, "The Harkis," p. 125. See, among many others, Bachaga Boualam, *Les harkis au service de la France* (Paris: France Empire, 1964); and Michel Roux, *Les harkis ou les oubliés de l'histoire 1954–1991* (Paris: La Découverte, 1991).

81. O'Ballance, *Algerian Insurrection*, p. 129n.

82. Carver, *War since 1945*, p. 149; Horne, *Savage War of Peace*, p. 538.

83. Alexander, Evans, and Keiger, "'War without a Name,'" p. 20.

4. São Paulo 1965–1971 and Montevideo 1963–1973

1. "Guevara's dismal failure, and the recognition that not all governments were as fragile as Batista's had been in Cuba, prompted insurgent intellectuals in Latin America to reassess strategic approaches, leading to the emergence of a new strategy of urban warfare in which terrorism [was] prominent." Bard E. O'Neill, *Insurgency and Terrorism: Inside Modern Revolutionary Warfare* (McLean, VA: Brassey's, 1990), p. 45.

2. Hugh Thomas, *Cuba: The Pursuit of Freedom* (New York: Harper and Row, 1977 [orig. 1971]), p. 215.

3. See Theodore Draper, *Castroism: Theory and Practice* (New York: Praeger, 1965); D. Chapelle, "How Castro Won," in *Modern Guerrilla Warfare*, ed. Franklin Mark Osanka (New York: Free Press, 1962); Louis A. Perez Jr., *Army Politics in Cuba, 1898–1958* (Pittsburgh, PA: University of Pittsburgh Press, 1976); Fulgencio Batista, *Cuba Betrayed* (New York: Vantage, 1962).

4. "Since the special circumstances of Cuba did not exist automatically elsewhere, those [self-proclaimed Castroite insurgencies] attempted in the 1960s in Argentina, Brazil, Bolivia, Colombia, the Dominican Republic, Ecuador, Guatemala, Peru, Paraguay, and Venezuela all failed." Ian F. W. Beckett, *Modern Insurgencies and Counterinsurgencies: Guerrillas and Their Opponents since 1750* (London: Routledge, 2001), p. 171. And of course, U.S. interest and involvement in these cases was much greater.

5. Ernesto Guevara, *Guerrilla Warfare* (New York: Vintage, 1969), p. 2.

6. From the early 1960s to the late 1990s, Lima's population grew from less than 1.2 million inhabitants to nearly 6 million; São Paulo went from less than 4 million to perhaps 13 million.

7. See Charles A. Russell, James A. Miller, and Robert E. Hildner, "The Urban Guerrilla in Latin America: A Select Bibliography," *Latin American Research Review*, vol. 9 (1974).

8. The best-known presentations of this approach are Regis Debray,

Revolution in the Revolution? (New York: Monthly Review, 1967); and Guevara, *Guerrilla Warfare*.

9. See James A. Miller "Urban Terrorism in Uruguay: The Tupamaros," in *Insurgency in the Modern World*, ed. Bard E. O'Neill, W. R. Heaton, and D. J. Alberts (Boulder, CO: Westview, 1980).

10. Howard J. Wiarda and Harvey F. Kline, *Latin American Politics and Development* (Boston: Houghton Mifflin, 1979), p. 62.

11. Samuel P. Huntington, *Political Order in Changing Societies* (New Haven, CT: Yale University Press, 1968), p. 226.

12. Alfred Stepan, *The Military in Politics: Changing Patterns in Brazil* (Princeton, NJ: Princeton University Press, 1971).

13. Anthony James Joes, *From the Barrel of a Gun: Armies and Revolutions* (Washington, DC: Pergamon-Brassey's, 1986), p. 172.

14. Ronald M. Schneider, *The Political System of Brazil: Emergence of a Modernizing Authoritarian Regime, 1964–1970* (New York: Columbia University Press, 1971), p. 80; see Thomas E. Skidmore, *The Politics of Military Rule in Brazil, 1964–1985* (New York: Oxford University Press, 1988), chapter 1, "The Origins of the 1964 Revolution." (Note that in the view of some experts, the coup eventually turned into a revolution.)

15. "From a technical point of view the coup was little short of a masterpiece." Schneider, *Political System of Brazil*, p. 103. See Stepan, *The Military in Politics*; Thomas E. Skidmore, *Politics in Brazil, 1930–1964* (New York: Oxford University Press, 1988); Alfred Stepan, "Political Leadership and Regime Breakdown: Brazil," in *The Breakdown of Democratic Regimes: Latin America*, ed. Juan Linz and Alfred Stepan (Baltimore, MD: Johns Hopkins University Press, 1978).

16. A. J. Languth, *Hidden Terrors* (New York: Pantheon, 1978).

17. Languth, *Hidden Terrors*, pp. 183ff.

18. Skidmore, *Politics of Military Rule in Brazil*, pp. 53–54.

19. Skidmore, *Politics of Military Rule in Brazil*, pp. 177ff, 156.

20. Skidmore, *Politics of Military Rule in Brazil*, p. 115.

21. See the highly respected work by Ronald H. Chilcote, *The Brazilian Communist Party: Conflict and Integration, 1922–1972* (New York: Oxford University Press, 1974).

22. Skidmore, *Politics of Military Rule in Brazil*, p. 125; see also Alzira Alves De Abreu, "Brazil's Guerrilla Trap," *History Today*, vol. 47 (1997).

23. Skidmore, *Politics of Military Rule in Brazil*, p. 103.

24. "In less democratic states, urban guerrilla warfare did not prove as potent and was more easily suppressed, since there was not the same self-imposed restraint on the part of the security forces." Beckett, *Modern Insurgencies*, p. 152.

25. Skidmore, *Politics of Military Rule in Brazil*, pp. 117, 125–28.

26. Skidmore, *Politics of Military Rule in Brazil*, p. 121.

27. James Kohl and John Litt, *Urban Guerrilla Warfare in Latin America* (Cambridge, MA: MIT Press, 1974), p. 51.

28. Skidmore, *Politics of Military Rule in Brazil*, p. 122.

29. Langguth, *Hidden Terrors*, p. 186. This source is especially friendly to Latin American guerrillas/terrorists.

30. Skidmore, *Politics of Military Rule in Brazil*, pp. 125, 100.

31. E. Bradford Burns, *A History of Brazil* (New York: Columbia University Press, 1970) (the two paragraphs are on p. 379); Timothy P. Wickham-Crowley, *Guerrillas and Revolution in Latin America: A Comparative Study of Insurgents and Regimes since 1956* (Princeton, NJ: Princeton University Press, 1992), p. 313.

32. Russell, Miller, and Hildner, "The Urban Guerrilla in Latin America," p. 70.

33. Chalmers Johnson, *Autopsy on People's War* (Berkeley: University of California Press, 1973), p. 5.

34. Geoffrey Fairbairn, *Revolutionary Guerrilla Warfare* (Harmondsworth, England: Penguin, 1974), p. 71. See also Joes, *Resisting Rebellion*, chapter 2.

35. See R. H. Fitzgibbon, *Uruguay: Portrait of a Democracy* (New Brunswick, NJ: Rutgers University Press, 1954) and S. G. Hanson, *Utopia in Uruguay* (New York: Oxford University Press, 1938).

36. Alain Labrousse, *The Tupamaros: Urban Insurgency in Uruguay* (Harmondsworth, England: Penguin, 1970), p. 23. This work is naively pro-Communist and anti-American.

37. Robert Moss, *Uruguay: Terrorism vs. Democracy* (London: Institute for the Study of Conflict, 1971), p. 211.

38. M. H. J. Finch, "Three Perspectives on the Crisis in Uruguay," *Journal of Latin American Studies*, vol. 3 (Nov. 1971), pp. 173–90.

39. Philip B. Taylor, *Government and Politics of Uruguay* (Westport, CT: Greenwood, 1981 [orig. 1961]), pp. 103, 156.

40. Robert Moss, *Uruguay*.

41. Robert Moss, "Urban Guerrillas in Uruguay," *Problems of Communism*, vol. 20 (1971), p. 213.

42. V. I. Lenin, "Left-Wing Communism," in *Selected Works* (Moscow: Progress Publishers, 1977), vol. 3, p. 343.

43. "Thirty Questions to a Tupamaro," in Labrousse, *The Tupamaros*; for Tupamaro insistence that "revolutionary action precipitates revolutionary situations" see Kohl and Litt, *Urban Guerrilla Warfare*, pp. 227 and passim, and Gordon H. McCormick, *From the Sierra to the Cities: The Urban Campaign of the Shining Path* (Santa Monica, CA: RAND, 1992).

44. Labrousse, *The Tupamaros*.

45. Kohl and Litt, *Urban Guerrilla Warfare*, p. 190.

46. Arturo Porzecanski, *Uruguay's Tupamaros* (New York: Praeger, 1973), p. 23.

47. Abraham Guillen, *Philosophy of the Urban Guerrilla*, ed. Donald C. Hodges (New York: Morrow, 1973).

48. Guillen, *Philosophy of the Urban Guerrilla*, p. vi.

49. Guillen, *Philosophy of the Urban Guerrilla*, p. 293.

50. Guillen, *Philosophy of the Urban Guerrilla*, p. 113.

51. Guillen, *Philosophy of the Urban Guerrilla*, p. 133.

52. Guillen, *Philosophy of the Urban Guerrilla*, p. 245.

53. Guillen, *Philosophy of the Urban Guerrilla*, p. 249.

54. See Wickham-Crowley, *Guerrillas and Revolutions*.

55. Guillen, *Philosophy of the Urban Guerrilla*, p. 289. "The Tupamaros [were] essentially a middle class movement recruited from the ranks of disaffected students, minor civil servants and professional men." Moss, *Uruguay*, p. 4. According to Labrousse, "Most of the Tupamaros come from the bourgeoisie"; *The Tupamaros*, p. 115. On criminal elements, see Alphonse Max, *The Tupamaros: A Pattern for Urban Guerrilla Warfare in Latin America* (The Hague: International Information and Documentation Centre, 1970).

56. Porzecanski, *Uruguay's Tupamaros*, pp. 29ff.

57. Walter Laqueur, *The New Terrorism*, p. 91.

58. See Max, *The Tupamaros;* many Tupamaros bore certain resemblances to the people described so vividly by Ralph Peters in "The New Warrior Class."

59. Moss, *Uruguay*.

60. Geoffrey Demarest, "Geopolitics and Urban Armed Conflict in Latin America," *Small Wars and Insurgencies*, vol. 6 (Spring 1995), p. 49.

61. Porzecanski, *Uruguay's Tupamaros*.

62. Max, *The Tupamaros*, p. 13.

63. Anthony Burton, *Urban Terrorism* (London: L. Cooper, 1975), p. 100.

64. F. A. Godfrey, "The Latin American Experience: The Tupamaros Campaign in Uruguay, 1963–1973," in *Armed Forces and Modern Counter-Insurgency*, ed. Ian F. W. Beckett and John Pimlott (London: Croom Helm, 1985), p. 132.

65. Godfrey, "The Latin American Experience."

66. Moss, *Uruguay*.

67. Edy Kaufman, *Uruguay in Transition* (New Brunswick, NJ: Transaction, 1979), p. 35.

68. Huntington, *Political Order in Changing Societies*, chapter 5.

69. J. Bowyer Bell, "Revolutionary Dynamics: The Inherent Inefficiency of the Underground," *Terrorism and Political Violence*, vol. 2 (1990), p. 203.

70. Indeed, in their minoritarian elitism and violence the Tupamaros had much in common with European fascist movements; see A. James Gregor, *The Fascist Persuasion in Radical Politics* (Princeton, NJ: Princeton University Press, 1974).

71. Kohl and Litt, *Urban Guerrilla Warfare*, p. 277.

72. Richard Gott, "Events since 1971," in Labrousse, *The Tupamaros*, p. 129.

73. Labrousse, *The Tupamaros*, p. 30.

74. Kaufman, *Uruguay in Transition*, pp. 32, 109.

75. Moss, *Uruguay*.

76. Burton, *Urban Terrorism*, p. 102.

5. Saigon 1968

1. *Washington Post*, April 6, 1969.

2. Don Oberdorfer, *Tet! The Turning Point in the Vietnam War* (New York: Da Capo, 1984 [orig. 1971]), p. 81.

3. Phillip B. Davidson, *Vietnam at War: The History, 1946–1975* (Novato, CA: Presidio, 1988), p. 483. Lieutenant General Davidson was chief intelligence adviser to both General Westmoreland and General Abrams.

4. Military History Institute of Vietnam, *Victory in Vietnam: The Official History of the People's Army of Vietnam, 1954–1975*, trans. Merle Pribbenow (Lawrence: University Press of Kansas, 2002), p. 214.

5. James J. Wirtz, *The Tet Offensive: Intelligence Failure in War* (Ithaca, NY: Cornell University Press, 1991), pp. 60, 23.

6. James R. Arnold, *The Tet Offensive: Turning Point in Vietnam* (London: Osprey, 1990), pp. 27–28.

7. Arnold, *Tet Offensive*, p. 21.

8. Ronald Spector, *Advice and Support: The Early Years 1941–1960* (Washington, DC: U.S. Army Center of Military History, 1983), p. 131; Ellen J. Hammer, *The Struggle for Indochina, 1940–1955* (Stanford, CA: Stanford University Press, 1956), p. 287; Henri Navarre, *Agonie de l'Indochine* (Paris: Plon, 1956), p. 46; Douglas Pike, *PAVN: People's Army of Vietnam* (Novato, CA: Presidio, 1986), p. 5.

9. Arnold, *Tet Offensive*, p. 15.

10. Allan E. Goodman, *An Institutional Profile of the South Vietnamese Officer Corps* (Santa Monica, CA: RAND, 1970), p. 9.

11. Olivier Todd, *Cruel April: The Fall of Saigon* (New York: Norton, 1990), p. 438.

12. Sir Robert Thompson, *Peace Is Not at Hand* (New York: David McKay, 1974), p. 169.

13. Jeffrey J. Clarke, *Advice and Support: The Final Years, 1965–1973* (Washington, DC: U.S. Army Center for Military History, 1988), p. 275.

14. Thomas C. Thayer, *War without Fronts: The American Experience in Vietnam* (Boulder, CO: Westview, 1986), 202; Pike, *PAVN*, p. 244; Guenter Lewy, *America in Vietnam* (New York: Oxford University Press, 1978), p. 172; William E. Le Gro, *Vietnam from Cease-Fire to Capitulation* (Washington, DC: U.S. Army Center of Military History, 1981), p. 34; William Westmoreland, *A Soldier Reports* (Garden City, NY: Doubleday, 1976), p. 252.

15. Bruce Catton, *The Army of the Potomac:* vol. 2, *Glory Road,* pp. 102, 255; Allan Nevins, *The War for the Union,* vol. 3, *The Organized War, 1863–1864* (New York: Scribner's, 1971), p. 131.

16. Davidson, *Vietnam at War,* p. 479.

17. Oberdorfer, *Tet!* p. 121.

18. Wirtz, *The Tet Offensive,* p. 84; but see also Ronnie E. Ford, *Tet 1968: Understanding the Surprise* (Portland, OR: Frank Cass, 1995).

19. Thucydides, *The Peloponnesian War,* in *The Landmark Thucydides,* ed. Robert B. Strassler (New York: Free Press, 1996), book 1, 84.

20. Machiavelli, *The Discourses,* chapter 48.

21. Clausewitz, *On War,* book 1, chapter 6.

22. Davidson, *Vietnam at War,* p. 483.

23. Wirtz, *The Tet Offensive,* p. 196.

24. Oberdorfer, *Tet!* p. 138.

25. See Pham Van Son, *Tet 1968* (Salisbury, NC: Documentary Publications, 1980 [orig. 1968]).

26. Large areas of Hue were taken over by NVA regulars, and fighting there ended with the successful siege of the ancient citadel by U.S. Marines. For the fighting in Hue, see Eric Hammel, *Fire in the Streets: The Battle for Hue, Tet 1968* (Chicago: Contemporary Books, 1991); Keith William Nolan, *Battle for Hue: Tet 1968* (Novato, CA: Presidio, 1983); George Smith, *The Siege at Hue* (Boulder, CO: Lynne Rienner, 1999); Nicholas Warr, *Phase Line Green* (Annapolis, MD: Naval Institute Press, 1997); and see the chapter "Death in Hue" in Oberdorfer, *Tet!*

27. Westmoreland, *A Soldier Reports,* p. 326.

28. For Hanoi's official description of VC actions around Saigon, see Military History Institute of Vietnam, *Victory in Vietnam,* pp. 219–23.

29. Davidson, *Vietnam at War,* p. 475; Ambassador Bunker cabled President Johnson that he believed thirty-three thousand had been killed and fifty-six hundred "detained." Ellsworth Bunker, *The Bunker Papers: Reports to the President from Vietnam, 1967–1973,* ed. Douglas Pike, 3 vols. (Berkeley: University of California Press, 1990), vol. 2, p. 334.

30. Davidson, *Vietnam at War,* p. 475.

31. Oberdorfer, *Tet!* p. 329. See also Tran Van Tra, *Concluding the Thirty-Years War* (Roslyn, VA: Foreign Broadcast Information Service, 1983), p. 35; William J. Duiker, *The Communist Road to Power in Vietnam* (Boulder, CO: Westview, 1981), p. 269; Lewy, *America in Vietnam*, p. 76; Thayer, *War without Fronts*, p. 92; Robert Shaplen, *Bitter Victory* (New York: Harper and Row, 1986), pp. 188–89; Douglas Blaufarb, *The Counterinsurgency Era: United States Doctrine and Performance 1950 to the Present* (New York: Free Press, 1977), pp. 261–62.

32. Wirtz, *The Tet Offensive*, p. 60.

33. Gabriel Kolko, *Anatomy of a War: Vietnam, the United States, and the Modern Historical Experience* (New York: Pantheon, 1985), p. 482.

34. Dave Richard Palmer, *Summons of the Trumpet* (San Rafael, CA: Presidio, 1978), p. 246; Wirtz, *The Tet Offensive*, p. 224; Hoang Ngoc Lung, *The General Offensives of 1968–1969* (Washington, DC: U.S. Army Center of Military History, 1981), pp. 22–23. "Perhaps one of the most significant failures of the enemy's Tet offensive was the absence of popular support for the enemy forces which penetrated the cities, support which he had evidently anticipated and counted on"(Bunker, *Bunker Papers*, vol. 2, p. 549).

35. Timothy Lomperis emphasizes this point in *The War Everyone Lost—and Won: American Intervention in Vietnam's Twin Struggles* (Baton Rouge: Louisiana State University Press, 1984), especially p. 169. As the official North Vietnamese Army history puts it: "When the battle did not progress favorably for our side and when we suffered casualties, rightist thoughts, pessimism, and hesitancy appeared among our forces." Military History Institute of Vietnam, *Victory in Vietnam*, p. 224. See also Victoria Pohle, *The Viet Cong in Saigon: Tactics and Objectives during the Tet Offensive* (Santa Monica, CA: RAND, 1969).

36. Westmoreland, *A Soldier Reports*, p. 332.

37. Davidson, *Vietnam at War*, p. 546.

38. Palmer, *Summons of the Trumpet*, p. 210.

39. Peter Braestrup, *Story: How the American Press and Television Reported and Interpreted the Crisis of Tet 1968 in Vietnam and Washington* (Boulder, CO: Westview, 1977), vol. 1, pp. 448–49. William Colby, CIA station chief in Saigon and chief of the CIA's Far Eastern division at the time of Tet, agrees; see his *Lost Victory* (Chicago: Contemporary Books, 1989), chapter 14.

40. James J. Wirtz, "The Battles of Saigon and Hue: Tet 1968," in *Soldiers in Cities: Military Operations on Urban Terrain*, ed. Michael C. Desch (Carlisle, PA: Strategic Studies Institute, 2001), p. 83. In Hue, the Communists had several days to bring in reinforcements and fortify their positions. Regular NVA formations began entering Hue on January 31 and were not completely defeated until February 23.

41. Oberdorfer, *Tet!* p. 155.

42. Samuel Popkin, "The Village War," in *Vietnam as History: Ten Years after the Paris Peace Accords,* ed. Peter Braestrup (Washington, DC: University Press of America, 1984), p. 102.

43. Blaufarb, *Counterinsurgency Era,* p. 271. See also Bunker, *Bunker Papers,* vol. 2, pp. 344, 346.

44. Kolko, *Anatomy of a War,* pp. 371, 334; Thayer, *War without Fronts,* p. 92.

45. Kolko, *Anatomy of a War,* p. 334.

46. Timothy J. Lomperis, *From People's War to People's Rule: Insurgency, Intervention, and the Lessons of Vietnam* (Chapel Hill: University of North Carolina Press, 1996), p. 341.

47. Bunker, *Bunker Papers,* vol. 2, p. 328.

48. Palmer, *Summons of the Trumpet,* p. 201.

49. See Truong Nhu Tang, *A Viet Cong Memoir* (New York: Harcourt, Brace, Jovanovich, 1985); also F. Charles Parker, *Vietnam: Strategy for a Stalemate* (New York: Paragon, 1989).

50. *New York Times,* October 1, 1994.

51. This is what *New York Times* and *Washington Post* reporter Peter Braestrup refers to as the "general unfamiliarity of the American press corps with Vietnam and the Vietnamese." *Big Story,* vol. 1, p. 445.

52. Maxwell D. Taylor, *Swords and Plowshares* (New York: Norton, 1972), p. 235.

53. *Foreign Relations of the United States, 1961–1963* (Washington, DC: U.S. Government Printing Office, 1988–91), vol. 3, p. 531 (hereafter *FRUS*).

54. See, for example, Ambassador Henry Cabot Lodge's message to President Kennedy, August 30, 1963, in *FRUS, 1961–63,* vol. 4, p. 58.

55. Frederick Nolting, *From Trust to Tragedy: The Political Memoirs of Frederick Nolting, Kennedy's Ambassador to Diem's Vietnam* (New York: Praeger, 1988), p. 116. See also Anne Blair, *Lodge in Vietnam* (New Haven, CT: Yale University Press, 1995); Philip E. Catton, *Diem's Final Failure: Prelude to America's War in Vietnam* (Lawrence: University Press of Kansas, 2002); Dennis J. Duncanson, *Government and Revolution in Vietnam* (New York: Oxford University Press, 1968), pp. 327–41; Ellen J. Hammer, *A Death in November: America in Vietnam, 1963* (New York: Dutton, 1987); Marguerite Higgins, *Our Vietnam Nightmare* (New York: Harper and Row, 1965); Mieczyslaw Maneli, *War of the Vanquished* (New York: Harper and Row 1971); William Prochau, *Once upon a Distant War: Young War Correspondents and the Early Vietnam Battles* (New York: Times Books, 1995); Francis X. Winters, *The Year of the Hare: America in Vietnam, January 25, 1963–February 15, 1964* (Athens: University of Georgia Press, 1997).

56. For the decisive role of the Ho Chi Minh Trail in the fall of South Vietnam, see Norman B. Hannah, *The Key to Failure: Laos and the Vietnam War* (Lanham,

MD: Madison Books, 1987); Harry Summers, *On Strategy: A Critical Analysis of the Vietnam War* (Novato, CA: Presidio, 1982); Sir Robert Thompson, "Regular Armies and Insurgency," in *Regular Armies and Insurgency*, ed. Ronald Haycock (London: Croom Helm, 1979).

57. Oberdorfer, *Tet!* p. 332.

58. Henry Kissinger, *Does America Need a Foreign Policy?* (New York: Simon and Schuster, 2001), p. 284.

59. Oberdorfer, *Tet!* p. 242.

60. Lewy, *America in Vietnam*, p. 434.

61. Davidson, *Vietnam at War*, p. 486.

62. Anthony James Joes, *America and Guerrilla Warfare* (Lexington: University Press of Kentucky, 2000), p. 232.

63. Peter Braestrup, *Big Story: How the American Press and Television Reported and Interpreted the Crisis of Tet 1968 in Vietnam and Washington*, 2 vols. (Boulder, CO: Westview, 1977), p. 492.

64. Braestrup, *Big Story*, vol. 1, pp. 162, 184, 531.

65. Braestrup, *Big Story*, vol. 1, p. 403.

66. Oberdorfer, *Tet!* pp. 30–31.

67. Elegant is quoted in Marc Leepson, "Vietnam War Reconsidered," *Editorial Research Reports* (March 1983), p. 195. See also Elegant's devastating article "How to Lose a War: The Press and Vietnam" in the August 1981 issue of *Encounter*.

68. The *Economist*, May 13, 1972, p. 34. See similar statements by Douglas Pike in Denis Warner, *Certain Victory: How Hanoi Won the War* (Kansas City, KS: Sheed, Andrews and McMeel, 1978), p. 183.

69. See the truly disedifying account in Lewy, *America in Vietnam*, pp. 400–401.

70. Todd, *Cruel April;* pp. 95, 253, 398; "The Reporter Was a Spy," *New York Times*, April 28, 1997.

71. Braestrup, *Big Story*, vol. 1, p. 705.

72. Davidson, *Vietnam at War*, p. 492.

73. "How could attrition possibly have worked when, in the final score, the North accepted more than 1 million killed and the United States could not accept 47,000?" Sir Robert Thompson, "Vietnam," in *War in Peace: Conventional and Guerrilla Warfare since 1945*, ed. Sir Robert Thompson (New York: Harmony, 1982), p. 197.

74. *Congressional Quarterly's Guide to U.S. Elections* (Washington, DC: Congressional Quarterly, 1975), p. 343; Philip E. Converse, Warren E. Miller, Jerrold G. Rusk, and Arthur C. Wolfe, "Continuity and Change in American Politics:

Parties and Issues in the 1968 Election," *American Political Science Review,* v. 53 (1960), pp. 1083–1105; Braestrup, *Big Story,* pp. 665–73.

75. Thompson, "Vietnam," p. 193.

6. Northern Ireland 1970–1998

1. J. Bowyer Bell, "Aspects of the Dragon World," *International Journal of Intelligence and Counterintelligence,* vol. 3 (Spring 1979), p. 20.

2. See, for example, Walker Connor, *Ethnonationalism: The Quest for Understanding* (Princeton, NJ: Princeton University Press, 1994).

3. See the very interesting treatment of Home Rule as it poisoned British politics for two generations in Roy Jenkins, *Gladstone* (London: Macmillan, 1995).

4. Tim Pat Coogan, *Eamon De Valera: The Man Who Was Ireland* (New York: HarperCollins, 1993). See also the Earl of Longford and Thomas P. O'Neill, *Eamon De Valera: A Biography* (Boston: Houghton Mifflin, 1971).

5. Frank Pakenham, *Peace by Ordeal: An Account, from First-hand Sources of the Negotiation and Signature of the Anglo-Irish Treaty, 1921* (London: Sidgwick and Jackson, 1972 [orig. 1935]).

6. Michael Hopkinson, *Green against Green: The Irish Civil War* (Dublin: Gill and Macmillan, 1988), pp. 110–11.

7. On Michael Collins, see Tim Pat Coogan, *The Man Who Made Ireland: The Life and Death of Michael Collins* (Niwot, CO: Roberts Rinehart, 1992).

8. M. L. R. Smith, *Fighting for Ireland? The Military Strategy of the Irish Republican Movement* (London: Routledge, 1995), pp. 51ff.

9. Coogan, *Man Who Made Ireland,* p. 389; see Eoin Neeson, *The Civil War, 1922–1923* (Dublin, Ireland: Poolbeg Press, 1989); and Calton Younger, *Ireland's Civil War* (Glasgow: Fontana, 1970).

10. Dermot Keogh, *The Vatican, the Bishops, and Irish Politics 1919–1939* (Cambridge, England: Cambridge University Press, 1986).

11. On the repeated failure of partition to resolve or reduce ethno-religious conflict, see Donald L. Horowitz, *Ethnic Groups in Conflict* (Berkeley: University of California Press, 2000).

12. J. Bowyer Bell, *The Irish Troubles: A Generation of Violence, 1967–1992* (New York: St. Martin's, 1993), pp. 40–41.

13. See Horowitz, *Ethnic Groups in Conflict,* chapter 7.

14. Bell, *Irish Troubles,* p. 39.

15. John Newsinger, *British Counterinsurgency: From Palestine to Northern Ireland* (New York: Palgrave, 2002), pp. 54–56.

16. Thomas Mockaitis, *British Counterinsurgency in the Post-Imperial Era* (Manchester, England: Manchester University Press, 1995), p. 97.

17. Newsinger, *British Counterinsurgency*, p. 155; Bell, *Irish Troubles*, p. 78.

18. Bell, *Irish Troubles*, pp. 79–80.

19. Newsinger, *British Counterinsurgency*, pp. 157–58.

20. Michael Dewar, *Brush Fire Wars: Minor Campaigns of the British Army since 1945* (New York: St. Martin's, 1984), p. 39.

21. Paul Dixon, "Counter-Insurgency in Northern Ireland and the Crisis of the British State," in *The Counter-Insurgent State: Guerrilla Warfare and State Building in the Twentieth Century*, ed. Paul B. Rich and Richard Stubbs (New York: St. Martin's, 1997), p. 188.

22. Anthony James Joes, *Guerrilla Warfare: A Historical, Biographical, and Bibliographical Sourcebook* (Westport, CT: Greenwood, 1996), p. 183.

23. See Joes, *Resisting Rebellion*, pp. 221–22 and passim.

24. Sir Robert Thompson, *Defeating Communist Insurgency: The Lessons of Malaya and Vietnam* (New York: Praeger, 1966), p. 110.

25. John Newsinger, "From Counterinsurgency to Internal Security: Northern Ireland 1969–1972," *Small Wars and Insurgencies*, vol. 6 (Spring 1995), p. 93.

26. Newsinger, *British Counterinsurgency*, p. 164.

27. British actions in subduing the Mau Mau rebellion in Kenya remain highly controversial; see, for example, David Anderson, *Histories of the Hanged: The Dirty War in Kenya and the End of Empire* (New York: Norton, 2005); and Caroline Elkins, *Imperial Reckoning: The Untold Story of Britain's Gulag in Kenya* (New York: Henry Holt, 2005).

28. Dewar, *Brush Fire Wars*, p. 228.

29. C. E. Callwell, *Small Wars: Their Principles and Practice* (London: Greenhill, 1990 [orig. 1896]), p. 143.

30. John Cloake, *Templer: Tiger of Malaya* (London: Harrap, 1985), p. 227.

31. Frank Kitson, *Low Intensity Operations: Subversion, Insurgency, Peacekeeping* (London: Faber, 1971), p. 95.

32. See Desmond Hamill, *Pig in the Middle: The Army in Northern Ireland, 1969–1984* (London: Methuen, 1985).

33. Newsinger, "From Counterinsurgency to Internal Security," p. 96.

34. Dewar, *Brush Fire Wars*, pp. 39–40.

35. Hamill, *Pig in the Middle*, p. 283.

36. Bell, *Irish Troubles*, p. 218.

37. Bell, *Irish Troubles*, p. 220.

38. Bell, *Irish Troubles*, p. xi.

39. Gerry Adams, *Before the Dawn: An Autobiography* (New York: Morrow, 1997), p. 126; Dixon, "Counter-Insurgency in Northern Ireland," p. 194.

40. Dixon, "Counter-Insurgency in Northern Ireland," p. 191.

41. Bell, *Irish Troubles*, pp. 216, 219.

42. Dewar, *Brush Fire Wars*, p. 54.

43. Dixon, "Counter-Insurgency in Northern Ireland," p. 192.

44. Anthony M. Burton, *Urban Terrorism: Theory, Practice, and Response* (London: L. Cooper, 1975), p. 179.

45. Newsinger, "From Counterinsurgency to Internal Security," p. 91; Bell, *Irish Troubles*, p. 126.

46. Bell, *Irish Troubles*, p. 187.

47. Mockaitis, *British Counterinsurgency*, p. 99.

48. Mockaitis, *British Counterinsurgency*, p. 100; Hamill, *Pig in the Middle*, p. 113.

49. Patrick Brogan, *World Conflicts* (Lanham, MD: Scarecrow, 1998), p. 419; Dewar, *Brush Fire Wars*, p. 232.

50. Brogan, *World Conflicts*, p. 418.

51. Newsinger, "From Counterinsurgency to Internal Security," p. 93.

52. Smith, *Fighting for Ireland?* p. 222.

53. Michael O'Riordan, head of the Irish Communist Party, wrote: "There has always existed more or less good relations between the IRA and the Irish Communists. We not only conduct a number of public and anti-imperialist activities together, but for more than a year a secret mechanism for consultations between the leadership of the IRA and the Joint Council of the Irish Workers' Party and the Communist Party of Northern Ireland has existed and is operating. *They unfailingly accept our advice with regard to tactical methods used in the joint struggle for civil rights and national independence for Ireland.*" Christopher Andrew, *The Sword and the Shield: The Mitrokhin Archive and the Secret History of the KGB* (New York: Basic Books, 1999), p. 377; my emphasis.

"In December 1969, shortly before the split which led to the emergence of the Provisionals, a secret meeting of the IRA leadership approved a proposal by [Cathal] Goulding [who became head of the Official wing] to establish a national liberation front including Sinn Fein, the Irish Communist Party, and other left-wing groups." Andrew, *The Sword and the Shield*, p. 639n. See Tim Pat Coogan, *The Troubles: Ireland's Ordeal 1966–1996 and the Search for Peace* (Boulder, CO: Roberts Rinehart, 1996), pp. 94–97.

54. Hamill, *Pig in the Middle*, p. 123.

55. Bell, *Irish Troubles*, p. 171.

56. Bell, *Irish Troubles*, p. 153.

57. Bell, *Irish Troubles*, pp. 642ff.

58. Tim Pat Coogan, *The IRA: A History* (Niwot, CO: Roberts Rinehart, 1993).

59. Mockaitis, *British Counterinsurgency*, p. 111.

60. Coogan, *The IRA*, p. 330.

61. For information on Libyan arms shipments to the Provos (at least one of them intercepted by the Irish navy), see Bell, *Irish Troubles*, and Burton, *Urban Terrorism*, pp. 188–89. On the ETA, see Sean MacStiofain, *Memoirs of a Revolutionary* (London: Gordon Cremonesi, 1978).

62. Richard English, *Armed Struggle: The History of the IRA* (New York: Oxford University Press, 2003).

63. Bell, *Irish Troubles*, p. 782.

64. Coogan, *The IRA*.

65. Jack Holland, *Hope against History: The Course of Conflict in Northern Ireland* (New York: Holt, 1999), p. 328.

66. See the prime minister's account of this mortar attack in John Major, *The Autobiography* (New York: HarperCollins, 1999), pp. 237–38.

67. Bell, *Irish Troubles*, p. 559.

68. Bell, *Irish Troubles*, p. 415.

69. Newsinger, "From Counterinsurgency to Internal Security," p. 104. Nevertheless, in March 1986 the RUC vigorously confronted Orange paramilitaries during the loyalist general strike, which failed.

70. Mockaitis, *British Counterinsurgency*, p. 116.

71. Bell, *Irish Troubles*, pp. 743, 806.

72. Smith, *Fighting for Ireland?*

73. Newsinger, *British Counterinsurgency*, pp. 171ff.

74. Bell, *Irish Troubles*, p. 320.

75. Bell, *Irish Troubles*, p. 675.

76. Edward Moxon-Browne, "The Water and the Fish: Public Opinion and the Provisional IRA in Northern Ireland," in *British Perspectives on Terrorism*, ed. Paul Wilkinson (London: Allen and Unwin, 1981).

77. For a less-than-complimentary portrait of Adams, see Ed Moloney, *A Secret History of the IRA* (New York: Norton, 2002).

78. Hamill, *Pig in the Middle*.

79. Bell, *Irish Troubles*, p. 660.

80. Paul Arthur and Keith Jeffery, *Northern Ireland since 1968* (London: Basil Blackwell, 1988), p. 70.

81. There were 160 traffic deaths in Northern Ireland in 1998, a year of relative peace.

82. Margaret Thatcher, *The Downing Street Years* (New York: HarperCollins, 1993), p. 58.

83. Mockaitis, *British Counterinsurgency*, p. 119.

84. Dewar, *Brush Fire Wars*, p. 232.

85. U.S. Census Bureau, *Statistical Abstract of the United States: 2003* (Washington, DC, 2003), p. 201.

86. Newsinger, *British Counterinsurgency*, p. 189.

87. David Pearson, "Low Intensity Operations in Northern Ireland," in *Soldiers in Cities: Military Operations on Urban Terrain*, ed. Michael C. Desch (Carlisle, PA: Strategic Studies Institute, 2001), p. 103.

88. Smith, *Fighting for Ireland*, p. 220.

89. Mockaitis, *British Counterinsurgency*, p. 145.

90. Burton, *Urban Terrorism*, p. 188.

91. In 1962, the directory of the Irish Republican Army publicly indicted the "attitude of the general public, which has been distracted from the supreme issue facing the Irish people—the unity and freedom of Ireland." Bell, *Irish Troubles*, p. 129.

92. Bell, *Irish Troubles*, p. 189.

7. Grozny 1994–1996

1. Anatol Lieven, *Chechnya: Tombstone of Russian Power* (New Haven, CT: Yale University Press, 1998), pp. 269–70.

2. Olga Oliker, *Russia's Chechen Wars, 1994–2000: Lessons for Urban Combat* (Santa Monica, CA: RAND, 2001), p. 14.

3. Lieven, *Chechnya*, p. 270.

4. Oliker, *Russia's Chechen Wars*, p. 2.

5. John F. Baddeley, *The Russian Conquest of the Caucasus* (New Haven, CT: Yale University Press, 1969 [orig 1908]): p. xxxv.

6. See W. E. D. Allen and Paul Muratoff, *Caucasian Battlefields: A History of the Wars on the Turko-Caucasian Frontier (1828–1921)* (Cambridge, England: Cambridge University Press, 1953); Baddeley, *The Russian Conquest of the Caucasus*; Marie Broxup, ed., *The North Caucasus Barrier: The Russian Advance towards the Muslim World* (New York: St. Martin's, 1992); Moshe Gammer, *Muslim Resistance to the Tsar: Shamil and the Conquest of Chechnya and Daghestan* (London: Frank Cass, 1994).

7. Lieven, *Chechnya*, p. 38; see Lesley Blanch, *The Sabres of Paradise* (London: John Murray, 1960).

8. Lieven, *Chechnya*, p. 324.

9. John B. Dunlop, *Russia Confronts Chechnya: Roots of a Separatist Conflict* (Oxford, England: Clarendon Press, 1998), pp. 58–69.

10. Dunlop, *Russia Confronts Chechnya*, pp. 58–61.

11. Khrushchev's notorious "Secret Speech" of 1956 presented many revealing details of this shameful episode.

12. Lieven, *Chechnya*, 321; see also Carlotta Gall and Thomas de Waal, *Chechnya: Calamity in the Caucasus* (New York: New York University Press, 1998).

13. Gall and de Waal, *Chechnya*, p. 165; Lieven, *Chechnya*, p. 85.

14. Lieven, *Chechnya*, p. 84.

15. Pavel Baev, *The Russian Army in a Time of Troubles* (London: Sage, 1996), p. 142.

16. Lieven says the original invasion force numbered 45,000, up to 55,000 by the spring of 1995 (*Chechnya*, pp. 4, 122); Oliker says that in February 1995 there were thirty thousand Russian troops in Chechnya, including elite spetsnaz and airborne units (*Russia's Chechen Wars*, p. 23). Stasys Knezys and Romanas Sedlickas estimate fifty thousand (*The War in Chechnya* [College Station: Texas A & M University Press, 1999], p. 129).

17. Robert Seely, *Russo-Chechen Conflict, 1800–2000: A Deadly Embrace* (Portland, OR: Frank Cass, 2001), p. 219.

18. Rajan Menon and Graham E. Fuller, "Russia's Ruinous Chechen War," *Foreign Affairs*, vol. 79 (March–April 2000), p. 39.

19. Oliker, *Russia's Chechen Wars*, p. 8.

20. U.S. Marine Corps Intelligence Activity, *Urban Warfare Case Study: City Case Studies Compilation* (Quantico, VA: U.S. Marine Corps, 1999), p. 9.

21. Seely, *Russo-Chechen Conflict*, p. 243.

22. Lieven, *Chechnya*, pp. 284–85.

23. Lieven, *Chechnya*, p. 290.

24. These appalling conditions, with their devastating consequences for troop morale, have not been effectively addressed; see the illuminating article by Mark Kramer, "The Perils of Counterinsurgency: Russia's War in Chechnya," *International Security*, vol. 29 (Winter 2004–5).

25. Lieven, *Chechnya*, p. 280.

26. Lester W. Grau, *Changing Russian Urban Tactics: The Aftermath of the Battle for Grozny* (Fort Leavenworth, KS: U.S. Army Foreign Military Studies Office, 1995), p. 1; Steven J. Blank and Earl H. Tilford, *Russia's Invasion of Chechnya: A Preliminary Assessment* (Carlisle, PA: Strategic Studies Institute, 1995).

27. Gall and de Waal, *Chechnya*, p. 241.

28. Oliker, *Russia's Chechen Wars*, p. 37.

29. Lieven, *Chechnya*, p. 280.

30. U.S. Marine Corps, *Military Operations on Urbanized Terrain: Marine Corps Warfighting Publication 3–35.3* (Washington, DC: U.S. Marine Corps, 1998), p. J-7.

31. Grau, *Changing Russian Urban Tactics*, p. 1.

32. Sean Edwards, *Mars Unmasked: The Changing Face of Urban Operations* (Santa Monica, CA: RAND, 2000), p. 33.

33. Lieven, *Chechnya,* p. 293.

34. Gregory J. Celestan, *Wounded Bear: The Ongoing Russian Military Operation in Chechnya* (Fort Leavenworth, KS: Foreign Military Studies Office, 1996), p. 7.

35. Gall and de Waal, *Chechnya,* p. 209.

36. U.S. Marine Corps, *Military Operations on Urbanized Terrain,* p. J-8.

37. Gall and de Waal, *Chechnya,* p. xiv.

38. Lieven, *Chechnya,* p. 286.

39. Seely, *Russo-Chechen Conflict,* p. 232.

40. Lieven, *Chechnya,* p. 285; see Graham H. Turbiville Jr., *Mafia in Uniform: The Criminalization of the Russian Armed Forces* (Fort Leavenworth, KS: Foreign Military Studies Office, 1995).

41. Robert Seely, *The Russo-Chechen Conflict,* p. 230.

42. U.S. Marine Corps, *Military Operations on Urbanized Terrain,* p. J-8.

43. Oliker, *Russia's Chechen Wars,* pp. 15–16.

44. Lieven, *Chechnya,* p. 279; see the damning report, probably issued by General Edvard Vorobjov, in Knezys and Sedlickas, *War in Chechnya,* pp. 81–85.

45. Lieven, *Chechnya,* pp. 120–21.

46. Blank and Tilford, *Russia's Invasion of Chechnya.*

47. Lieven, *Chechnya,* p. 269.

48. Dunlop, *Russia Confronts Chechnya,* pp. 210, 221.

49. Lieven, *Chechnya,* p. 338.

50. Lieven, *Chechnya,* p. 337.

51. Seely, *Russo-Chechen Conflict,* p. 221.

52. Oliker, *Russia's Chechen Wars,* pp. 9ff.

53. Dunlop, *Russia Confronts Chechnya,* p. 222.

54. Oliker, *Russia's Chechen Wars,* p. 11.

55. Edwards, *Mars Unmasked* (Santa Monica, CA: RAND, 2000), p. 26.

56. Gall and de Waal, *Chechnya,* p. 174.

57. Lieven, *Chechnya,* p. 109.

58. John R. Pilloni, "Burning Corpses in the Streets: Russia's Doctrinal Flaws in the 1995 Fight for Grozny," *Journal of Slavic Military Studies,* vol. 13 (June 2000), p. 63n47.

59. Timothy Thomas, "The Battle for Grozny: Deadly Classroom for Urban Combat," *Parameters,* vol. 29 (Summer 1999), p. 89.

60. Celestan, *Wounded Bear,* p. 2.

61. Pilloni, "Burning Corpses in the Streets," p. 39.

62. Edwards, *Mars Unmasked,* p. 26; Lieven, *Chechnya,* p. 109.

63. Thomas, *Battle for Grozny,* p. 101.

64. Oliker, *Russia's Chechen Wars*, p. 17.

65. Baev, *The Russian Army in a Time of Troubles*, p. 142.

66. Lieven, *Chechnya*, p. 325.

67. Lieven, *Chechnya*, p. 119.

68. Knezys and Sedlickas, *War in Chechnya*, pp. 94–96.

69. Edwards, *Mars Unmasked*, p. 23.

70. Knezys and Sedlickas, *War in Chechnya*, p. 109.

71. Celestan, *Wounded Bear*, p. 7.

72. Aslan Maskhadov, elected president of Chechnya in 1997, was killed by Russian troops March 8, 2005.

73. Raymond C. Finch, *Why the Russian Military Failed in Chechnya* (Fort Leavenworth, KS: Foreign Military Studies Office, 1998), p. 10n.

74. Gall and de Waal, *Chechnya*, p. 205.

75. Celestan, *Wounded Bear*, p. 11.

76. Lieven, *Chechnya*, p. 130. See also David P. Dilegge, "View from the Wolves' Den: The Chechens and Urban Operations," *Small Wars Journal* (2005), http://www.Smallwarsjournal.com.

77. Oliker, *Russia's Chechen Wars*, p. 62.

78. U.S. Marine Corps, *Military Operations on Urbanized Terrain*, p. J-6.

79. Gall and de Waal, *Chechnya*, p. 206.

80. U.S. Marine Corps, *Military Operations on Urbanized Terrain*, p. J-5.

81. U.S. Marine Corps, *Military Operations on Urbanized Terrain*, p. J-5.

82. Oliker, *Russia's Chechen Wars*, p. 13; my emphasis.

83. Edwards, *Mars Unmasked*, p. 29n.

84. Knezys and Sedlickas, *War in Chechnya*, p. 123. In the Second Chechen War (1999–2000), the Russians again lost many tanks on city streets and again failed to enclose Grozny completely. Russian soldiers easily became hostages because of their poor base security (Oliker, *Russia's Chechen Wars*, p. 68).

85. Pilloni, "Burning Corpses in the Streets," p. 57.

86. Gall and de Waal, *Chechnya*, p. xi.

87. The same sad process occurred two centuries before, when the French Revolutionary regime depopulated the Vendée and Brittany, and in the 1930s, during the Japanese invasion of China.

88. Lieven, *Chechnya*, p. 133.

89. Finch, *Why the Russian Military Failed*, p. 5.

90. Celestan, *Wounded Bear*, p. 4. In South Vietnam, the Communist Viet Cong and the North Vietnamese army greatly increased the use of artillery against inhabited places, once they realized that a majority of the southern population was indifferent or hostile to them.

91. U.S. Marine Corps, *Military Operations on Urbanized Terrain*, p. J-1.

92. Finch, *Why The Russian Military Failed*, p. 7.

93. Celestan, *Wounded Bear*, p. 6.

94. Lieven, *Chechnya*, p. 46.

95. Lester W. Grau and Timothy L. Thomas, *"Soft Log" and Concrete Canyons: Russian Urban Combat Logistics in Grozny* (Fort Leavenworth , KS: Foreign Military Studies Office, 2000).

96. Gall and de Waal, *Chechnya*, p. 247.

97. Pilloni, "Burning Corpses in the Streets," p. 54.

98. John Erickson, *The Road to Berlin: Stalin's War with Germany* (New Haven, CT: Yale University Press, 1999 [orig. 1983]), p. 629.

99. Seely, *Russo-Chechen Conflict*, p. 262.

100. Pilloni, "Burning Corpses in the Streets," p. 59n3.

101. Lieven says that up to January 1997, forty-four hundred Russian soldiers were killed, seven hundred were missing, seven hundred deserted; see his *Chechnya*, p. 108.

102. Gall and de Waal, *Chechnya*, p. 227; Seely, *Russo-Chechen Conflict*, pp. 261–62.

103. Knezys and Sedlickas, *War in Chechnya*, p. 303.

104. Edwards, *Mars Unmasked*, p. 31.

105. Edwards, *Mars Unmasked*, p. 31.

106. Gall and de Waal, *Chechnya*, p. 335; Oliker, *Russia's Chechen Wars*, p. 30.

107. Knezys and Sedlickas, *War in Chechnya*, p. 287.

108. Oliker, *Russia's Chechen Wars*, p. 31; Lieven, *Chechnya*, 141–42.

109. Brogan, *World Conflicts*, p. 397.

110. Baev, *The Russian Army in a Time of Troubles*, p. 146.

111. Pilloni, "Burning Corpses in the Streets," p. 48.

112. Oliker, *Russia's Chechen Wars*, p. 33.

113. Finch, *Why the Russian Military Failed*, p. 6.

114. Grau, *Changing Russian Urban Tactics*, p. 1.

115. Oliker, *Russia's Chechen Wars*, p. 35.

116. Anatol Lieven, "Lessons of the War in Chechnya, 1994–1996," in *Soldiers in Cities: Military Operations on Urban Terrain*, ed. Michael C. Desch (Carlisle, PA: Strategic Studies Institute, 2001), p. 60; Lieven, *Chechnya*, p. 113.

117. Lieven, *Chechnya*, p. 270.

118. Lieven, *Chechnya*, p. 106; Gall and de Waal, *Chechnya*, pp. 177ff.

119. Oliker, *Russia's Chechen Wars*, p. 35.

120. Lieven, *Chechnya*, p. 250.

121. Blank and Tilford, *Russia's Invasion of Chechnya*.

122. Dunlop, *Russia Confronts Chechnya*, p. 213.

123. Oliker, *Russia's Chechen Wars*, p. 14.

124. Blank and Tilford, *Russia's Invasion of Chechnya*, p. 4.

125. Lieven, *Chechnya*, p. 3. Fighting in Chechnya continued for years, with thousands of Russian casualties, even though the Russian troops there enjoyed a numerical ratio of more than 40 to 1 over the local insurgents. See Kramer, "Perils of Counterinsurgency."

Conclusion

1. Horne, *A Savage War of Peace*, p. 239.

2. U.S. Marine Corps, *Military Operations on Urbanized Terrain*, p. J-6.

3. U.S. Marine Corps, *Military Operations on Urbanized Terrain*, p. J-5. U.S. Abrams tanks are considerably less vulnerable to ground fire than Russian tanks in Grozny; Kendall D. Gott, *Breaking the Mold: Tanks in Cities* (Fort Leavenworth, KS: Combat Studies Institute Press, 2006), p. 105.

4. One might argue that the Bolshevik rising of October 1917 in Petrograd is an exception. That, however, took place in one night, against a totally undefended government, and is commonly referred to by non-Communist writers as a coup d'état.

5. See Gordon McCormick, *From the Sierra to the Cities: The Urban Campaign of The Shining Path* (Santa Monica, CA: RAND, 1992).

6. Daniel Henninger, "Troops in Fallujah Are the Best since World War II," *Wall Street Journal*, November 18, 2004.

7. Jonathan F. Keiler, "Who Won the Battle of Fallujah?" *Proceedings of the U.S. Naval Institute*, vol. 131 (January 2005).

8. "The Message from Fallujah," *Christian Science Monitor*, November 15, 2004. See also "Victory in Fallujah," *Wall Street Journal*, November 17, 2004; F. J. West, "The Fall of Fallujah," *Marine Corps Gazette*, vol. 89 (July, 2005), and F. J. West, *No True Glory: A Frontline Account of the Battle for Fallujah* (New York: Bantam, 2005).). Gott gives the number of American fatalities as thirty-eight; *Breaking the Mold*, p. 103.

9. Hence, "the city became, as Castro had predicted, a graveyard of the revolutionary." Beckett, *Modern Insurgencies*, p. 176.

10. Of course, the leaders of the Warsaw Rising had reasonable hopes that Nazi encirclement would be broken by the approaching Soviet armies or neutralized by Allied airdrops, or both.

11. Bell, "Revolutionary Dynamics," pp. 194, 195, 197, 209.

12. De Abreu, "Brazil's Guerrilla Trap."

13. Oliker, *Russia's Chechen Wars*, p. xv.

14. Lieven, "Lessons of the War in Chechnya," p. 61. Jennifer M. Taw and Bruce Hoffman, *The Urbanization of Insurgency: A Potential Challenge to U.S. Army Operations* (Santa Monica, CA: RAND, 1994). The destruction of such slums

and the transfer of their inhabitants to other areas would greatly assist security forces, but at a perhaps unacceptably high political cost.

15. "Urban combat is vertical in nature, whereas conventional combat is horizontal." U.S. Marine Corps, *Urban Warfare Study: City Case Studies Compilation* (Quantico, VA: U.S. Marine Corps, 1999).

16. "Urban combat is extremely manpower-intensive and produces significant attrition among men and matériel." U.S. Marine Corps, *Urban Warfare Study*, p. 2. "Urban combat is the domain of old-fashioned infantry;" Barry R. Posen, "Urban Operations: Tactical Realities and Strategic Ambiguities," in Desch, *Soldiers in Cities*, p. 153.

17. "[The enemy] may gain an advantage against superior [U.S. and allied] forces by capitalizing on a perceived weakness of many Western nations: the inability to endure continuous losses or casualties for other than vital national interests or losses for which they are psychologically unprepared." Field Manual 3-06, *Urban Operations* (Washington, DC: Headquarters, Department of the Army, 2003), chapter 3, section 13.

18. Wirtz, "The Battles of Saigon and Hue" p. 85.

19. Metz and Millen, *Insurgency and Counterinsurgency in the Twenty-first Century*, p. 16.

20. Colin S. Gray, "Strategy in the Nuclear Age," in *The Making of Strategy: Rulers, States and War*, ed. Williamson Murray, MacGregor Knox, and Alvin Bernstein (Cambridge, England: Cambridge University Press, 1994), p. 603.

21. Eliot A. Cohen, "The Strategy of Innocence," in Murray, Knox, and Bernstein, *The Making of Strategy*, p. 464.

22. Gray, "Strategy in the Nuclear Age," p. 613; and see his *Irregular Enemies and the Essence of Strategy: Can the American Way of War Adapt?* (Carlisle, PA: Strategic Studies Institute, 2006).

23. Bell, *The Irish Troubles*, p. 662.

24. Posen, "Urban Operations," p. 162.

25. William L. Shirer, *The Rise and Fall of the Third Reich* (New York: Simon and Schuster, 1960), p. 645.

26. Sun Tzu, *The Art of War*, trans. Samuel B. Griffith (New York: Oxford University Press, 1963), p. 78.

27. U.S. Marine Corps, *Urban Warfare Study*, pp. 1–17. "Cities that are descending into chaos quickly must be isolated from the surrounding countryside"; Wirtz, "The Battles of Saigon and Hue," p. 83.

28. On the Morice Line, see Thompson, *War in Peace*, pp. 128–29.

29. Callwell, *Small Wars*, p. 143.

30. Lieven, "Lessons of the War in Chechnya," p. 58. On getting useful information *about* the enemy *from* the enemy, see Richard L. Clutterbuck, *The Long, Long War: Counterinsurgency in Malaya and Vietnam* (New York: Praeger, 1966), p. 106.

31. U.S. Marine Corps, *Urban Warfare Study,* p. 2. This Marine Corps study of course was not *advocating* such a lack of concern.

32. Laqueur, *The New Terrorism,* p. 281.

33. See Harvey Rishikof and Michael Schrage, "Technology vs. Torture," *Slate* (August 18, 2004), http://slate.msn.com/id2105332/.

Selected Bibliography

Adams, Gerry. *Before the Dawn: An Autobiography.* New York: Morrow, 1996.
———. *Falls Memories.* Niwot, CO: Roberts Rinehart, 1994.
Alexander, Martin S., and J. F. V. Keiger, eds. *France and the Algerian War: Strategy, Operations and Diplomacy.* London: Frank Cass, 2002.
Alexander, Martin S., Martin Evans, and J. F. V. Keiger, eds. *The Algerian War and the French Army, 1954–1962: Experiences, Images, Testimonies.* New York: Palgrave Macmillan, 2002.
Alexander, Martin, and J. F. V. Keiger. "France and the Algerian War: Strategy, Operations and Diplomacy." *Journal of Strategic Studies,* vol. 25 (June 2002).
Allen,. W. E. D., and Paul Muratoff. *Caucasian Battlefields: A History of the Wars on the Turko-Caucasian Frontier (1828–1921).* Cambridge, England: Cambridge University Press, 1953.
Anders, Wladyslaw. *An Army in Exile: The Story of the Second Polish Corps.* London: Macmillan, 1949.
Anderson, David. *Histories of the Hanged: The Dirty War in Kenya and the End of Empire.* New York: Norton, 2005.
Arnold, James R. *The Tet Offensive: Turning Point in Vietnam.* London: Osprey, 1990.
Arthur, Max. *Northern Ireland: Soldiers Talking, 1969 to Today.* London: Sidgwick and Jackson, 1987.
Arthur, Paul, and Keith Jeffery. *Northern Ireland since 1968.* London: Basil Blackwell, 1988.
Aussaresses, Paul. *Battle of the Casbah: Terrorism and Counterterrorism in Algiers, 1955–1957.* New York: Enigma, 2002.
Baev, Pavel. *The Russian Army in a Time of Troubles.* London: Sage, 1996.

Baddeley, John F. *Russian Conquest of the Caucasus*. New York: Russell and Russell, 1969 [orig. 1908].

Baldwin, Hanson. *Battles Lost and Won: Great Campaigns of World War II*. New York: Harper and Row, 1966.

Barnett, Thomas P. M. *The Pentagon's New Map: War and Peace in the Twenty-First Century*. New York: Putnam's, 2004.

Beaufre, André. *La guerre révolutionnaire: Les formes nouvelles de la guerre*. Paris: Fayard, 1972.

Baumann, Robert F. *Russian/Soviet Unconventional Wars in the Caucasus, Central Asia, and Afghanistan*. Fort Leavenworth, KS: Leavenworth Papers no. 20 (1993).

Beckett, Ian F. W. *Encyclopedia of Guerrilla Warfare*. Santa Barbara, CA: ABC-Clio, 1999.

———. "The Future of Insurgency." *Small Wars and Insurgencies*, vol. 16 (December 2005).

———. *Modern Insurgencies and Counterinsurgencies: Guerrillas and Their Opponents since 1750*. London: Routledge, 2001.

———. "The Soviet Experience." In *The Roots of Counterinsurgency: Armies and Guerrilla Warfare, 1900–1945*. Ed. Ian F. W. Beckett. London: Blandford, 1988.

———, ed. *The Roots of Counterinsurgency: Armies and Guerrilla Warfare, 1900–1945*. London: Blandford, 1988.

Beckett, Ian F. W., and John Pimlott, eds. *Armed Forces and Modern Counter-Insurgency*. New York: St. Martin's, 1985.

Behr, Edward. *The Algerian Problem*. London: Hodder & Stoughton, 1961.

Bell, J. Bowyer. "Aspects of the Dragonworld: Covert Communications and the Rebel Ecosystem." *International Journal of Intelligence and Counterintelligence*, vol. 3 (Spring 1979).

———. *The Gun in Politics: An Analysis of Irish Political Conflict, 1916–1986*. New Brunswick, NJ: Transaction, 1987.

———. *The Irish Troubles: A Generation of Violence, 1967–1992*. New York: St. Martin's, 1993.

———. "Revolutionary Dynamics: The Inherent Inefficiency of the Underground." *Terrorism and Political Violence*, vol. 2 (1990).

———. *The Secret Army: A History of the IRA*. London: Blond, 1970 .

Bennigsen, Alexandre, and Marie Broxup. *The Islamic Threat to the Soviet State*. New York: St. Martin's, 1983.

Bew, Paul, Peter Gibbon, and Henry Patterson. *Northern Ireland, 1921–1996: Political Forces and Social Classes*. London: Serif, 1996.

Bishop, Patrick, and Eamonn Mallie. *The Provisional IRA*. London: Heinemann, 1987.

Blanch, Lesley. *The Sabres of Paradise*. London: John Murray, 1960.

Blank, Steven J., and Earl H. Tilford. *Russia's Invasion of Chechnya: A Preliminary Assessment*. Carlisle, PA: Strategic Studies Institute, 1995.

Bocca, Geoffrey. *The Secret Army*. Englewood Cliffs, NJ: Prentice-Hall, 1968.

Borsody, Stephen. *The Triumph of Tyranny: The Nazi and Soviet Conquest of Central Europe*. London: Cape, 1960.

Boualam, Bachaga. *Les harkis au service de la France*. Paris: France Empire, 1964.

Boyer de la Tour, Pierre. *De l'Indochine à l'Algérie: Le martyre de l'armée française*. Paris: Presses du mail, 1962.

Braestrup, Peter. *Big Story: How the American Press and Television Reported and Interpreted the Crisis of Tet 1968 in Vietnam and Washington*. 2 vols. Boulder, CO: Westview, 1977.

———. *Vietnam as History: Ten Years after the Paris Peace Accords*. Washington, DC: University Press of America, 1984.

Brewer, John D., and Kathleen Magee, *Inside the RUC: Routine Policing in a Divided Society*. Oxford: Clarendon Press, 1991.

Bromberger, Serge. *Les rebelles Algériens*. Paris: Plon, 1958.

Broxup, Marie, ed. *The North Caucasus Barrier: The Russian Advance toward the Muslim World*. New York: St. Martin's, 1992.

Buczek, Roman. *Stanislaw Mikolajczyk*. 2 vols. Toronto: Century Publications, 1996.

Bunker, Ellsworth. *The Bunker Papers: Reports to the President from Vietnam, 1967–1973*. Ed. Douglas Pike. Berkeley: University of California Press, 1990.

Burton, Anthony. *Urban Terrorism: Theory, Practice, and Response*. London: L. Cooper, 1975.

Callwell, C. E. *Small Wars: Their Principles and Practice*. London: Greenhill, 1990 [orig. 1896].

Carr, E. H. *The Bolshevik Revolution, 1917–1923*. New York: Macmillan, 1961.

Carver, Michael. *War since 1945*. New York: Putnam's, 1981.

Catton, Philip E. *Diem's Final Failure: Prelude to America's War in Vietnam*. Lawrence: University Press of Kansas, 2002.

Charters, David A. "From Palestine to Northern Ireland: British Adaptation to Low-Intensity Operations." In *Armies in Low-Intensity Conflict: A Comparative Analysis*. Ed. David Charters and Maurice Tugwell. London: Brassey's, 1989.

Celestan, Gregory J. *Wounded Bear: The Ongoing Russian Military Operation in Chechnya*. Fort Leavenworth, KS: Foreign Military Studies Office, 1996.

Chamberlin, William Henry. *The Russian Revolution, 1917–1921*. 2 vols. New York: Macmillan, 1935.

Ciechanowski, Jan M. *The Warsaw Rising of 1944*. New York: Cambridge University Press, 1974.

Clark, Michael K. *Algeria in Turmoil: A History of the Rebellion*. New York: Praeger, 1959.

Clausewitz, Carl von. *On War*. Ed. and trans. Michael Howard and Peter Paret. Princeton, NJ: Princeton University Press, 1976.

Cloake, John. *Templer: Tiger of Malaya*. London: Harrap, 1985.

Conquest, Robert. *The Nation Killers*, 2d ed. New York: Macmillan, 1970.

Cohen, Eliot. "The Strategy of Innocence." In *The Making of Strategy: Rulers, States and War*. Ed. Williamson Murray, MacGregor Knox, and Alvin Bernstein. Cambridge, England: Cambridge University Press, 1994.

Coogan, Tim Pat. *Eamon De Valera: The Man Who Was Ireland*. New York: HarperCollins, 1993.

———. *The IRA: A History*. Niwot, CO: Roberts Rinehart, 1993.

———. *The Man Who Made Ireland: The Life and Death of Michael Collins*. Niwot, CO: Roberts Rinehart, 1992.

D'Abernon, Edgar, Lord. *The Eighteenth Decisive Battle of World History: Warsaw 1920*. London: Hodder and Stoughton, 1931.

Davidson, Phillip B. *Vietnam at War: The History, 1946–1975*. Novato, CA: Presidio, 1988.

Davies, Norman. *Rising '44: The Battle for Warsaw*. New York: Viking, 2003.

———. *White Eagle, Red Star: The Polish-Soviet War 1919–1920*. New York: St. Martin's, 1972.

De Abreu, Alzira Alves. "Brazil's Guerrilla Trap." *History Today*, vol. 47 (1997).

Debray, Régis. *Revolution in the Revolution?* New York: Grove, 1967.

De Gaulle, Charles. *Memoirs of Hope: Renewal and Endeavor*. New York: Simon and Schuster, 1971.

Delmas, Claude. *La guerre révolutionnaire*. 3d ed. Paris: Presses universitaires de France, 1972 [orig. 1959].

Demarest, Geoffrey. "Geopolitics and Urban Armed Conflict in Latin America." *Small Wars and Insurgencies*, vol. 6 (Spring 1995).

Demarest, Geoffrey, and Lester W. Grau. "Maginot Line or Fort Apache? Using Forts to Shape the Counterinsurgency Battlefield." *Military Review* (November–December 2005).

Derradji, Abder-Rahmane. *The Algerian Guerrilla Campaign: Strategy and Tactics*. Lewiston, NY: Edwin Mellen, 1997.

Desch, Michael C., ed. *Soldiers in Cities: Military Operations on Urban Terrain*. Carlisle, PA: Strategic Studies Institute, 2001.

Devlin, Bernadette. *The Price of My Soul*. New York: Knopf, 1969.

Dewar, Michael. *The British Army in Northern Ireland*. London: Arms and Armour, 1985.

———. *Brush Fire Wars: Minor Campaigns of the British Army since 1945*. New York: St. Martin's, 1984.

Dillon, Martin, and Dennis Lehane. *Political Murder in Northern Ireland.* Harmondsworth, England: Penguin, 1973.

Dixon, Paul. "Counter-Insurgency in Northern Ireland and the Crisis of the British State." In *The Counter-Insurgent State: Guerrilla Warfare and State Building in the Twentieth Century.* Ed. Paul B. Rich and Richard Stubbs. New York: St. Martin's, 1997.

Duggan, John P. *History of the Irish Army.* Dublin: Gill and Macmillan, 1991.

Dunlop, John B. *Russia Confronts Chechnya: Roots of a Separatist Conflict.* Oxford, England: Clarendon Press, 1998.

Edwards, Sean J. A. *Mars Unmasked: The Changing Face of Urban Operations.* Santa Monica, CA: RAND, 2000.

Elkins, Caroline. *Imperial Reckoning: The Untold Story of Britain's Gulag in Kenya.* New York: Henry Holt, 2005.

Erickson, John. *The Road to Berlin: Stalin's War with Germany.* New Haven, CT: Yale University Press, 1999 [orig. 1983].

Evans, Martin. "The Harkis: The Experience and Memory of France's Muslim Auxiliaries." In *The Algerian War and the French Army 1954–1962: Experiences, Images, Testimonies.* Ed. Martin S. Alexander, Martin Evans, and J. F. V. Keiger. New York: Palgrave Macmillan, 2002.

Farrell, Michael. *Northern Ireland: The Orange State.* London: Pluto, 1976.

Fauriol, Georges, ed. *Latin American Insurgencies.* Washington, DC: Georgetown Center for Strategic and International Studies and the National Defense University, 1985.

Fejto, Francois. *Behind the Rape of Hungary.* New York: McKay, 1957.

Fiddick, Thomas. *Russia's Retreat from Poland, 1920.* New York: St. Martin's, 1990.

Field Manual 3-06, *Urban Operations.* Washington, DC: Headquarters, Department of the Army, 2003.

Finch, M. H. J. "Three Perspectives on the Crisis in Uruguay." *Journal of Latin American Studies,* vol. 3 (1972).

Finch, Raymond C. *Why the Russian Military Failed in Chechnya.* Fort Leavenworth, KS: U.S. Army, Foreign Military Studies Office, 1998.

Ford, Ronnie E. *Tet 1968: Understanding the Surprise.* Portland, OR: Frank Cass, 1995.

Friedman, George. *America's Secret War: Inside the Hidden Worldwide Struggle between America and Its Enemies..* New York: Doubleday, 2004.

Fryer, Peter. *The Hungarian Tragedy.* London: D. Donson, 1957.

Gaddis, John Lewis. *The United States and the Origins of the Cold War: 1941–1947.* New York: Columbia University Press, 1972.

Gadney, Reg. *Cry Hungary! Uprising 1956.* New York: Atheneum, 1986.

Gall, Carlotta, and Thomas de Waal. *Chechnya: Calamity in the Caucasus.* New York: New York University Press, 1998.

Gammer. Moshe. *Muslim Resistance to the Tsar: Shamil and the Conquest of Chechnya and Daghestan.* London: Frank Cass, 1994.

Garlinski , Jozef. "The Polish Underground State (1939–1945)." *Journal of Contemporary History,* vol. 10 (1975).

Garton Ash, Timothy. *The Uses of Adversity: Essays on the Fate of Central Europe.* New York: Vintage, 1990.

Gati, Charles. *Hungary and the Soviet Bloc.* Durham, NC: Duke University Press, 1986.

Gerwehr, Scott, and Russell W. Glenn. *Sharpening the Sword: A Review of Military Field Experimentation.* Santa Monica, CA: RAND, 2003.

———. *Unweaving the Web: Deception and Adaptation in Future Urban Operations.* Santa Monica, CA: RAND, 2002.

Gilbert, Marc Jason, and William Head, eds. *The Tet Offensive.* Westport, CT: Praeger, 1996.

Glenn, Russell W., et al. *Honing the Keys to the City: Refining the United States Marine Corps Reconnaissance Force for Urban Ground Combat Operations.* Santa Monica, CA: RAND, 2005.

Glenn, Russell W., and Gina Kingston. *Urban Battle Command in the Twenty-first Century.* Santa Monica, CA: RAND, 2005.

Godard, Yves. *Les paras dans la ville.* Paris: Fayard, 1972.

Godfrey, F. A. "The Latin American Experience: The Tupamaros Campaign in Uruguay, 1963–1973." In *Armed Forces and Modern Counter-Insurgency.* Ed. Ian F. W. Beckett and John Pimlott. New York: St. Martin's, 1985.

Goltz, Thomas. *Chechnya Diary.* New York: Thomas Dunne, 2003.

Goodman, Allen E. *An Institutional Profile of the South Vietnamese Officer Corps.* Santa Monica, CA: RAND, 1970.

Gordon, David C. *The Passing of French Algeria.* New York: Oxford University Press, 1966.

Gott, Kendall D. *Breaking the Mold: Tanks in Cities.* Fort Leavenworth, KS: Combat Studies Institute Press, 2006.

Gougeon, François-Marie. "The Challe Plan: Vain Yet Indispensable Victory." *Small Wars and Insurgencies,* vol. 16 (December 2005).

Grau, Lester W. *Changing Russian Urban Tactics: The Aftermath of the Battle for Grozny.* Fort Leavenworth, KS: U.S. Army Foreign Military Studies Office, 1995.

Gray, Colin S. *Irregular Enemies and the Essence of Strategy: Can the American Way of War Adapt?* Carlisle, PA: Strategic Studies Institute, 2006.

———. *Modern Strategy.* Oxford: Oxford University Press, 1999.

Grivas, George. *General Grivas on Guerrilla Warfare.* New York: Praeger, 1965.

Grosser, Alfred. *French Foreign Policy under De Gaulle.* Boston: Little, Brown, 1967.

Guevara, Ernesto. *Guerrilla Warfare*. New York: Vintage, 1969.

Guillen, Abraham. *Philosophy of the Urban Guerrilla*. Ed. Donald C. Hodges. New York: Morrow, 1973.

Gutman, Israel. *The Jews of Warsaw: Ghetto, Underground, Revolt*. Bloomington: Indiana University Press, 1982.

———. *Resistance: The Warsaw Ghetto Uprising*. New York: Houghton Mifflin, 1994.

Hamill, Desmond. *Pig in the Middle: The Army in Northern Ireland, 1969–1984*. London: Methuen, 1985.

Handbook for Joint Urban Operations. Washington, DC: Joint Staff, 2000.

Hanson, Joanna K. M. *The Civilian Population and the Warsaw Uprising of 1944*. Cambridge, England: Cambridge University Press, 1982.

Haraszti-Taylor, Eva. *The Hungarian Revolution of 1956: A Collection of Documents from the British Foreign Office*. Nottingham, England: Astra, 1995.

Harbi, Mohammed. *Aux origines du FLN*. Paris: Editions Bourgeois, 1975.

———. *1954: La guerre commence en Algérie*. Brussels: Éditions complexe, 1954.

Hashim, Ahmed. "The Insurgency in Iraq." *Small Wars and Insurgencies*, vol. 14 (Autumn 2003).

Haycock, Ronald, ed. *Regular Armies and Insurgency*. London: Croom Helm, 1979.

Heggoy, Alf Andrew. *Insurgency and Counterinsurgency in Algeria*. Bloomington: Indiana University Press, 1972.

Heller, Andor. *No More Comrades*. Chicago: Regnery, 1957.

Henissart, Paul. *Wolves in the City: The Death of French Algeria*. New York: Simon and Schuster, 1970.

Hills, A. "Hearts and Minds or Search and Destroy?" *Small Wars and Insurgencies*, vol. 13, (Spring 2002).

Hoensch, Jorg K. *A History of Modern Hungary, 1867–1994*. London: Longman, 1988.

Hoffman, Bruce. *Insurgency and Counterinsurgency in Iraq*. Santa Monica, CA: RAND, 2004.

Hoffman, Bruce, and Jennifer Morrison. "Urbanization of Insurgency." *Small Wars and Insurgencies*, vol. 6 (1995).

Hoffman, Bruce, and Jennifer M. Taw. *Defence Policy and Low Intensity Conflict: The Development of Britain's "Small Wars" Doctrine during the 1950s*. Santa Monica, CA: RAND, 1991.

———. *Strategic Framework for Countering Terrorism and Insurgency*. Santa Monica, CA: RAND, 1992.

Hogard, Jacques. "Guerre révolutionnaire et pacification." *Revue militaire d'information* (January 1957).

———. "Stratégie et tactique dans la guerre révolutionnaire." *Revue militaire d'information* (June 1958).

Holland, Jack. *Hope against History: The Course of Conflict in Northern Ireland.* New York: Holt, 1999.

Hopkinson. Michael. *Green against Green: The Irish Civil War.* New York: St. Martin's, 1988.

Horne, Alistair. *The French Army and Politics 1870–1970.* London: Macmillan, 1984.

———. *A Savage War of Peace: Algeria, 1954–1962.* Rev. ed. New York: Penguin, 1987.

Huntington, Samuel P. *Political Order in Changing Societies.* New Haven, CT: Yale University Press, 1968.

Horthy, Miklos [Nicholas]. *Memoirs.* London: Hutchinson, 1956.

Hutchinson, Martha Crenshaw. *Revolutionary Terrorism: The FLN in Algeria 1954–1962.* Stanford, CA: Hoover Institution, 1978.

Irving, David J. C. *Uprising.* London: Hodder and Stoughton, 1981.

Jedrzejewicz, Waclaw. *Pilsudski: A Life for Poland.* Introduction by Zbigniew Brzezinski. New York: Hippocrene, 1982.

Jeffery, Keith. "Intelligence and Counterinsurgency Operations: Some Reflections on the British Experience." *Intelligence and National Security,* vol. 2 (1987).

Jenkins, Brian. *The Five Stages of Urban Guerrilla Warfare.* Santa Monica, CA: RAND, 1971.

———. *Soldiers versus Gunmen: The Challenge of Urban Guerrilla Warfare.* Santa Monica, CA: RAND, 1974.

———. *An Urban Strategy for Guerrillas and Governments.* RAND, 1972.

Joes, Anthony James. *From the Barrel of a Gun: Armies and Revolution.* Washington, DC: Pergamon-Brassey's, 1986.

———. *Resisting Rebellion: The History and Politics of Counterinsurgency.* Lexington: University Press of Kentucky, 2004.

Kahn, Robert A. *A History of the Habsburg Empire, 1526–1918.* Berkeley: University of California Press, 1974.

Karoly, Mihaly. *Memoirs.* London: J. Cape, 1956.

Karski, Jan (Jan Kozielewski). *The Great Powers and Poland: From Versailles to Yalta.* Lanham, MD: University Press of America, 1985.

———. *Story of a Secret State.* Boston: Houghton Mifflin, 1944.

Kaufer, Rémi. *Histoire de la guerre franco-française.* Paris: Seuil, 2002.

Kaufman, Edy. *Uruguay in Transition.* New Brunswick, NJ: Transaction, 1979.

Keegan, John. *Six Armies in Normandy: From D-Day to the Liberation of Paris.* New York: Viking, 1982.

Kelly, George. *Lost Soldiers: The French Army and Empire in Crisis.* Cambridge, MA: MIT Press, 1965.

Keogh, Dermot. *The Vatican, the Bishops, and Irish Politics 1919–1939.* Cambridge, England: Cambridge University Press, 1986.

Keiler, Jonathan F. "Who Won the Battle of Fallujah?" *Proceedings of the U.S. Naval Institute,* vol. 131 (January 2005).

Kersten, Krystyna. *The Establishment of Communist Rule in Poland, 1943–1948.* Berkeley: University of California Press, 1991.

Khrushchev, Nikita. *Khrushchev Remembers.* Boston: Little, Brown, 1970.

Kiraly, Bela. "Hungary's Army: Its Part in the Revolt," *East Europe,* vol. 7 (June 1958).

Kiraly, Bela, and Paul Jonas, eds. *The Hungarian Revolution of 1956 in Retrospect.* Boulder, CO: East European Quarterly, 1978.

Kissane, Bill. *The Politics of the Irish Civil War.* New York: Oxford University Press, 2005.

Kissinger, Henry. *Does America Need a Foreign Policy?* New York: Simon and Schuster, 2001.

Kitson, Frank. *Low Intensity Operations: Subversion, Insurgency, Peacekeeping.* London: Faber, 1971.

Knezys, Stasys, and Romanas Sedlickas. *The War in Chechnya.* College Station: Texas A&M University, 1999.

Kohl, James, and John Litt. *Urban Guerrilla Warfare in Latin America.* Cambridge, MA: MIT Press, 1974.

Kolko, Gabriel. *Anatomy of a War: Vietnam, the United States, and the Modern Historical Experience.* New York: Pantheon, 1985.

Komorowski [Bor], Tadeusz. *The Secret Army.* New York: Macmillan, 1951.

Kopacsi, Sandor. *In the Name of the Working Class.* London: Fontana/Collins, 1989.

Korbonski, Stefan. *Fighting Warsaw: The Story of the Polish Underground State.* New York: Minerva Press, 1968.

Kovacs, Imre. *Facts about Hungary.* New York: Hungarian Committee, 1959.

Kraft, Joseph. *Struggle for Algeria.* Garden City, NY: Doubleday, 1961.

Krakowski, Shmuel. *The War of the Doomed: Jewish Armed Resistance in Poland, 1942–1944.* New York: Holmes and Meier, 1984.

Kramer, Mark. "The Soviet Union and the 1956 Crises in Poland and Hungary: Reassessments and New Findings." *Journal of Contemporary History,* vol. 33 (1998).

———. "The Perils of Counterinsurgency: Russia's War in Chechnya." *International Security,* vol. 29 (Winter 2004–5).

Kurzman, Dan. *The Bravest Battle: The Twenty-eight Days of the Warsaw Ghetto Uprising.* New York: Da Capo, 1993 [orig. 1976].

La Gorce, Paul-Marie de. *The French Army: A Military-Political History.* New York: George Braziller, 1963.

Labrousse, Alain. *The Tupamaros: Urban Insurgency in Uruguay.* Introduction by Richard Gott. Harmondsworth, England: Penguin, 1970.

Langguth, A. J. *Hidden Terrors.* New York: Pantheon, 1978.

Lapidus, Gail. "Contested Sovereignty: The Tragedy of Chechnya." *International Security,* vol. 23 (1998).

Laqueur, Walter. *The New Terrorism: Fanaticism and the Arms of Mass Destruction.* New York: Oxford University Press, 1999.

Lasky, Melvin J. *The Hungarian Revolution: A White Book.* New York: Praeger, 1957.

Lieven, Anatol. *Chechnya: Tombstone of Russian Power.* New Haven, CT: Yale University Press, 1998.

———. "Lessons of the War in Chechnya, 1994–1996." In *Soldiers in Cities: Military Operations on Urban Terrain.* Ed. Michael C. Desch. Carlisle, PA: Strategic Studies Institute, 2001.

———. "The World Turned Upside Down." *Armed Forces Journal,* August 1998.

Linden, Eugene. "The Exploding Cities of the Developing World." *Foreign Affairs,* vol. 75 (January–February 1996).

Litvan, Gyorgy. *The Hungarian Revolution of 1956: Reform, Revolt, and Repression, 1953–1963.* London: Longman, 1996.

Longford, Earl of [Frank Pakenham], and Thomas P. O'Neill. *Eamon De Valera: A Biography.* Boston: Houghton Mifflin, 1971.

Lomperis, Timothy J. *From People's War to People's Rule: Insurgency, Intervention, and the Lessons of Vietnam.* Chapel Hill: University of North Carolina, 1996.

Lukas, Richard C. *The Forgotten Holocaust: The Poles under German Occupation.* Lexington: University Press of Kentucky, 1986.

Macartney, C. A. *A History of Hungary, 1929–1945,* 2 vols. New York: Praeger, 1957.

Major, John. *John Major: The Autobiography.* New York: HarperCollins, 1999.

Mallin, Jay, ed. *Terror and Urban Guerrillas.* Coral Gables, FL: University of Miami Press, 1971.

Manwaring, Max G. *Shadows of Things Past and Images of the Future: Lessons for the Insurgencies in Our Midst.* Carlisle, PA: Strategic Studies Institute, 2004.

———. *Street Gangs: The New Urban Insurgency* . Carlisle, PA: Strategic Studies Institute, 2005.

Mao Tse-tung. *Basic Tactics* [orig. 1937]; *On Guerrilla Warfare* [orig. 1937]; *On Protracted War* [orig. 1938]; *Problems of Strategy in Guerrilla War against Japan* [orig. 1938]. In *Selected Works of Mao Tse-tung,* vol. 2. Peking: Foreign Languages Press 1965.

————. *Selected Military Writings*. Peking: Foreign Languages Press, 1963.

Marighella, Carlos. *For the Liberation of Brazil*. Harmondsworth, England: Penguin, 1971.

————. *Manual of the Urban Guerrilla*. Trans. Gene Hanrahan. Chapel Hill, NC: Documentary Publications, 1985.

Marks, Thomas A. "Urban Insurgency." *Small Wars and Insurgencies*, vol. 14 (Autumn 2003).

Massu, Jacques. *La vraie bataille d'Alger*. Paris: Plon, 1971.

Max, Alphonse. *Tupamaros: A Pattern for Urban Guerrilla Warfare in Latin America*. The Hague: International Information and Documentation Centre, 1970.

McCormick, Gordon H. *From the Sierra to the Cities: The Urban Campaign of the Shining Path*. Santa Monica, CA: RAND, 1992.

McElroy, Gerald. *The Catholic Church and the Northern Ireland Crisis, 1968–1986*. Dublin: Gill and Macmillan, 1991.

McGuffin, John. *Internment*. Tralee, Ireland: Anvil, 1973.

Medby, Jamison Jo, and Russell W. Glenn. *Street Smart Intelligence: Preparation of the Battlefield for Urban Operations*. Santa Monica, CA: RAND, 2005.

Menon, Rajan, and Graham E. Fuller. "Russia's Ruinous Chechen War." *Foreign Affairs*, vol. 79 (March–April 2000).

Meray, Tibor. *Thirteen Days That Shook the Kremlin*. London: Thames and Hudson, 1958.

Metz, Steven, and Raymond Millen. *Insurgency and Counterinsurgency in the Twenty-first Century: Reconceptualizing Threat and Response*. Carlisle, PA: Strategic Studies Institute, 2004.

Mikes, George [Gyorgy]. *A Study in Infamy: The Operations of the Hungarian Secret Police*. London: A. Deutsch, 1959.

————. *The Hungarian Revolution*. London: A. Deutsch, 1957.

Mikolajczyk, Stanislaw. *The Rape of Poland*. New York: McGraw Hill, 1948.

Military History Institute of Vietnam. *Victory in Vietnam: The Official History of the People's Army of Vietnam 1954–1975*. Trans. Merle L. Pribbenow. Lawrence: University Press of Kansas, 2002.

Military Operations in Low Intensity Conflict. Washington, DC: Headquarters, Departments of the Army and the Air Force, 1990.

Mockaitis, Thomas. *British Counterinsurgency, 1919–60*. New York: St. Martin's, 1990.

————. *British Counterinsurgency in the Post-Imperial Era*. Manchester, England: University of Manchester Press, 1995.

Moine, André. *Ma guerre d'Algérie*. Paris: Hachette/Carrere, 1995

Molnar, Miklos. *Budapest 1956: A History of the Hungarian Revolution*. London: Allen and Unwin, 1971.

Morgan, Ted. *My Battle of Algiers*. New York: Collins, 2006.

Morrison, Jennifer, and Bruce Hoffman. "The Urbanisation of Insurgency: Potential Challenge to U.S. Army Operations." *Small Wars and Insurgencies*, vol. 6 (Spring 1995).

Moss, Robert. *Urban Guerrillas: The New Face of Political Violence*. London: Temple Smith, 1972.

————. "Urban Guerrillas in Uruguay." *Problems of Communism*, vol. 20 (1971).

————. *Uruguay: Terrorism vs. Democracy*. London: Institute for the Study of Conflict, 1971.

Moxon-Browne, Edward. *Nation, Class, and Creed in Northern Ireland*. Aldershot, England: Gower, 1983.

————. "The Water and the Fish: Public Opinion and the Provisional IRA in Northern Ireland." In *British Perspectives on Terrorism*. Ed. Paul Wilkinson. London: Allen and Unwin, 1981.

Neeson, Eoin. *The Civil War, 1922–1923*. Dublin, Ireland: Poolbeg Press, 1989.

Newsinger, John. *British Counterinsurgency: From Palestine to Northern Ireland*. New York: Palgrave, 2002.

————. "From Counter-Insurgency to Internal Security: Northern Ireland, 1969–1972." *Small Wars and Insurgencies*, vol. 6 (Spring 1995).

Nichols, Johanna. "Who Are the Chechens?" *Central Asian Survey*, vol. 14 (1995).

Nivat, Anne. *Chienne de Guerre: A Woman Reporter behind the Lines of the War in Chechnya*. New York: Public Affairs, 2001.

O'Ballance, Edgar. *The Algerian Insurrection, 1954–1962*. Hamden, CT: Archon, 1967.

————. *Terror in Ireland*. Novato, CA: Presidio, 1981.

Oberdorfer, Don. *Tet! The Turning Point in the Vietnam War*. New York, Da Capo, 1984 [orig. 1971].

O'Connell, James W. *Is the United States Prepared to Conduct Military Operations on Urbanized Terrain?* Newport, RI: Naval War College, 1992.

O'Leary, Brendan, and John McGarry. *The Politics of Antagonism: Understanding Northern Ireland*. Atlantic Highlands, NJ: Athlone, 1996.

Oliker, Olga. *Russia's Chechen Wars 1994–2000: Lessons for Urban Combat*. Santa Monica, CA: RAND, 2001.

Oliveira, Sergio d'. "Uruguay and the Tupamaro Myth." *Military Review*, vol. 53 (1973).

Olson, Lynne, and Stanley Cloud. *A Question of Honor: The Kosciuszko Squadron; Forgotten Heroes of World War II*. New York: Alfred Knopf, 2003.

O'Neill, Bard. *Insurgency and Terrorism: From Revolution to Apocalypse*. 2d ed. Washington, DC: Potomac Books, 2005.

O'Neill, Bard, W. R. Heaton, and D. J. Alberts, ed. *Insurgency in the Modern World*. Boulder, CO: Westview, 1980.

O'Sullivan, Patrick. "A Geographical Analysis of Guerrilla Warfare." *Political Geography Quarterly*, vol. 2 (1983).

Paget, Julian. *Counterinsurgency Campaigning*. London; Faber, 1967.

Pakenham, Frank. *Peace by Ordeal: An Account, from First-hand Sources of the Negotiation and Signature of the Anglo-Irish Treaty, 1921*. London: Sidgwick and Jackson, 1972 [orig. 1935].

Pape, Robert A. *Bombing to Win: Airpower and Coercion in War*. Ithaca, NY: Cornell University Press, 1996.

Paret, Peter. *French Revolutionary Warfare from Indochina to Algeria: An Analysis of a Political and Military Doctrine*. New York: Praeger, 1964.

Paul, Allen. *Katyn: The Untold Story of Stalin's Polish Massacre*. New York: Scribner's, 1991.

Pearson, David. "Low Intensity Operations in Northern Ireland." In *Soldiers in Cities: Military Operations on Urban Terrain*. Ed. Michael C. Desch. Carlisle, PA: Strategic Studies Institute, 2001.

Peters, Ralph. "The New Warrior Class Revisited." *Small Wars and Insurgencies*, vol. 13 (Spring 2002).

———. "After the Revolution." *Parameters*, vol. 25 (Summer 1995).

———. "Heavy Peace." *Parameters*, vol. 29 (Spring 1999).

———. "Our Soldiers, Their Cities." *Parameters*, vol. 26 (Spring 1996).

———. "The New Warrior Class." *Parameters*, vol. 24 (Summer 1994).

Pham Van Son. *Tet 1968*. Salisbury, NC: Documentary Publishers, 1980 [orig. 1968].

Pike, Douglas. *PAVN: People's Army of Vietnam*. Novato, CA: Presidio, 1986.

Pilloni, John R. "Burning Corpses in the Streets: Russia's Doctrinal Flaws in the 1995 Fight for Grozny." *Journal of Slavic Military Studies*, vol. 13 (June 2000).

Pilsudska, Alexandra. *Pilsudski: A Biography by His Wife*. New York: Dodd, Mead, 1941.

Pilsudski, Jozef. *Memories of a Polish Revolutionary and Soldier*. London: Faber and Faber, 1931.

———. *Year 1920 and Its Climax: Battle of Warsaw during the Polish-Soviet War*. New York: Pilsudski Institute of America, 1972.

Pohle, Victoria. *The Viet Cong in Saigon: Tactics and Objectives during the Tet Offensive*. Santa Monica, CA: RAND, 1969.

Politkovskaya, Anna. *A Dirty War: A Russian Reporter in Chechnya*. London: Harville, 2001.

Polonsky, Antony. *Politics in Independent Poland, 1921–1939: The Crisis of Constitutional Government*. Oxford, England: Clarendon Press, 1972.

Porzecanski, Arturo. *Uruguay's Tupamaros*. New York: Praeger, 1973.

Posen, Barry R. "Urban Operations: Tactical Realities and Strategic Ambiguities." In *Soldiers in Cities: Military Operations on Urban Terrain*. Ed. Michael C. Desch. Carlisle, PA: Strategic Studies Institute, 2001.

Pryce-Jones, David. *The Hungarian Revolution*. New York: Horizon 1970.

Raevsky, Andrei. "Russian Military Performance in Chechnya: An Initial Evaluation." *Journal of Slavic Military Studies*, vol. 8 (December 1995).

Reese, Roger R. *Stalin's Reluctant Soldiers: A Social History of the Red Army 1925–1941*. Lawrence: University Press of Kansas, 1996.

Rishikoff, Harvey, and Michael Schrage. "Technology vs. Torture." *Slate* (August 18, 2004). http://slate.msn.com/id2105332/.

Roux, Michel. *Les harkis, ou les oubliés de l'histoire 1954–1990*. Paris: La Découverte, 1991.

Roy, Jules. *J'accuse le General Massu*. Paris: Seuil, 1972.

Rozek, E. *Allied Wartime Diplomacy: A Pattern in Poland*. New York: Wiley, 1958

Russell, Charles A., James A. Miller, and Robert E. Hildner. "The Urban Guerrilla in Latin America: A Select Bibliography." *Latin American Research Review*, vol. 9 (1974).

Russell, John. "Mujahedeen, Mafia, Madmen: Russian Perceptions of Chechens during the Wars in Chechnya, 1994–1996 and 1999–2001." *Journal of Communist Studies and Transition Politics*, vol. 18 (March 2002).

Ryder, Chris. *The Ulster Defence Regiment: An Instrument of Peace?* London: Methuen, 1991.

Salan, Raoul. *Algérie française*. Paris: Presses de la Cité, 1972.

Sarkesian, Sam. *Unconventional Conflicts in a New Security Era: Lessons from Malaya and Vietnam*. Westport, CT: Greenwood, 1993.

Schneider, Ronald M. The *Political System of Brazil: The Emergence of a Modernizing Authoritarian Regime, 1964–1970*. New York: Columbia University Press, 1971.

Sebestyen, Victor. *Twelve Days: The Story of the Hungarian Revolution*. New York: Pantheon, 2006.

Seely, Robert. *Russo-Chechen Conflict, 1800–2000: A Deadly Embrace*. Portland, OR: Frank Cass, 2001.

Servan-Schreiber, Jean-Jacques. *Lieutenant en Algérie*. Paris: R. Julliard, 1957.

Seton-Watson, Hugh. *The East European Revolution*. Boulder, CO: Westview, 1985.

———. *The Russian Empire, 1801–1917*. Oxford, England: Clarendon Press, 1967.

Sherwood, Robert E. *Roosevelt and Hopkins: An Intimate History*. New York: Harper's, 1948.

Skidmore, Thomas E. *Politics in Brazil, 1930–1964: An Experiment in Democracy*. New York: Oxford University Press, 1967.

———. *The Politics of Military Rule in Brazil, 1964–1985*. New York: Oxford University Press, 1988.

Smith, David J., and Gerald Chambers. *Inequality in Northern Ireland*. Oxford, England: Clarendon Press, 1991.

Smith, M. L. R. *Fighting for Ireland? The Military Strategy of the Irish Republican Movement*. London: Routledge, 1995.

Smith, Sebastian. *Allah's Mountains: Politics and War in the Russian Caucasus*. London: Tauris, 2001.

Souyris, André. "Les conditions de la parade et la riposte à la guerre révolutionnaire." *Revue militaire d'information*, February–March 1957.

Stepan, Alfred. *The Military in Politics: Changing Patterns in Brazil*. Princeton, NJ: Princeton University Press, 1971.

Sun Tzu. *The Art of War*. Trans. Samuel B. Griffith. New York: Oxford University Press, 1963.

Talbott, John. "French Public Opinion and the Algerian War." *French Historical Studies*, vol. 9 (1975).

———. The *War without a Name: France in Algeria 1954–1962*. New York: Knopf, 1980.

Taw, Jennifer M., and Bruce Hoffman. *The Urbanization of Insurgency: Potential Challenge to U.S. Army Operations*. Santa Monica, CA: RAND, 1994.

Taylor, A. J. P. *The Habsburg Monarchy, 1809–1918*. Chicago: University of Chicago Press, 1976.

Taylor, Maxwell D. *Swords and Plowshares*. New York: Norton, 1972.

Taylor, Peter. *Beating the Terrorists? Interrogation at Omagh, Gough, and Castlereagh*. New York: Penguin, 1980.

———. *Behind the Mask: The IRA and Sinn Fein*. New York: TV Books, 1997.

———. *Provos: The IRA and Sinn Fein*. London: Bloomsbury, 1987.

Taylor, Philip B. *Government and Politics of Uruguay*. Westport, CT: Greenwood, 1961.

Tec, Nechama. *When Light Pierced the Darkness: Righteous Christians and the Polish Jews*. New York: Oxford University Press, 1988.

Thatcher, Margaret. *The Downing Street Years*. New York: HarperCollins, 1993.

Thomas, Timothy L. "The Battle of Grozny: Deadly Classroom for Urban Combat." *Parameters*, vol. 29 (Summer 1999).

———. "Grozny 2000: Urban Combat Lessons Learned." *Military Review*, (July / August 2000).

———. "The Russian Armed Forces Confront Chechnya: II. Military Activities, 11–31 December 1994." *Journal of Slavic Military Studies*, vol. 8 (June 1995).

Thompson, Sir Robert. *Defeating Communist Insurgency: The Lessons of Malaya and Vietnam*. New York: Praeger, 1966.

———, ed. *War in Peace: Conventional and Guerrilla Warfare since 1945.* New York: Harmony, 1982.

———. "Vietnam." In *War in Peace: Conventional and Guerrilla Warfare since 1945.* Ed. Sir Robert Thompson. New York: Harmony, 1982.

Tishkov, Valery. *Chechnya: Life in a War-Torn Society.* Berkeley: University of California Press, 2004.

Tokes, Rudolph. *Bela Kun and the Hungarian Soviet Republic.* New York: Praeger, 1967.

Tran Van Tra. *Concluding the Thirty-Years War.* Roslyn, VA: Foreign Broadcast Information Service, 1983.

Trinquier, Roger. *Modern War: A French View of Counterinsurgency.* Trans. Daniel Lee. Introduction by Bernard Fall. New York: Praeger, 1964 [orig. 1961

Tripier, Philippe. *Autopsie de la guerre d'Algérie.* Paris: Editions France-Empire, 1972.

Truong Nhu Tang. *A Viet Cong Memoir.* San Diego, CA: Harcourt, Brace, Jovanovich, 1985.

Turbiville, Graham H., Jr., *Mafia in Uniform: The Criminalization of the Russian Armed Forces.* Fort Leavenworth, KS: Foreign Military Studies Office, 1995.

Tushnet, Leonard. *To Die with Honor: The Uprising of the Jews in the Warsaw Ghetto.* New York: Citadel, 1965.

U.S. Marine Corps. *Military Operations on Urbanized Terrain.* Marine Corps Warfighting Publication 3–35.3. Washington, DC.: U.S. Marine Corps, 1998.

Urban, G. R. *The Nineteen Days.* London: Heinemann, 1957.

Urban, Mark. *Big Boys' Rules: The Secret Struggle against the IRA.* London: Faber, 1992.

Vali, Ferenc A. *Rift and Revolution in Hungary.* Cambridge, MA: Harvard University Press, 1961.

Van Dyke, Carl. "Kabul to Grozny: A Critique of Soviet (Russian) Counterinsurgency Doctrine." *Journal of Slavic Military Studies,* vol. 9 (1996).

Vidal-Naquet, Pierre. *Torture: Cancer of Democracy.* Harmondsworth, England: Penguin, 1963.

Wall, I. M. *France, the United States, and the Algerian War.* Berkeley: University of California Press, 2001.

Volgyes, Ivan, ed. *Hungary in Revolution, 1918–1919.* Lincoln: University of Nebraska, 1971.

West, F. J. *No True Glory: A Frontline Account of the Battle for Fallujah.* New York: Bantam, 2005.

———. "The Fall of Fallujah." *Marine Corps Gazette,* vol. 89 (July 2005).

Westmoreland. William. *A Soldier Reports.* Garden City, NY: Doubleday, 1976.

Weygand, Maxime. *Memoirs*. 2 vols. Paris: Flammarion, 1950–57.

White, Robert W. *The Provisional Irish Republicans*. Westport, CT: Greenwood, 1993.

White, Robert W., and Terry F. White. "Revolution in the City: On the Resources of Urban Guerrillas." *Terrorism and Political Violence*, vol. 3 (1991).

Whyte, John. *Interpreting Northern Ireland*. Oxford, England: Clarendon Press, 1990.

Wiarda, Howard J., and Harvey F. Kline. *Latin American Politics and Development*. Boston: Houghton Mifflin, 1979.

Wickham-Crowley, Timothy. *Guerrillas and Revolution in Latin America: A Comparative Study of Insurgents and Regimes since 1956*. Princeton, NJ: Princeton University Press, 1992.

Williams, Philip M. *Crisis and Compromise: Politics in the Fourth Republic*. London: Longman, 1964.

Winters, Francis X. *The Year of the Hare: America in Vietnam, January 25, 1963–February 15, 1964*. Athens: University of Georgia Press, 1997.

Wirtz, James J. "The Battles of Saigon and Hue: Tet 1968." In *Soldiers in Cities: Military Operations on Urban Terrain*. Ed. Michael C. Desch. Carlisle, PA: Strategic Studies Institute, 2001.

———. *The Tet Offensive: Intelligence Failure in War*. Ithaca, NY: Cornell University Press, 1991.

Wolf , Eric. *Peasant Wars of the Twentieth Century*. New York: Harper and Row, 1969.

Wright, Frank. *Northern Ireland: A Comparative Analysis*. Dublin: Gill and Macmillan, 1987.

Ximenes [pseud.] "Essai sur la guerre révolutionnaire." *Revue militaire d'information*, February–March 1957.

Younger, Calton. *Ireland's Civil War*. Glasgow: Fontana, 1970.

Zamoyski, Adam. *The Forgotten Few: The Polish Air Force in World War II*. Barnsley, England: Pen and Sword, 2004.

Zawodny, J. K. *Death in the Forest*. South Bend, IN: University of Notre Dame Press, 1962.

Zelkina, Anna. *In Quest for God and Freedom: The Sufi Response to the Russian Advance in the North Caucasus*. New York: New York University Press, 2000.

Zervoudakis, Alexander J. "From Indochina to Algeria: Counterinsurgency Lessons." In *The Algerian War and the French Army 1954–1962: Experiences, Images, Testimonies*. Ed. Martin S. Alexander, Martin Evans, and J. F. V. Keiger. New York: Palgrave Macmillan, 2002.

Zhukov, Georgi. *Memoirs of Marshal Zhukov*. New York: Delacorte, 1971.

Index